T0135754

Technische Universität Braunschweig
Carl-Friedrich-Gauß-Fakultät
Institut für Betriebssysteme und Rechnerverbund

Dynamic Network Selection for Optimized Use of
Mobile Internet

Von der Carl-Friedrich-Gauß-Fakultät
Technische Universität Carolo-Wilhelmina zu Braunschweig

zur Erlangung des Grades

Doktor-Ingenieur (Dr.-Ing.)

genehmigte

Dissertation

von Sven Lahde,
geboren am 05.05.1980
in Zeven

Eingereicht am 29.10.2010
Mündliche Prüfung am 21.12.2010
Referent: Prof. Dr.-Ing. Lars Wolf
Korreferent: Prof. Dr. rer. nat. Martin Mauve

2011

Bibliografische Information der Deutschen Nationalbibliothek

Die Deutsche Nationalbibliothek verzeichnet diese Publikation in der
Deutschen Nationalbibliografie; detaillierte bibliografische Daten sind
im Internet über http://dnb.d-nb.de abrufbar.

Diss., Technische Universität Carolo-Wilhelmina zu Braunschweig, 2010

ISBN 978-3-8325-2767-9

Logos Verlag Berlin GmbH
Comeniushof, Gubener Str. 47,
10243 Berlin
Tel.: +49 (0)30 42 85 10 90
Fax: +49 (0)30 42 85 10 92
INTERNET: http://www.logos-verlag.de

Kurzfassung

Die mobile Nutzung des Internets hat in den letzten Jahren einen enormen Bedeutungszuwachs erfahren. Leistungsfähige Geräte und bezahlbare Datentarife haben eine starke Nachfrage nach Smartphones mit innovativen Bedienkonzepten ausgelöst und völlige neue Geschäftsfelder für Anwendungen und Dienste eröffnet. Zusätzlich existiert eine große Vielfalt heterogener Kommunikationsnetze und -technologien die für einen Zugang zum Internet genutzt werden können. Neben Mobilfunknetzen wie UMTS und GSM, gibt es unter anderem eine Vielzahl von WLAN Hotspots oder auch WiMAX Netze mit denen sich ein Benutzer verbinden kann. Auch neuartige Vernetzungskonzepte, wie die Fahrzeug-zu-Fahrzeug Kommunikation oder unterbrechungstolerante Netze lassen sich eventuell für den Internetzugang nutzen. Obwohl diese Optionen deutlich unterschiedliche Kommunikationseigenschaften aufweisen, bieten sie in ihrer Gesamtheit ein hohes Potential für die Nutzung von Internet in mobilen Umgebungen. Eine Integration dieser unterschiedlichen Netze und ihre effiziente Nutzung sind die zentralen Herausforderungen für die nächste Mobilfunkgeneration. Aktuelle mobile Geräte unterstützen meist bereits mehrere Kommunikationstechnologien. Dennoch werden die dadurch entstehenden Möglichkeiten heutzutage nicht vollends ausgenutzt. Im Allgemeinen muss immer noch der Benutzer entscheiden welches Netz er verwendet. Ebenso muss er mögliche Unterbrechungen der Verbindung zum Internet handhaben. Der Benutzer selbst hat daran allerdings gar kein Interesse. Er möchte lediglich seine Anwendungen nutzen, unabhängig davon wie diese auf das Internet zugreifen.

In dieser Arbeit stellen wir ein System für die dynamische Auswahl von Netzen in heterogenen Kommunikationsumgebungen vor. Es bildet die Grundlage für benutzerzentrierte Dienste, die die Auswahl des Zugangsweges zum Internet transparent gegenüber den Benutzern und Anwendungen realisieren. Unser Hauptaugenmerk liegt auf der Entwicklung einer neuartigen Strategie zur Auswahl des „besten"Netzes für jede einzelne Anwendung. Hierfür haben wir ein zweistufiges Konzept erarbeitet, das sowohl die individuellen Anforderungen der einzelnen Anwendungen, als auch anwendungsübergreifende Zielvorgaben und Beschränkungen der verfügbaren Ressourcen berücksichtigt. Unser Ansatz ermöglicht die Bündelung von Netzen um eine höhere Leistung zu erreichen. Weiterhin bietet er die Option auf alternative Zugangsmöglichkeiten zum Internet zu warten, die vermutlich in naher Zukunft verfügbar sein werden. Darüber hinaus haben wir ein Konzept zur

Verwaltung der verschiedenen Verbindungswege entwickelt, welches sowohl vertikale Verbindungsübergaben zwischen Netzen verschiedener Technologien, als auch die gleichzeitige Nutzung mehrere Wege durch das Internet beinhaltet. In unterschiedlichsten Szenarien haben wir die Leistungsfähigkeit dieser Mechanismen untersucht, um deren Stärken und Grenzen zu ermitteln. Die Ergebnisse dieser Arbeit sollen einen Beitrag dazu leisten die verfügbaren Kommunikationsmöglichkeiten in heterogenen Netzen besser auszunutzen und gleichzeitig die Dienstgüte für den Benutzer zu erhöhen.

Abstract

The use of Internet access on mobile devices gained a strong popularity during the last years. Powerful devices and affordable data rates triggered a huge demand on smartphones with innovative user interfaces and opened up completely new business models for application services. In addition, there exists a variety of heterogeneous access networks and technologies that might be used for Internet access. Besides cellular networks like UMTS and GSM, there are, for instance, plenty of WLAN hotspots or WiMAX networks one can connect to. Moreover, a user may get Internet access via novel networking concepts like Vehicular Ad-hoc Networks or Delay Tolerant Networks as well. All of them feature clearly different communication characteristics, but in combination they offer a high potential for Internet access in the mobile domain. The integration of such heterogeneous access networks and the efficient use of the available communication resources are key challenges for the next generation of mobile communications. Although today's mobile devices are equipped with multiple interfaces for accessing different networking technologies, they do not make full use of these capabilities. In general, it is still the user that has to decide which network to use and to deal with network disruptions while being on the move. But, users simply want to use their common applications, regardless of how they access the Internet.

In this thesis, we propose a framework for dynamic network selection in heterogeneous communication environments. It provides the basis for user-centric services that make the selection of access networks transparent to users and to applications. Our primary focus is on the design of a novel strategy for selecting the "best" network for each individual application. We propose a two-tier concept that considers the needs of individual applications as well as cross-application objectives and resource limitations. Our approach allows for bundling different network paths to achieve a higher performance and for deferring application requests, for instance, to wait for access networks that are expected to appear in the future. Furthermore, we implemented a path management concept including mechanisms for vertical handovers and for concurrent multipath transfer. We investigated the performance of them in various heterogeneous networking scenarios, to analyze their potentials and their limitations. The results of this thesis are intended to make a better use of the available communication capabilities in heterogeneous networking environments and to increase the overall service quality that is experienced by the user.

Acknowledgements

My work on this thesis has been a long journey and an exciting time with plenty of new experiences, challenging problems, interesting people, lively discussions, but also lots of hard work. It was also a time that changed my life completely and will always be treasured in my mind. I have never been alone on this journey. There have always been companions around me, at least for a short leg. It was their support that helped me to accomplish this work and to get back on track in times where I was lost in ideas, concepts, measurement results or written pages. Now, as I finally reached the destination, it is time to express my deepest gratitude to those people that made my journey a success.

First, I would like to thank Prof. Dr.-Ing. Lars Wolf for encouraging me to go on this journey and to work on my research project at his institute. He always provided feedback and suggestions that helped me to improve this work. During my time at the institute, he was available for discussions on my ideas, questions or concerns every time and provided me with the personal freedom to manage my work in the institute and my family life at home. Second, I would like to thank Prof. Dr. rer. nat. Martin Mauve for agreeing to be the assessor of my thesis. Special thanks go to the Deutsche Telekom Stiftung for their support of my research work. In particular, I would like to thank Christiane Frense-Heck for being always willing to listen to my questions and organizing all the seminars and events. I enjoyed the discussions with doctoral students from other fields in a very open and familiar atmosphere. I also thank René Obermann for agreeing to be my mentor during that time.

I fondly remember to numerous meetings, discussions, events, and evenings at Hubert's with my colleagues at the Institute for Operating Systems and Computer Networks that were essential parts of the pleasant working environment. I would like to thank Dr. Marc Bechler for his support during my first steps as a researcher and introducing me to the institute. In particular, I would like to thank Dr. Jens Brandt, Oliver Wellnitz and Michael Doering for their friendship and fruitful discussions as well as their comments that helped me throughout my work. Special thanks belong to Jens for proofreading this work and providing me with valuable comments and suggestions that pushed me to come to an end. But, I would also like to thank all my other colleagues that provided me always a great support. In addition, there have been numerous students that supported my research work in student or diploma theses. Here, special thanks go to Michael Doering, Irina Gaponova and Martin Wegner.

Finally, I owe my deepest gratitude to my family that supported me at all times on my journey. In particular, I thank my wife Nina who was a great support and had the enormous strength to care about our lovely sons during the week while still managing her own studies. But also my parents and my parents-in-law provided us with an immense support and were always available to help any time they were needed to allow me to complete this work.

Sven Lahde, October 2010

This research work was supported by Deutsche Telekom Stiftung.

Contents

List of Figures

List of Tables

Chapter 1

Motivation

The use of Internet access on mobile devices has rapidly evolved in the past years. The German provider Deutsche Telekom expects the global mobile data traffic to grow from 0.03 Exabytes per month in 2008 to more than 2 Exabytes per month in 2013, which would be a compound annual growth of more than 130 % [3]. For Germany, Deutsche Telekom already increased its revenue in mobile data transfer by 46 % in 2009. These facts make clear that mobile Internet services and wireless broadband access will be the key success factors for telecommunication providers during the next years.

Basically, there are three major drivers for the increased importance of mobile Internet access. The first one goes back to the advent of broadband Internet access at home. With the time flat rates for Internet access became affordable and popular, the Internet gained an essential part of the users' daily life. Users became "always-on" and a variety of novel applications and business models appeared. An ever increasing amount of services was shifted into the web and this process is still ongoing. Manifold companies fully rely on web-based services. Furthermore, new applications that focus on collaboration or social networking have emerged quickly. According to a study by the Federal Association for Information Technology, Telecommunications and New Media (BITKOM), 81 % of the Germans in the age of 14 to 49 years cannot imagine a life without Internet [4].

In the last years, this process encroached on the mobile domain. People no longer want to use the novel services solely at home, but at any arbitrary place inside or outside of their domicile. Thus, a variety of wireless networking technologies have been evolved. They are the second driver for mobile Internet access, as they became almost ubiquitous in the past years. The density of different access networks increased dramatically. Besides cellular networks like UMTS and GSM, more and more local area and metropolitan area technologies gained some importance for mobile Internet access. In October 2010, JiWire [5] counted 340,049 registered WLAN hotspots in 144 countries and presumably, the actual number of available hotspots is still a multiple of that value. Further technologies like WiMAX, DVB-H, Vehicular Ad-hoc Networks (VANETs) [6] or Delay Tolerant Networks (DTNs) [7] may provide additional communication capabilities. Today, there are continuous enhancements in developing novel or enhanced wireless communication standards for different application areas. All of these networks show clearly different communication characteristics, for instance, in terms of throughput, delay, availability and costs. However, in combination they offer a high communication performance.

Finally, the third driver that literally boosted the demand on mobile Internet access is the development of novel mobile devices, as for instance the Apple iPhone [8], that come with innovative operational concepts and user interfaces. The display sizes and the processing power of these devices are ever increasing, which makes the use of common (Internet) applications much more convenient to the user. The devices often come with multiple network interfaces for different technologies. Thus, in general the user would already be able to benefit from the heterogeneous communication environment that was mentioned before. The high popularity and consumer acceptance of the novel mobile devices as well as the availability of affordable rates for mobile data transfer resulted in a barrage of novel applications that are tailored to these devices and give people the opportunity to access the Internet at almost any place. The Mobile Metrics Report by AdMob [9] showed an increase in the Internet traffic of smartphones by 193 % from February 2009 to February 2010.

1.1 Problem Statement and Objectives

Although mobile users may have the option to choose between a wide range of communication technologies to access the Internet, a large amount of this communication potential is actually wasted. Traditionally, users have to select one of the available access networks manually. Figure 1.1 illustrates the scenario of using mobile Internet as it can be found today. Users either stay always connected to the network of their mobile telecommunications provider or may occasionally choose to use a WLAN hotspot in their vicinity. This way, it is not possible to make full use of the potentials that are provided by the heterogeneous communications ecosystem. Especially the mobility of the device, the diverse characteristics of different networking technologies, and the fluctuating availability of networks make it a challenging task to choose always the best network for communications. This cannot be managed by the users themselves. Most users will also be overstrained in selecting the best path for their communication needs and do not have the knowledge to be able to balance the advantages and disadvantages of different networks. Only some devices do already support very rudimentary strategies for switching between different networking technologies while being on the move. However, these techniques are often based on trivial strategies that, for instance, use the mobile telecommunications system by default and switch to WLAN if a known hotspot becomes available. In general, such a handover is not seamless and results in the break of existing connections.

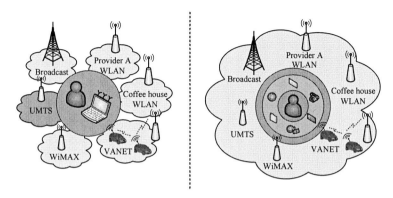

Figure 1.1: From today's manual selection of Internet access to Always Best Connected

To overcome these limitations, we require an integrated approach for managing Internet access via different networks that is transparent to the user and to the applications as it is depicted on the right side of figure 1.1. Key features for such an approach are a seamless and application-oriented handling of mobility as well as an efficient strategy for dynamic access network selection that makes individual decisions for each application based on the specific set of application and user requirements. This concept is known as "Always Best Connected" (ABC) and describes a user-centric framework for the selection of access networks [1]. However, existing ABC approaches do often make sub-optimal use of the communications ecosystem. For instance, they either connect to only one network at the time or optimize the network selection with respect to isolated applications. Moreover, they often use only few dedicated parameters and do not provide the flexibility to support arbitrarily complex decision objectives.

In this thesis we aim at improving these issues by proposing a novel framework for an ABC service that meets the following objectives:

1. The service should utilize the available communication resources to the best and may also distribute data across multiple networks. Moreover, it should not only decide on candidate networks that are available at the moment, but also on ones that are expected to appear in the future.

2. The system has to be independent of any specific networking technologies. In addition, it should not be bound to any specific mechanisms or infrastructure components that have to be implemented by network operators.

3. Changes of access networks that are used should be transparent to the user and to the applications.

4. The decision concept should provide a modular and flexible design to support arbitrary objectives and networking technologies.

5. The network selection strategy should find a global optimum for both specific requirements of the individual applications and cross-application policies that may be defined by the user. For this, it has to provide a high level of flexibility to find reasonable tradeoffs for conflicting objectives.

The outcome of our research is muXer, a flexible and modular architecture for dynamic network selection that is designed to cope with challenging communications ecosystems. It tries to overcome the deficiencies of the existing ways of using mobile Internet access. The core component in muXer is a novel two-tier decision process using arbitration. For each application that requires network access, it rates the suitability of different candidate networks and allocates the available network resources with respect to cross-application requirements. One of the highlighted features of our concept is that it does not assume applications to have a continuous connection to the Internet. One cannot expect to be always-on as even nationwide mobile telecommunications networks have coverage gaps and make Internet access, for instance on a train ride, very challenging. Various applications like e-mail or a file download in the background even do not require an immediate network access. Moreover, a user may accept longer data transmission periods if, for instance, the data transfer is free of charge, instead of using a pricey GPRS link. Second, the decision process allows for spreading application data traffic across several heterogeneous networks and integrates this feature as a reasonable decision option. This way, it is possible to use network capacities more efficiently and to serve even demanding applications in scenarios with limited resources. Finally, our network selection strategy follows an integrated approach that considers the individual requirements of applications on the one hand as well as cross-application objectives and limitations on the other hand. Thus, it aims at finding a global optimum for the user and for all applications, while minimizing mutual interferences at the same time. This feature differentiates muXer from other existing proposals that focus either on selecting the networks purely with respect to individual application requirements or on choosing one single network for the mobile device.

To manage the mobility of a device as well as the functionalities for vertical handovers and concurrent multipath transfer, we have implemented a path management module that interacts with transport layer functionalities and provides support for legacy applications. Here, our main interest is on evaluating the performance of these mechanisms in heterogeneous communication environments. In particular, we analyze the effects of the aforementioned functionalities on the throughput of the application and the experienced end-to-end delay in various mobile communications scenarios.

1.2   Contributions and Scope

This thesis proposes a novel concept for dynamic network selection. The main contribution of our work is a highly flexible arbitration concept that allows for an application-oriented selection of networks, but considers cross-application objectives as well. This network selection concept is embedded in an architectural framework for an ABC service. Further contributions relate to a path management concept and to the evaluation of transport-layer mechanisms for vertical handovers and concurrent multipath transfer in heterogeneous communication environments. The particular contributions that have been made by our work are as follows:

Architecture for dynamic network selection: In this thesis, we propose a novel architecture called muXer that is designed to provide a high flexibility for integrating arbitrary communication technologies and decision objectives for the network selection process. An important issue in designing the architecture was to minimize the dependence on additional infrastructure components and to keep the system independent of specific protocols or functionalities that have to be supported by network or service providers. This aspect eases a later deployment of the framework, increases the efficiency of utilizing available network resources, and comes with the benefit that the user may have contracts with arbitrary communications providers. In particular, we implemented prototypes of three modules within this architecture. First, the core module is the decision engine that runs the actual network selection process. Second, we provide a path management module that interacts with the transport protocol for managing the mobility of the device and enforcing the decisions that were released by the decision engine. Finally, we implemented a conceptual prototype for a network monitoring module that is able to collect information about network characteristics as inputs for the network selection process. The basic concepts of our muXer architecture have been presented in [10].

Transport layer handover management: Our aforementioned path management module interacts with the transport layer protocol to trigger handovers between different networks. We presented this approach in [11]. It is based on the Stream Control Transmission Protocol (SCTP) [12]. To support legacy applications that use, for instance, TCP, we provide a wrapper that enables the use of SCTP for these applications and implements the additional triggers for changes of the networking configurations. In particular, we evaluated the effects of vertical handover events on the network performance perceived by the applications and compare the results of our SCTP-based approach to those of a related approach that uses TCP.

Concurrent Multipath Transfer in challenging environments: We evaluate the challenges of Concurrent Multipath Transfer (CMT) in highly heterogeneous communication environments and propose optimizations to transport layer mechanisms for increasing the efficiency of CMT in the context of clear differences in the characteristics of the paths to be bundled. In addition, we evaluate this concept in various communication scenarios with respect to the application data throughput and the experienced end-to-end delay in order to analyze the potential benefits and the limitations of CMT in heterogeneous communication scenarios.

Arbitration-based decision concept: Finally, we propose a two-tier concept for dynamic network selection that is featured by an extremely high modularity and flexibility. In contrast to existing approaches, it combines application-centric and cross-application views on the decision problem. Thus, it aims at satisfying application and user requirements on the one hand, but also accounts for resource limitations and cross-application objectives on the other hand. Further features of the proposed concept are additional decision options to bundle networks for meeting the application demands or to defer application requests. We implement this concept and provide a scenario-based demonstration of the first tier as well as a simulation-based evaluation of the second tier. Parts of our results have been presented in [13].

In this thesis, we discuss numerous core issues and concepts for dynamic network selection to make efficient use of available communication characteristics. However, there are still some aspects in the field of Always Best Connected that cannot be covered within this thesis. Nevertheless, they can help to improve the general concepts and approaches that are proposed in this work.

QoS guarantees: If an application is scheduled to a certain network, we do not establish any Quality of Service (QoS) reservations along the path from the mobile device to the remote peer. Such QoS guarantees or service level agreements may help to improve the Quality of User Experience. However, this is a challenging task due to, for instance, fluctuating network characteristics and the mobility of the mobile device. Additionally, it may require support from intermediate systems on the path through the Internet. Research on these issues is beyond the scope of our work.

Content adaptation: To improve the perceived quality of using an application in challenging communications situations, one might use content adaptation techniques. As an example, it is possible to reduce the quality of a video stream dynamically, if the available resources do not allow for serving the original stream. However, these techniques do highly depend on the individual applications and are out of our scope.

Objectives for individual applications: For every application there might be different notions on which decision objectives are more important than others. The importance
or design of certain applications may even depend on the current context or the deployment scenario. The parameterization of application-oriented decision objectives
and their relative importance require extensive research on the actual effects of certain
parameters on the application performance. However, in this thesis we focus on the
general concepts and procedures for implementing a flexible decision process. Thus,
the application-oriented parameterizations and the tuning of application-oriented decision concepts cannot be covered within this work.

1.3 Outline

This thesis is structured into six chapters that are organized as self-contained modules, each
focusing on one specific part of our research problem. Figure 1.2 illustrates the organization
of these modules.

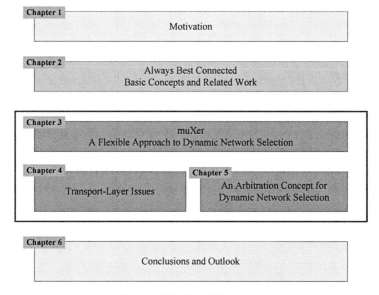

Figure 1.2: Outline of this thesis

Chapter 2 addresses the background of this work. It starts with an overview on the variety of different options to get Internet access on a mobile device and points out their different characteristics. Afterwards, we present the general concept behind the idea of Always Best Connected. Here, we describe the different functionalities that relate to a seamless and dynamic selection of networks. We introduce basic technologies and protocols with a focus on the problems that are addressed in this thesis and give an overview of approaches to different path management issues. Afterwards, related work on algorithms for dynamic network selection is presented. Finally, we discuss several related projects in the context of our work.

In *chapter 3*, we present our approach to a dynamic network selection framework. First, we define our target scenario and derive the requirements and design issues for an efficient network selection approach. Afterwards, we introduce the muXer architecture and describe the basic procedures and concepts. Here, we concentrate on three major aspects. We start with the general concept to obtain generic input parameters for the decision process that makes it possible to compare networks with highly heterogeneous characteristics. Following, we introduce the general principle of our arbitration-based decision concept, before we finally address our approach to path management.

Chapter 4 deals with the analysis of mechanisms for vertical handover and concurrent multipath transfer at the transport layer. The chapter starts with an introduction to the Stream Control Transmission Protocol (SCTP) that provides the basis for our implementations. The advantage of SCTP compared to TCP is the inherent support of using multiple IP addresses at both ends of a transport layer connection. Next, we turn to the implementation of handover functionalities. For this, we use a standardized enhancement of the SCTP protocol. Afterwards, we present our optimized approach to network bundling in heterogeneous networking scenarios that allows for aggregating the bandwidth of multiple access networks at the transport layer. Finally, the focus of this chapter is on the evaluation of the path management functionality in heterogeneous communication environments. For this, we analyze the performance of the proposed mechanisms in different networking scenarios.

In *chapter 5* we turn to the main focus of this work, which is the actual decision concept. In the first part, we discuss different categories of QoS parameters and their relevance to either individual applications or to all applications as a whole. In addition, we point out that the different objectives in the context of dynamic network selection do always require some tradeoff between conflicting optimization goals. Afterwards, we introduce the details of the muXer decision concept that relies on two tiers. The first tier implements the application-oriented arbitration and provides, for instance, a rating of the candidate networks with respect to their accordance to the decision objectives. These results go into the second tier that is responsible for the allocation of network resources to the applications. Following, we describe our basic prototype of the first tier that implements a module for rating networks with respect to the QoS requirements of the applications and a further module for determining an overall priority of each application. Both modules are only intended for a general proof-of-concept. We demonstrate the working of our approach in two different communication scenarios. For the second tier, we propose the muXer Global Resource Allocation Process (GAP) that schedules applications either to none, one, or multiple networks. We analyze the performance of GAP in a variety of scenarios and compare it to alternative algorithms.

Finally, *chapter 6* concludes this thesis and provides a summary of the contributions and the results. In addition, we give an outlook on future research issues that are opened up by our architecture, but exceed the scope of this work.

Chapter 2

Always Best Connected – Basic Concepts and Related Work

Today, users can choose between a wide range of communication technologies when they want to access the Internet. Besides wired access technologies like Ethernet, DSL or cable there are various wireless technologies covering, for instance, GSM, 3G, IEEE 802.11a/b/g/n Wireless LAN, WiMAX, DVB-H/T or satellite systems that can be used for data transmission. It can be expected that the number of mobile communication technologies will increase even further in the future.

Although up-to-date mobile devices often come with interfaces for several communication technologies, it is still the user that has to decide which network he wants to use for Internet access. Seamless roaming is often only possible within the same technology and/or the same provider domain. Thus, the different candidate networks that might be used offer only "communication isles", but cannot be understood as an integrated heterogeneous network. To overcome these limitations and to utilize the potential performance of such a heterogeneous communications ecosystem, the network and especially the access selection needs to become transparent to users and to applications. In general, users do not want to care about which network is best at a certain moment. They would be satisfied if they can configure some general boundary conditions, while the actual network selection is managed by their device.

The easiest way would be to use a mobile telecommunications network at any time. They provide almost seamless mobile connectivity across frontiers and provider boundaries. In 2009, 1,050 GSM networks where available in 222 countries world-wide [14]. For Germany, GSM connectivity is almost nationwide available, which also holds for most other European countries. However, being always connected does not necessarily imply that such a network provides the highest performance at the same time. In several application scenarios, the use of other available communication technologies would provide a higher performance and/or lower costs to the user. Additionally, GPRS and especially UMTS networks have distinct coverage gaps even in Germany [15].

From this context, the concept of Always Best Connected (ABC) arose [1]. It defines a user-centric network selection approach that provides seamless connectivity and always the best communication performance at any time. A central aspect in this concept is the autonomous access selection that hides the process of network selection from the applications and the user.

This chapter aims at introducing the vision of Always Best Connected as well as the challenges and tasks it imposes on the technical realization. We start with an overview of different networking technologies in section 2.1, followed by the description of different communication scenarios for mobile devices in section 2.2. Afterwards, section 2.3 introduces the concept of Always Best Connected. In the following, we turn to related work in this area. First, we present existing approaches on managing vertical handoffs, concurrent multipath transfer and disruption tolerance in section 2.4. Second, section 2.5 overviews various strategies for network selection that have been proposed in the literature. Third, we present other projects that aim at designing related frameworks for providing Always Best Connected services in section 2.6. Finally, the chapter closes with a summary.

2.1 Networking Technologies for (Mobile) Internet Access

Today, there is variety of different networking technologies that might be used to get Internet access. All of them have different communication characteristics, coverage areas and costs. Figure 2.1 gives an overview on several communication technologies that are categorized with respect to the area that might be served by a network.

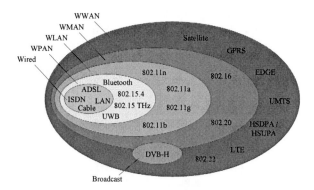

Figure 2.1: Technologies for Internet access

First, the figure shows wired technologies like ISDN, ADSL, Cable or other LAN approaches. These technologies are listed here, as they typically provide the backbone for other wireless systems. For instance, many people use a WLAN router at home that is connected to their ADSL line. This way, the performance of the Internet access may be limited by the performance of the ADSL connection rather than the WLAN link.

The next level comprises wireless technologies for personal area networks (WPANs). Those have often a coverage lower than 10 m. Most of the technologies that belong to this group aim at providing high data rates at low energy consumption and costs. A popular representative of WPAN technologies is Bluetooth that offers a gross data rate of up to 3 Mbit in version 2.1 [16] and up to 54 Mbit/s in version 3.0 [17] by integrating techniques from IEEE 802.11g WLANs. Ultra Wideband (UWB) [18] has been proposed as an extension to Bluetooth or for realizing Wireless USB. It provides data rates of up to 480 Mbit/s. Both standards are mainly driven by industry consortia. However, the IEEE works on WPAN standards as well. For instance, they proposed the 802.15.4 standard that provides the basis for Zigbee. It has gained importance for automation applications or sensor networks and is designed with a clear focus on extreme low energy consumption and implementation complexity. IEEE 802.15.4 provides maximum data rates between 20 and 250 kbit/s depending on the frequency band being used. Finally, there is an IEEE 802.15 THz Interest Group [19] that started to work on a standard for Terahertz (THz) communications. Here, data rates of at least 1 Gbit/s, but probably even more than 10 Gbit/s are expected in the future.

In the class of Wireless Local Area Networks (WLANs) especially the IEEE 802.11 standards have gained an extremely high popularity in the past years [20]. Today, various products as, for instance, embedded devices, smartphones, notebooks or even busses and trams use WLAN network access to exchange data. In October 2010, JiWire [5] counted 340,049 registered WLAN hotspots in 144 countries. It can be expected that this number is only a small fraction of the number of networks that really exist. In addition to private WLAN hotspots, various restaurants, hotels or chains of coffee houses provide Internet access via WLAN. Beyond this, there are numerous initiatives building-up larger WLAN networks in cities. Examples are Wireless Wolfsburg (Germany) [21], Google WiFi Mountain View (USA) [22], Paris WiFi (France) [23] or several communities in Denmark, like the city of Copenhagen.

The coverage area of WLANs is often several hundred meters. There has been a lot of work on improving the performance of IEEE 802.11 since the first standard was released in 1997. Today, IEEE 802.11g is commonly used and provides maximum data rates between 1 and 54 Mbit/s depending on the signal quality. This bandwidth has to be shared with all other users in the local vicinity. Implementations of to the latest IEEE 802.11n standard, that has been published in 2009, may even reach data rates of up to 600 Mbit/s [24]. Moreover, there are multiple extensions to the core IEEE 802.11 standards that introduce, for instance, security features like WPA [25] and Quality of Service features [26].

The next class in our scheme comprises Wireless Metropolitan Area Networks (WMANs) that may cover areas of multiple kilometers. Here, one popular example technology is WiMAX that bases on the IEEE 802.16 standard [27]. Today, WiMAX networks are available in cities like Amsterdam (Netherlands, WorldMax Aerea), Baltimore (USA, XOHM) or Portland (USA, Clearwire). The mobile WiMAX variant that is defined in IEEE 802.16e provides maximum data rates of up to 63 Mbit/s in downlink direction as well as up to 28.22 Mbit/s in uplink direction [28]. However, the actual performance depends on the channel configuration, asymmetries in up- and downlink, as well as the number of users. Performance measurements by Paolini [29] in Portland showed throughputs of about 3.031 Mbit/s in the downlink and 425 kbit/s in the uplink. In addition to WiMAX, there are also other approaches like IEEE 802.20 [30] that offers a peak data rate per cell of more than 16 Mbit/s in downlink and more than 3.2 Mbit/s in uplink direction [31]. Per user, these values reduce to 4 Mbit/s and 1.2 Mbit/s respectively.

Finally, there is a variety of 2G (GPRS, EDGE), 3G (UMTS, HSDPA/HSUPA) and Super 3G (LTE) mobile telecommunications technologies that provide Internet access with nation- or even worldwide roaming. Today, the actual deployment stage of the individual technologies often decreases with their capacity. In Germany, GPRS has the highest coverage and is even available in rural areas. However, there are still numerous unchartered territories, were even GPRS is not available. In contrast, HSDPA and HSUPA are mostly only available in urban centers. LTE has even not been deployed so far. From the aforementioned systems, GPRS provides the lowest data rate with a downstream of 53.6 kbit/s and an upstream of 13.4 kbit/s. HSDPA provides a maximum downlink data rate of 14.4 Mbit/s, but often only 7.2 Mbit/s or even 3.6 Mbit/s are supported. LTE is expected to achieve peak data rates of up to 300 Mbit/s in downlink and 75 Mbit/s in uplink direction. Another technology for WWANs is standardized in IEEE 802.22. It has been designed to operate in the traditional TV spectrum. Here, capacities become available due to the change-over from analog to digital TV broadcast. The coverage area of a base station can be up to 100 km [32]. The maximum data rate per cell ranges between 18 and 24 Mbit/s. Per user, a maximum data rate of 1.5 Mbit/s in downlink and 384 kbit/s in uplink direction can be expected. Finally, there are also further technologies as, for instance, satellite systems or broadcast approaches like DVB-H that might be used to deliver data to mobile users.

In summary, we can state that this huge amount of different networking technologies with different availabilities at different locations constitutes a highly heterogeneous communication environment. It provides immense capabilities for network access. Our survey showed that the particular technologies feature clearly different characteristics. With some exceptions, one might state that the higher the area covered by a technology the lower the data rate that might be available for the user. One the one hand, a higher coverage area increases the probability of staying connected to the network when being mobile. But, there are also other differences between the technologies besides data rate and coverage as, for instance, delay, jitter, any guarantees on the available bandwidth per user, the support of mobility, or costs. Thus, each technology has its own specific advantages and disadvantages in certain scenarios and with respect to certain applications. Of course, there may be a higher number of potential candidate networks using different technologies in metropolitan areas than in rural areas, as the higher population density makes the expansion of communication networks in such areas more profitable. Even if the data rates will increase further and the deployment of wireless broadband technologies will continue, we can expect that very high data rates will still not be available across large areas in the foreseeable future.

Today, the potential of the whole communications ecosystem is not used fully used. Devices connect only to one access network at a particular time and implement at most very trivial strategies to decide on which network to use. One key challenge for improving the efficiency of Internet access is to implement a framework for dynamic network selection that provides a high flexibility in managing the full variety of existing and future networking technologies.

2.2   Scenarios

In general, there are multiple possible networking scenarios on how a mobile device may get Internet access. In this work, we focus on the target scenario that is shown in figure 2.2. Here, the mobile device is multihomed, which means that it is equipped with a set of interface cards for different networking technologies. Via each of these interfaces, the mobile device may connect to an infrastructure network that provides access to the Internet. A second option would be use an ad hoc network that provides an Internet gateway. This ad hoc network may provide an end-to-end connection to the Internet via multiple hops, as it has been proposed by Bechler in [33] for vehicular integration scenarios. Moreover, data might also be forwarded in a store-carry-forward manner. We proposed such a Disruption Tolerant Networking (DTN) approach using busses as data vehicles in [34].

However, there are other potential communication scenarios as well. Two important examples are described in the following. The first one is illustrated in figure 2.3. Here, a *mobile router* that may be installed, for instance, in a vehicle provides Internet access to other passengers inside. In this case, the application services and network interfaces to the Internet do not share the same device. Thus, the network selection process must run in a distributed manner. Application and user requirements or network characteristics have to be exchanged between the router and the mobile devices. The available resources do not only have to be shared between concurrent applications at one device, but also across multiple devices.

Finally, the *swarm scenario* that is depicted in figure 2.4 features an even higher complexity than the mobile router concept. Here, mobile device with Internet access share their

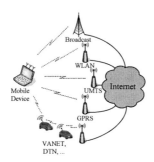

Figure 2.2: Target scenario: Multihomed device

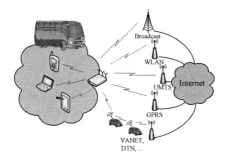

Figure 2.3: Alternative scenario: Mobile router

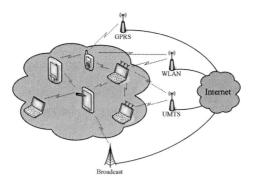

Figure 2.4: Alternative scenario: Swarm

resources with any other devices via an ad hoc network. It requires a fully distributed decision concept and protocols for managing traffic flows within the ad-hoc network as well as service discovery mechanisms. Furthermore, one has to think about an incentive system for users that share their Internet access with others.

Although these alternative communication scenarios are out of the scope in this place, they should still be supported by our ABC framework. However, the management of cooperative decisions or the exchange of information between the different components opens up further research questions that need to be addressed in future research work. For the remainder of this work, we concentrate on the target scenarios shown in figure 2.2.

2.3   Always Best Connected

Today, a user has to choose the network he wants to use manually by proactively plugging a cable into his device or connecting to a wireless network. If the user moves, the network connection may break down and he has to choose a new network by himself. Meanwhile, the data connections of the applications on the mobile device will break down as well and have to be recovered after the reconnection. The continuity of communication sessions is typically not ensured, as the device may get a different IP address when accessing the new network. There are only few examples for products that provide at least a limited functionality of handovers between different access networks. These are, for instance, the Apple iPhone [8] or Swisscom Mobile Unlimited [35]. However, these solutions are often restricted to specific network technologies like GSM/UMTS and WLAN or require some support by the network provider.

2.3.1   Reference Model

To overcome these deficiencies, Gustafsson and Jonsson introduced the concept of "Always Best Connected" (ABC) [1]. The term is defined as "[...] to being not only always connected, but also being connected in the best possible way [...]". It refers to a paradigm for mobile networking with efficient usage of network capacity beyond the existing limits between different communication technologies. The aim of the ABC concept is to provide always the best quality of service (QoS) to the user by exploiting the network heterogeneity and switching between network technologies. However, there are different notions on what the "best" network actually is. For instance, this depends on the interests of different players in the communications ecosystem that are illustrated in figure 2.5.

First, the users typically want to have the best service at the lowest costs. The user's satisfaction with a service depends on a variety of parameters [36]. Foremost, it relies on the expected and experienced behavior of the applications that are used. Second, network

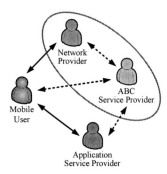

Figure 2.5: ABC players

providers have their own interests. They want to use their networks as efficient as possible and aim at reducing their operational costs. Today, several providers offer Internet access via different access technologies to their customers. To give an example, in Germany Deutsche Telekom operates a GSM and UMTS network as well as WLAN hotspots. Thus, if we assume that transferring data via the UMTS network is more expensive to the provider than using a WLAN hotspot, he may benefit from an ABC strategy that switches to WLAN networks whenever possible. On the one hand, ABC services might be offered directly by a network operator, but there may also be a separate ABC service provider as a third player in our ecosystem. It may manage the selection of networks independent of the access networks being used and may offer additional services like content adaptation. Such a concept provides a higher flexibility to the user as he is not bound to the access networks of one specific network provider. Finally, the last players in our ecosystem are service providers that offer differentiated services to the user or provide content adaptation services. Thus, if a user is connected via multiple and frequently changing access networks, the service provider may offer to adapt the delivered content directly to the capabilities of the available networks, to achieve a high Quality of User Experience.

The idea of ABC turns away from the existing vertical integration concept for heterogeneous networks and states a horizontal integration as it is shown in figure 2.6. One important issue in this concept is the abstraction of network management and network selection from the user and the application. First and foremost, a user just wants to use a specific application and expects it to work properly. If this application requires Internet access, the network should provide sufficient QoS characteristics to meet the application requirements, even if the user moves with his device and communication characteristics change over time. This transparency of the network access is an essential part of the ABC concept. The user

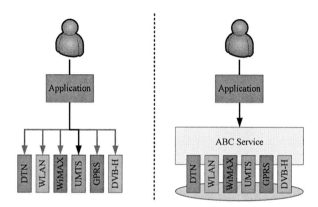

Figure 2.6: Vertical vs. horizontal integration of networks

itself has no longer to deal with questions on which network to use. Instead, the ABC service aims at maximizing the Quality of User Experience (QoE) by selecting those networks that provide sufficient performance and, for instance, minimize the user's costs at the same time.

The implementation of such an ABC service requires several components that provide the required functionalities for managing the different networks and for deciding on which ones to use. In the following, we will introduce these functional components.

2.3.2 Functional Components

Gustafsson and Jonsson identified a set of seven general modules that are required for implementing an ABC service. Following, we give an overview of these modules, that are illustrated in figure 2.7, and describe their functionalities.

Network Monitoring

To be able to decide on how to access the Internet, one requires information about the available networks and their communication characteristics. Service level agreements and costs with respect to certain providers might be of interest as well. The task of the *Network Monitoring* component is to collect this information for different networks and to provide an information pool for the decision process. The challenges in this context are twofold. First, different networking technologies have often very different characteristics and offer heterogeneous interfaces and metrics to describe the network performance. Thus, one has to find a

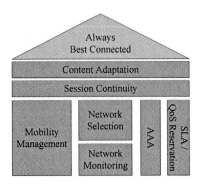

Figure 2.7: Functional elements of ABC services according to Gustafsson and Jonsson [1]

concept that allows for making the different networks comparable on a common basis. This approach appears to be almost straightforward for typical parameters like throughput, delay or packet loss. But, differences in, for instance, the networks' up- and downlink characteristics or in whether the medium access mechanisms allow for a concurrent or guaranteed use of the networks make the modeling of suitable parameters complex. Moreover, one has to consider cross-layer effects. To give an example, the notion of the available bandwidth depends strongly on the protocol layer where the measurement is done. The second challenge is to develop mechanisms that allow for measuring the required parameters without causing high overheads in terms of data traffic.

Network Selection

The core element of an ABC service is the network selection algorithm. In general, it operates on a set of objectives it has to adhere to and decides on which network to use. For this, it uses the parameters that are provided by the *Network Monitoring* module. Basically, the decision can be made either at the *mobile device* or in the *network*. The former case is a more user-centric approach where the mobile device can select networks independently and on the basis of its local requirements. This way, the user has a higher flexibility in which service provider and network technology to use. Moreover, decisions are optimized on the user's personal requirements. The latter option is a rather provider-centric approach, where the network provider may advise mobile devices to use a specific network. From the provider's perspective such mechanisms are well suited to increase the efficiency of network usage in terms of operating costs as well as for providing differentiated services to the users. If a network is used to its full capacity, users with lower service levels might be hand over to another network or get completely disconnected from the network. Thus, it is possible to guarantee users with higher service levels a specific service quality. In addition, providers that operate multiple access networks as, for instance, GSM, UMTS and WLAN hotspots, will typically have different costs for providing Internet access to customers via each of these technologies. Thus, mobile devices that require Internet access at a certain location may be distributed across these networks to maximize the provider's network utilization and minimizing its costs at the same time. From the user's perspective, the major disadvantage of a provider-centric approach is that it neglects the specific needs of him and those of the applications he is running. Of course, there are also hybrid approaches where device-centric and network-centric selection mechanisms cooperatively select the networks to be used [37]. Here, the advantage is that the network selection may consider the interests of both players. However, such a solution is again limited to specific providers that support this mechanism or it requires standardized mechanisms for the negotiation of access networks.

However, the location where decisions are being made is only one differentiating factor between existing implementations of network selection mechanisms. Another aspect is the granularity of handling application requirements. One option is that the network selection module releases one decision that holds for all applications running on the device. Thus, all applications have to use the selected network for communication. Such a method is easy to implement, but features no differentiation between individual application requirements. Moreover, it brings no real advantages of utilizing the communication capabilities in heterogeneous communication environments. Alternatively, the algorithm may separate between specific classes as, for instance, real-time and non-real-time applications. This approach brings improvements, but the assignment of applications to specific classes requires again certain concessions with respect to the actual requirements of certain applications and the individual importance of specific parameters to them. Finally, the third option that provides the highest granularity is to make individual decisions for each application. This is the most flexible one in modeling and matching application requirements and might meet the requirements for our scenario best. However, this comes at the costs of a higher complexity in handling the different requirements and managing applications-flows separately from each other.

A major challenge in designing an algorithm for network selection is to find a flexible and modular decision concept that is able to handle highly heterogeneous objectives and decision parameters. Additionally, one needs a suitable approach to find reasonable tradeoffs between conflictive decision objectives. It must be possible to parameterize the algorithm to the needs of any application. Another important issue is that the approach should be independent of specific characteristics of any networking technologies to be able to support as many access networks as possible. Finally, one has to deal with the problem of applications that use the same network concurrently and thus may interfere with each other in competing for the available resources.

Mobility Management and Session Continuity

Although our overview in figure 2.7 lists mobility management and session continuity as two separate blocks, we discuss them here together as both components have a strong functional correlation. The mobility management has to put the decisions of the network selection module into action. In general, two aspects of mobility management can be distinguished. First, an ABC service depends on path management functionalities that enable handovers between different network technologies. The second aspect is the location management for addressing mobile device from the Internet. Especially in dynamic communication scenarios with higher mobility, a mobile device may need to change access networks frequently. However, basic handover functionality is not enough to meet the aforementioned target of a transparent horizontal integration of access networks. The ABC service has to provide session continuity to avoid the break of active communication sessions. A second aspect in this context is the tolerance to times of networks disruptions. It can be expected that there will be times where the mobile device has no access to any network or where the available communication capacity is not sufficient to serve all applications that request for network resources. In such scenarios, disruption tolerance is an important feature to bridge these time gaps [7]. Depending on the requirements, it is possible to implement the aforementioned aspects at different layers of the ISO/OSI protocol stack.

Authentication, Authorization and Accounting (AAA)

In some cases, a user has to authenticate before it gains access to a network. Even today users often have multiple subscriptions to, for instance, operators of different WLAN hotspots. To manage these different subscriptions, the ABC service needs an AAA component. This component might either be implemented in an isolated module or as an integrated AAA framework. In the former case, the mobile device handles the subscriptions to multiple operators locally. The second option requires a standardized mechanism which is supported by the different operators and relies on roaming agreements between them.

Content Adaptation

An ABC service may have additional possibilities to adapt the application content to changing communication characteristics. This can be useful in either saving network resources or in increasing the Quality of User Experience. One example for this is the adaptation of a video stream that is sent to the mobile device, but features a higher resolution than actually can be displayed there. Thus, the video might be adapted to the capabilities of the mobile device using transcoding techniques [38]. Such a mechanism may also be useful in scenarios where it is not possible to serve all requests of the applications. It can help to avoid that communication would either be not possible or that the user would be dissatisfied with the service. An ABC service may provide mechanisms to adapt to challenging network characteristics dynamically by, for instance, reducing the amount of data to be transferred. In this case, the user may experience a worse quality of the video stream in situations where resources are limited, but the application itself will work as intended.

End-to-End QoS guarantees

Finally, another aspect that raises up in the context of ABC relates to end-to-end QoS guarantees. Such challenges are a severe problem for ABC services. The nature of wireless networks that feature fluctuating characteristics paired with the ability to switch between different networks and providers make the maintenance of QoS reservations in the network highly difficult and will typically require support by infrastructure components in the network.

2.3.3 Summary

The reference concept of ABC provides a framework including various services and mechanisms that are needed to make the network "invisible" to the users. Some of these components like the mobility management and the network selection mechanism are essential parts of this framework, while others may provide subsidiary services that can be used to further improve the experienced QoS. As we already mentioned in the introduction, we will not be able to address all of the aforementioned aspects within this work. Instead, we concentrate on the design of a suitable network selection process and the transparent mobility management functionalities. As an aside, we also briefly touch on a concept for network monitoring and for integrating disruption tolerance. In the following, we present related work on the mobility management issues and on existing approaches for implementing the network selection process. Afterwards, we will discuss several related frameworks for integrating heterogeneous networks.

2.4 Mobility Management

In our target scenario, a mobile device will experience frequent changes of the availability and of the characteristics of access networks. To be still able to provide an always best connected Internet access, one requires functionalities to manage these changes and to enforce any decisions being made by the access selection module. In the context of our objectives stated in section 1.1, we have to address three major issues:

▶ First, we need a vertical handover mechanism that allows for handing the connection of an application over to a different network without interrupting the service.

▶ Second, we aim at using multiple networks concurrently for the data transfer of an application. Thus, we must provide a suitable approach that schedules the data traffic efficiently onto the bundled links.

▶ Finally, we want to make use of a proactive deferment of application requests in our ABC decision concept. Therefore, it must be possible to integrate protocols that handle these times of disruption with respect to the application.

Today, Internet protocols do not feature these functionalities. Initially, they were not designed with mobility issues in mind. Nevertheless, there is already some related research work in this area.

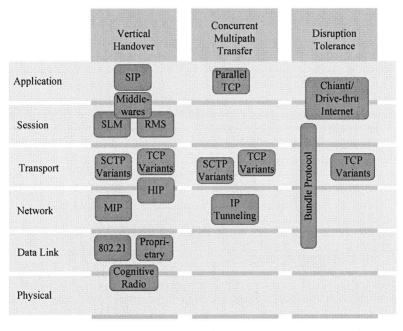

Figure 2.8: Overview on related work at different ISO/OSI layers

All of the aforementioned aspects can be implemented at different layers of the ISO/OSI protocol stack. Figure 2.8 gives a generalized overview on approaches that can be found in the literature for either of the three issues we have to deal with. In the following, we will present some exemplary approaches and discuss the advantages and disadvantages of implementing the required functionalities at each of the layers.

2.4.1 Vertical Handover

A handover is the transition of a network connection from one access network or cell to another one. If the networks that are involved in the handover process use the same technologies and probably even belong to the same administrative domain, the handover is named horizontal. However, in the context of our target scenario, we have to be able to manage vertical handovers between different communications systems. Here, we may further distinguish three different scenarios:

▶ handovers between networks with similar capacity,

▶ handovers from a low capacity network to a high capacity network, and

▶ handovers from a high capacity network to a low capacity network.

The former two scenarios are less problematic. In the first case, upper layer protocols may only experience a very short disruption at the time the handover is executed. Similarly, when switching from a low capacity network like UMTS to a high capacity network like WLAN more bandwidth becomes available and upper layer protocols may gradually converge to the new limit. The third scenario results in a drop of the available bandwidth that poses challenges to, for instance, congestion control mechanisms and will typically result in performance degradations. For our approach, the handover should not lead to a service interruption for the user or the application. Thus, it has to be executed in a seamless way. The interpretation of what seamlessness means to an application is highly dependent on the actual service. While some applications as, for instance, e-mail are highly disruption tolerant in general, other ones like video conferencing may tolerate only very short times of disruptions. Another important requirement for a vertical handover mechanism in the context of our work is the ability to perform handovers for individual applications. As each application may have its own specific requirements, it must be possible to manage all application connections separately from each other. In related work, multiple approaches for vertical handovers have already been proposed. Following, we present some exemplary proposals ordered by the ISO/OSI layer they belong to.

Application Layer

Schulzrinne and Wedlund propose an application-layer concept on the basis of SIP [39] to manage the mobility of mobile devices [40]. They pointed out that their approach is well-suited for streaming or conferencing applications, but requires transport layer support for implementing seamless handovers for TCP or SCTP-based applications. Zhang et al. provide enhancements to this approach that aim at overcoming the problem of very long handover delays [41]. Here, streaming applications are focused as well. Thus, for the largest part of Internet applications SIP might be used to implement location management of multihomed devices, but has to be combined with additional handover mechanisms at other protocol layers. Both aforementioned approaches describe only concepts for managing the mobility of the device, but not the mobility of individual applications. In fact, this is another disadvantage, as for an application-oriented handover management one has to integrate the mechanisms directly into existing applications or application protocols. Thus, the functionality is less transparent to them. On the other hand, it might be possible to optimize the handover mechanisms to the needs of certain applications.

Session Layer

At the session layer one can find examples for vertical handover mechanisms as well. Langenfeld et al. propose SLM, a mobility management framework that makes use of TCP [42]. To execute a handover, SLM switches the application data stream from one TCP connection to another one. The concept might be combined with transport protocol enhancements that provide a higher performance in wireless networks. Kristiansson and Parnes propose another approach based on Resilient Mobile Sockets (RMS) [43]. Here, the RMS encapsulates multiple UDP sockets and manages handovers between them. In addition, one can find also proposals for approaches that introduce novel middlewares with specific APIs [44]. The major advantage of a session layer approach is its relative low implementation complexity. Basically, it has to manage multiple transport layer associations and might be combined with any transport protocol. However, in today's Internet protocols stack, there is typically no session layer protocol. Thus, implementing the handover functionalities at the session layer may require changes of the network API and thus modifications of applications that want to use network services.

Transport Layer

Most work focuses on extensions of either the Transmission Control Protocol (TCP) or the Stream Control Transmission Protocol (SCTP). Obviously, the reason to use TCP is its dominance in the Internet. In [45], Maltz et al. propose MSOCKS that uses a Performance Enhancing Proxy [46] in the Internet to split the connection between the mobile device and the correspondent node. For a handover, the mobile device closes its connection to the proxy first and reestablishes it via the new access network. The connection between proxy and correspondent node is not affected by the handover process. Similar approaches are used for I-TCP [47] or M-TCP [48]. Migrate TCP [49] uses tokens that are associated with certain connections. Thus, when the mobile node closes and reestablishes the connection, the token can be used to migrate the old connection to the new one.

In contrast to TCP, SCTP comes with the advantage that it provides an inherent support of multihoming. Thus, it allows for implementing smooth handovers. Mobile SCTP [50] makes use of an SCTP extension to change the IP addresses that are bound to the communication association between both peers. Thus, the handover is executed by switching the addresses that are actively used for communication. The same approach is used by TraSH/Sigma [51, 52]. Cellular SCTP [53] provides performance enhancements for mSCTP.

Like the aforementioned approaches, transport-layer solutions can be used to implement application-oriented handovers. They do not require the support of any infrastructure components for executing handovers, but rely on the support of external services for location management. Another advantage is that changes of applications or lower layer protocols are not necessary. Nevertheless, not all applications may use the specific transport protocol that is extended with handover mechanisms. In this case one might use a wrapper application or a Performance Enhancing Proxy to extend the application with handover functionalities.

Host Identity Protocol

The Host Identity Protocol (HIP) introduces a new layer that resides between the transport and the network layer [54, 55]. It is based on the approach of separating the location of a device in the network from its identity. For this, HIP introduce, so called, Host Identities that are independent of the device's IP addresses. Now, upper layer protocols may use these Host Identities for addressing other peers in the network. The mapping of host identities to IP addresses is done dynamically by HIP. The advantage of this approach is that it does not require any changes at the network layer protocol mechanisms. However, for the introduction of Host Identities, upper layer protocols may have to be changed. Moreover, HIP comes with an additional overhead, as it needs a separate packet header.

Network Layer

The most prominent approach to handle mobility at the network layer is MobileIP [56, 57]. The implementation of MobileIP requires additional infrastructure support in the network. First, a so-called Home Agent has to be placed in the home network of the mobile device. Each mobile device requires a dedicated global IP address in its home network. If the device moves to a foreign network, it will receive an additional care-of-address (COA) there. Afterwards, it registers the COA at its Home Agent. Depending on whether the COA is co-located or not, MobileIP requires an additional Foreign Agent (FA) in the foreign network that forwards packets to the mobile device. Now, whenever a correspondent node sends packets to the home address of the mobile device, the Home Agent will intercept these packets and tunnel them to the registered COA. Thus, the mobile device remains always reachable via its home address. However, up to now MobileIP has not become a success in the Internet. This relates to its main drawbacks that are the required infrastructure components and the high protocol overhead due to tunneling and triangular routing. One example for an architecture that uses MobileIP for vertical handovers between WLAN and GPRS is OmniCom [58]. This approach proposes to implement a special FA for the use of the GRPS network. This FA has to be located outside of the provider's GPRS network, as the authors do not expect MobileIP to be supported by network providers. Furthermore, it assumes that the mobile device will not obtain a public IP address in the GPRS networks due to the use of Network Address Translation (NAT). Thus, OmniCon uses an IP-over-TCP tunnel instead of pure IP encapsulation. The NEMO project [59] deals with the development of a mobile router for heterogeneous communication environments. Here, the handover is based on MobileIPv6 that is extended with NEMO Basic Support [60] as it has been standardized by the IETF. A different network-layer approach is proposed by Chen et al. in [61]. The so-called Universal Seamless Handover Architecture (USHA) works with the help of virtual IP tunnels. It requires a Handover Server in the Internet that acts as tunnel endpoint for the mobile device. If a handover is triggered, the mobile device switches the network interfaces of the tunnel endpoint. Bechler et al. propose a similar approach that implements seamless handover on the basis of IP-in-IP tunneling [62].

Network layer approaches come with the advantage that they are implemented at the waist of the protocol stack and thus have the highest impact in supporting the variety of existing upper and lower layer protocols. However, they require changes in the network infrastructure and may result in suboptimal routing of data, as the initial concept of the Internet was not designed for mobility.

Sub-Network Layer

Finally, there are multiple approaches for implementing vertical handovers below the network layer. They can be basically categorized into two groups. On the one hand, there are proposals that describe handover procedures between two dedicated technologies. Examples for these handover approaches can be found for WLAN and UMTS [63, 64], WLAN and CDMA [65] as well as WLAN and WiMAX [66] among others. In general, they come up with proprietary modifications of the signaling protocols to allow for session transfers and fast registration to the new network.

On the other hand, there are standardization efforts by the IEEE as well as the 3GPP. The IEEE proposes a standard for Media Independent Handover Services [67] that has been named IEEE 802.21. It is intended to support all kinds of IEEE 802 networks as well as 3G networks. Moreover, there is also work on integrating broadcast networks. The core of the IEEE 802.21 reference model is a Media Independent Handover Function (MIHF) between the network layer and the data link layer. The MIHF provides a well-defined interface to the upper layer protocols and hides the technology specific handover mechanisms from them.

In addition, it provides functions to trigger handover events and offers information about the characteristics of available networks. Thus, in general IEEE 802.21 does not initiate handovers by itself. Instead, it provides only the necessary functionality to assist decisions that were made at higher layers. The main drawbacks of IEEE 802.21 are that the implementation of the service still requires extensions to the link layer standards and implementations to integrate new service access points that provide the required functionality for IEEE 802.21. In addition, it still depends on upper layer mobility management functionalities to ensure the continuity of application sessions. A comparable approach to IEEE 802.21 was also standardized by the 3rd Generation Partnership Project (3GPP) and is called Generic Access Network (GAN) or Unlicensed Mobile Access (UMA) [68]. GAN is implemented in several of today's mobile phones [69]. It requires the network operator to install a centralized GAN controller into its core network that manages roaming services between the cellular network and other communication technologies. For this, the mobile device has to establish an IPsec tunnel to the GAN controller if it connects to, for instance, a WLAN network. Again, GAN provides only the pure handover functionality. Thus, it requires additional protocols to support service continuity. In addition, it needs to be supported by the user's provider.

Finally, there are also approaches based on cognitive radios [70]. Here, handovers are managed within the radio itself by switching between different frequencies. These approaches require special hardware and are not able to handle data flows in an application-oriented way.

Summary

Actually, a large variety of solutions for vertical handovers is available. Approaches that are implemented *below* the transport layer have several problems with respect to our target scenario. First, they do not support an application-oriented management of handovers without any cross-layer support. Second, they require considerable changes in the existing Internet architecture in terms of additional infrastructure components and modifications of intermediate systems. Third, for a seamless transition between two networks, those approaches require additional support by upper layer protocols to handle packet losses and changes in the characteristics of the end-to-end path. Sub-network layer approaches are even often designed to support only a certain combination of networks. Also here, there is an inevitable need for further protocol modifications at upper layers.

Proposal for handover mechanisms *above* the network layer come with the advantage that they leave the existing structure of the Internet untouched. Changes are only necessary at the communicating peers, which eases the integration of the mechanisms. Most approaches that are located at either the application or the session layer require modifications of the applications. For application layer approaches, one has to implement the actual handover mechanism in the applications. This deficiency is avoided by session-layer approaches. But, as the session layer is not used in today's Internet applications as an explicit layer, there will be the need for API modifications. Finally, there is the option to implement handover mechanisms at the transport layer. This option shares the same advantages as the previous ones. It does not need any support of the Internet infrastructure and is able to handle handovers in an application-oriented way. Moreover, there is no need for protocol modification at other layers and intermediate systems to provide seamless handovers. Basically, there are only two drawbacks. One the one hand, there are multiple transport protocols being used in the Internet. Thus, changes of multiple protocols may be necessary to make all applications handover capable. The second limitation relates to an aspect that has been neglected so far in this discussion. A transport layer approach has to rely on external location management services for a multihomed device. However, there are multiple approaches that address this issue [50]. We will not discuss any of them here, as our primary interest is on the basic handover functionality. Thus, in the end, the transport layer solution appears to be the best option. Especially SCTP provides a good basis for integration these mechanisms, as it comes with multihoming support that is missing in TCP. But, even existing proposals in the literature generally lack on sustainable performance evaluations on the network characteristics that are experience by applications during and after a handover event.

2.4.2 Concurrent Multipath Transfer

Concurrent Multipath Transfer (CMT) enables the parallel use of multiple, potentially independent, paths through the network to achieve a higher throughput. In heterogeneous scenarios, the major challenge of this approach is the design of a scheduling and data delivery strategy that copes well with high path asymmetries and reduces the reordering of delivered data packets at the receiving peer. In the literature, one can find different approaches for realizing CMT functionalities either on the application, the transport or the network layer.

Application Layer

Application layer approaches for multipath transfer use, for instance, parallel TCP connections and distribute the data along these connections. The mechanisms presented by Hacker et al. [71] and Sivakumar et al. [72] are mainly designed for high speed networks and try to overcome performance issues with TCP in such scenarios. Thus, they do not share data between independent communication paths with different communication characteristics. Instead, all connections are established over the same path. In general, any application layer multipath solution has several disadvantages. One major issue is that it puts the task of scheduling data appropriately along the bundled paths to the applications. Thus, the applications have to be modified and their complexity increases as they have to monitor the different paths and need to take care of data reordering by their own. An alternative approach might be to source the required functionalities out into a middleware that hides these tasks from the actual application. Nevertheless, even this would come with additional overhead and complexity. Moreover, it still requires some modifications of applications to integrate the support of this middleware.

Transport Layer

Much work deals with the implementation of concurrent multipath transfer at the transport layer. The reason for this is that the transport layer already provides several metrics and functionalities that are needed for striping data efficiently across the bundled paths. The approaches that can be found in the literature do again mainly rely on modifications of TCP and SCTP. Hsieh and Raghupathy propose a mechanism called parallel TCP (pTCP) [73]. It uses several "virtual" TCP connections between sender and receiver that are used to aggregate bandwidth. A so-called Striped Connection Manager handles these connections and allocates data to them based on the ratio of congestion window (cwnd) size and round-trip time (RTT). However, the authors do not discuss the effects of reordering at the receiver. Furthermore, the evaluation assumes equal RTTs for the bundled paths. In addition, potential path failures are another aspect that has not been addressed in this work. An alternative TCP-based approach is mTCP [74] that tries to overcome some of the problems with pTCP. It introduces mechanisms for path recovery and the detection of shared bottlenecks. The scheduling of data packets is done with the help of a score function that determines the ratio of outstanding packets to be sent and the size of the congestion window of each single path. Based on this, mTCP chooses always the path with the lowest score at the moment for data transfer. One clear disadvantage of mTCP is that it requires the use of Resilient Overlay Networks (RON) [75] to set up multiple paths between source and destination. In addition, data acknowledgements are always sent along one primary path. This makes the detection of path failures along this path complex and reduces the failover performance.

A general disadvantage of all TCP-based approaches is TCP's lack of multihoming support. Thus, there is always the need for substantial changes in the protocol implementation at both, the sending and the receiving peer. Thus, a lot of work deals with extending SCTP with CMT capabilities, as SCTP meets several fundamental requirements any CMT techniques are in need of. In particular, its multihoming support allows for binding several source and destination addresses to one joint transport layer association. Thus, fewer changes to the standard protocol are needed. Iyengar et al. propose an SCTP-based CMT algorithm that aims to reduce reordering at the receiver [76, 77]. For this, it schedules data packets to a path as soon as there is capacity available in the congestion window. If more than one option is possible, the path is chosen arbitrarily. In general, the full congestion window of a path is used before the scheduler switches to another path. In their work, the authors compare different retransmission strategies for CMT with the result that strategies taking packet losses along paths into account perform better than those that do not consider them. Another mechanism that is presented by Argyriou and Madisetti [78] also spreads packets along the paths on the basis of the sizes of their congestion windows. They enhance this concept with a shared detection of network bottlenecks. However, the description of the mechanism is quite vague and the evaluation assumes that both paths have the same bandwidth-delay products. IPCC-SCTP [79] uses a congestion-window driven scheduler and introduces per-path congestion control. The sender maintains a mapping of which packets are sent along which paths. But, the approach requires a very large receiver window to deal with reordering at the receiver. Finally, LS-SCTP implements multipath transfer by using per-path congestion control and explicit path sequence numbers that are included in each chunk [80]. Data is assigned to the paths according to the ratio of the size of their congestion window and the measured RTT. A clear disadvantage of this approach is the need for modifications of the SCTP packet format. Perotto et al. introduce approaches called Sender-Based Packet Pair (SBPP) and Westwood SCTP [81]. Both variants use a Faster-Path-First scheduling approach for assigning packets to different paths. Thus, they determine the estimated reception time of a new data packet and schedule it along the path with the lowest value. SBPP-SCPT and W-SCTP differ in the way how they estimate the path's bandwidth. The former mechanism uses pairs of heartbeat packets sent every 30 seconds on each path to probe the bandwidth. The latter mechanism employs the bandwidth estimation technique used in TCP Westwood+ [82]. Both proposals neglect any differences in the propagation delays between sender and receiver. Fiore et al. use the same concept and applied it to real-time applications with the help of SCTP's partial reliability feature [83, 84]. However, the approach they present focuses only on scenarios where no full reliability of the data transfer is required and outdated information becomes useless for the receiver.

Network Layer

In the end, there are also some approaches to realize multipath transfer at the network layer. Phatak and Goff use IP-in-IP tunneling together with additional IP and/or TCP modifications [85]. Here, the share of data that is sent along one path depends on its share on the total bandwidth being available at the moment. The actual scheduling is done probabilistically keeping the determined share in mind. To do this, the scheduler adapts the size of packets sent on each particular path. However, this approach comes with additional overhead for the IP-in-IP tunneling and needs dedicated support by the network infrastructure. Moreover, the proposal assumes that the end-to-end delays are dominated by constant transmission times, which is not always given in the context of our target scenario.

Summary

In general, the presented approaches for CMT are not designed to cope well in heterogeneous communication scenarios. Almost all of them rely on certain assumptions or limitations that are not met in our target scenario. To give an example, they simplify network characteristics or assume unlimited buffer sizes at the receiver. Most mechanisms only consider the size of the congestion window or the bandwidth for their scheduling decisions, but neglect parameters especially like the propagation delay. In addition, packet losses are often ignored. Therefore, the approaches can be expected to perform less efficient in real scenarios, where bandwidth and delay characteristic of the paths differ. Our review on related CMT approaches impels us to the final conclusion that, as in our discussion on vertical handover mechanisms, a transport layer approach turns out to be the most suitable option for the same reasons. Moreover, a combined implementation of handover and CMT mechanism in one application reduces the number of changes at the communication peers and thus eases the integration of both functionalities.

2.4.3 Disruption Tolerance

Today's transport and application-layer protocols are mainly designed with the assumption that there is a permanent end-to-end connection between the communicating peers for the time of the communication session. However, in mobile scenarios this assumption is no longer true, as there are several situations where the mobile device will have no access to any network. Furthermore, it may not always be possible to serve all applications with the requested resources, due to limitations of the available network resources. In related work, one can find some approaches that address the issue of improving the performance of existing protocols with respect to disruption tolerance. In the following, we give an overview of some prominent proposals.

Application / Session Layer

First, there is work on implementing disruption tolerance at the session layer. One example is the Drive-thru Internet architecture that provides persistent connections for TCP in scenarios with challenging and intermittent connectivity [7, 86]. The research on Drive-thru Internet proceeds within the Chianti project [87]. Here, the objective is to design a system architecture for robust mobile Internet access with a focus on providing disruption tolerant services. Both approaches are based on the idea of having two dedicated proxies, one at the mobile client and one in the Internet or at the receiving peer. Thus, applications or the correspondent node may run standard Internet protocols, while an optimized protocol is used between the proxies. Additionally, they work on application-layer protocol optimizations to make applications more robust against network disruptions.

Transport Layer

Moreover, there are multiple approaches for integrating disruption tolerance at the transport layer. Several of them aim at improving the performance of TCP. The problem with TCP is that its congestion control mechanisms assume missing packets to be lost by congestion in the network. Thus, TCP reduces its sending rate and tries to retransmit the missing packet in exponentially increasing intervals up to at least 60 s [88]. One exemplary approach that aims at overcoming these shortcomings is Freeze-TCP [89]. Here, the receiving peer notifies the sending one if it expects an imminent disconnection and forces the sender into zero window probing mode [90]. Thus, it keeps the last state of the congestion window. M-TCP [91] proposes an approach where a performance enhancing proxy is used to split the connection in to two parts. Thus, one can use an optimized wireless transport protocol for the wireless link, while standard TCP is used through the Internet to the corresponding node. MCTP combines these approaches with further optimizations for Internet access via Vehicular Ad-hoc Networks (VANETs) [92]. We were able to show that such an approach gains a significant increase in terms of throughput in a highway scenario where Internet access is provided occasionally by WLAN hotspots along the road.

Bundle Protocol

Finally, there are also approaches for completely new protocols. Especially the Bundle Protocol [93] that has already been standardized by the IETF has gained increasing importance for delay and disruption tolerant communications in the past years. The protocol defines so-called bundles that are messages with portions of user data. Those bundles are routed independently from each other to their destination and might be cached at intermediate nodes. Thus, mobile nodes may carry bundles with them in order to bring them closer to their destination. One particular advantage of the Bundle Protocol is that it does not have to be implemented at one specific layer to make the network stack disruption tolerant. It might be used at the session layer as well as at the network layer. In the latter case, the Bundle Protocol can be used in combination with IP or is even able to replace it.

Summary

The overview on different approaches for supporting delay tolerance shows, that transport layer approaches have been researched well in the past and might be used in our target scenario. However, session and application layer approaches provide new interesting concepts as they are able to bring higher opportunities in using the characteristics of delay tolerant applications. A problem with most of today's applications is that they were not designed to cope with disruptions well, although they might be disruption tolerant in general. Thus, additional application protocol modifications are needed. But, such aspects go beyond the scope of this work.

2.4.4 Discussion

In the previous section we presented approaches for mobility management issues across the network protocol stack. Of course, our overview is not exhaustive and describes only several prominent examples. Actually, various work deals with the question of which layer is best suited to implement mobility management functionalities [94–97]. A general difference between approaches at the different layers is the level of abstraction from existing protocols and the granularity of managing data flows. Further differentiating factors relate to the possibilities of adapting protocol mechanisms to the dynamic networking characteristics in mobile and heterogeneous communication environments. Figure 2.9 illustrates these relationships.

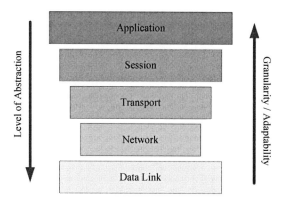

Figure 2.9: General characteristics of mobility management at different layers

Basically, the lower the layer where mobility management functionalities are integrated, the higher is the abstraction of these functionalities from existing protocols being used in the Internet. Thus, no or at least few changes are required especially in the applications. However, this comes often with a higher protocol and signaling overhead as well as with the need of additional infrastructure support in the network. The other way round, the higher mobility management is located in the protocol stack, the finer is the information on individual data flows, making it possible to adapt to the specific requirements of individual applications. One argument for implementing mobility functionalities at the network layer

	Application Orientation	Protocol Integration	Infrastructure Support	Transparency/ Seamlessness
Application	++	+	++	-
Session	++	o	+	++
Transport	++	+	++	++
Network	-	o	-	o
Sub-network	-	-	-	o

Table 2.1: Evaluation of mobility and path management approaches

is often the high importance IP gained in the past and the evolution to all-IP networks. Thus, the protocol stack may have a variety of protocols above and below the network layer, but IP is used to transfer any data via any network. This aspect is often referred to as hourglass model of the protocol stack and has been indicated in figure 2.9.

In table 2.1, we summarize the findings of our review on related work for mobility and path management issues. We evaluated approaches on different layers with respect to four metrics that have a high importance with respect to our overall objective:

▶ **Application Orientation**
First, the mechanisms need to be able to differentiate between single applications.

▶ **Protocol Integration**
Second, there should be as few changes to existing protocols and mechanisms as possible to ease the system's integration.

▶ **Infrastructure Support**
Third, the proposed approach should not rely on additional infrastructure that has to be provided by a network and service provider.

▶ **Transparency/Seamlessness**
Finally, the mechanisms should hide the effects of the mechanisms as good as possible from upper layer protocols and the applications.

An application-oriented mobility management at the *network layer* will require additional cross-layer support to be able to identify single data flows. Thus, this aspect is rated with '-'. As nearly all applications are IP-based, one might expect that the implementation at the network layer has the highest benefit with respect to supporting a variety of existing protocols without severe changes. But, there are strong drawbacks with respect to suboptimal routing, higher overhead, complexity as well as practical issues that prevented MobileIP from becoming largely deployed. Thus, in summary we decided on rating the protocol integration aspect with 'o'. Additionally, network layer approaches require additional infrastructure components that have to be deployed in the Internet and need to be supported by the home network as well as all networks the mobile node wants to visit. Finally, drastic changes of the network characteristics at lower layers will typically affect transport layer mechanisms and lead to performance degradation. Thus, network layer approaches receive an average rating with respect to transparency and seamlessness.

Sub-network layer solutions do often rely on specific procedures for certain configuration of networks to be considered. They share the same problems as network layer solutions, but feature an even higher dependence on support by upper layer protocols.

Application and session layer approaches have a high granularity, as they allow for handling the mobility of individual application services. These approaches overcome the limitations of network layer mechanisms as they keep the routing of the Internet traffic untouched and are independent of any additional infrastructure components. In addition, the implemented mechanisms might be tuned directly to the specific requirements of certain applications. Approaches at the application layer rely only on external location management services and require no further changes of other network protocols. Thus, protocol integration is rated with '+'. However, transparency and seamlessness are rated with '-', as they shift the full complexity of mobility management functionalities immediately into the applications. The session layer abstracts this complexity from the applications, but it is generally not used in the Internet today. Thus, there may still be the need to adapt applications and the way on how they access network services.

From our point of view, the most promising location to implement mobility management functionalities for an ABC service is the *transport layer*. It shares almost the same advantages with the session and application layer approaches, but provides a transparent interface to upper layer protocols. The inherent transport layer functionalities that are available in, for instance, TCP and SCTP provide already a good basis of information to make efficient use of the available network capabilities by controlling the flow of data. A further reason for a transport-layer integration approach is the fact that several proposed mechanisms at other layers would require transport layer enhancements as well. But, lower layer protocols at the network layer or the data link layer require no modifications at all if mobility management is realized at the transport layer. In general the use of SCTP might be preferred compared to TCP as it is already capable of handling multiple network layer addresses. Of course, this requires some kind of support for TCP-based applications that dominate the Internet today. Moreover, a transport-layer approach requires external services for location management.

2.5   Network Selection Strategies

A core element in ABC frameworks is the strategy for the selection of access networks. Several different approaches have been proposed for this task in previous work. The existing approaches differ significantly in the complexity and flexibility of the decision criterions being considered. The spectrum of possible solutions ranges from trivial approaches that always select the network with the best signal strength to highly complex selection strategies based on, for instance, policy-based architectures or fuzzy-controllers that use neural networks and learning techniques to adapt dynamically to changing environments and conditions. Thus, there is a wide range of possible methods that have been proposed to tackle the problem, each featuring individual strengths and weaknesses. Figure 2.10 shows five categories of network selection strategies that gain the highest importance in the literature.

Figure 2.10: Categorization of related work on dynamic network selection

In the following sections, we discuss the fundamental characteristics of these categories and present exemplary solutions to the problem of selecting the best network.

2.5.1   Trivial Strategies

The first category comprises very trivial strategies to decide on which network to use. Most of these solutions make only use of lower layer criterions. For instance, they simply use a measure for the radio signal quality like the Received Signal Strength Indication (RSSI) [58, 98–101]. Thereby, most of these approaches compare the signal strengths of several access networks directly and always select the one which has the highest signal strength at the time the decision is made. Other algorithms take additional hysteresis margins or thresholds into account for eliminating temporary fluctuations of the signal level and for avoiding ping-pong effects. The functioning of these approaches is comparable to a horizontal Power-Budget-Handover in GSM Networks [102], where the basestation initiates a handover if the received signal level of the current cell is lower than the signal level of a neighbored one plus a handover margin. The use of averaging windows or dwell timers [103–105] are further mechanisms aiming on the same objective [106]. Besides the received signal strength, additional metrics like the signal-to-noise interference or the error rate are used as well. Even though these mechanisms work well in horizontal handover scenarios, they generally perform worse in vertical ones, due to the different characteristics and coverage areas of each possible network technology.

Jong et al. propose the use of context information on the speed of a mobile device in a WLAN-CDMA handover scenario [107]. The goal is to reduce the number of unnecessary handovers. This way, the decision strategy is able to assess whether a handover is advantageous or not, by comparing a velocity threshold to the current speed of the mobile device. The threshold is determined on the basis of call dropping and call blocking probabilities. Basically, this means that mobile devices moving at higher speeds will be more likely to use the CDMA system, while slower nodes prefer the WLAN system.

Another decision strategy based on radio signal strengths (RSS) is presented by Zahran et al. [108]. Here, the authors propose the use of an application-based signal strength threshold (ASST) in order to map application requirements on a RSS value. Afterwards, this value is used to determine the remaining time the network will provide a QoS level which is sufficient for the application. The authors assume that the WLAN network is usually the preferred network due to the higher performance in terms of throughput and costs.

Finally, WiSE and AISLE propose SCTP-based approaches that make use of bandwidth estimation techniques to determine the possible throughputs for all available networks. They aim at maximizing the throughput of a mobile node, while still providing a high level fairness to other nodes using the same access network [109, 110].

In summary it can be said that these trivial strategies are very simple to implement as only very few values have to be compared to come to a decision. However, they suffer from various disadvantages when dealing with vertical handovers between networks that feature highly heterogeneous communication characteristics. Since neither information on the performance provided by the available networks nor information on the quality of service needed by the applications is considered in the decision process, it cannot be guaranteed that the application is still operating in a satisfactory manner after the handover. For example a video streaming application that requires a bandwidth of 2 Mbit/s may run well over an 802.11 WLAN link, but will have clear problems to transfer the same amount of data when handing the connection over to GPRS. Only the approach presented by Zahran et al. addresses this fact [108]. However, this algorithm assumes that there is always a preferred network and handovers are initiated between this one and another network. Moreover, in the case of leaving the preferred network, the algorithm does not ensure that the throughput provided by the new network is sufficient for the application.

Another problem of only using metrics from lower layers as a basis for the decision is that they are difficult to compare for networks using different communication technologies. Although, for instance, the radio signal strength measured in dbm is a valid metric for the availability of a specific network, it is not possible to compare the values that were obtained for different networks directly, since the systems being used operate with different receiver sensitivities and transmitting powers. The same argument holds for other potential criterions as well. Thus, although trivial approaches may be a reasonable option for managing handovers in homogenous environments, they do not meet the requirements of heterogeneous communication environments.

2.5.2 Class-based Approaches

The class-based decision strategies try to overcome the limitations of trivial approaches by defining a specific set of traffic or service classes. Each of these classes represents a different type of service that may be provided to the application. The concept relates to the mechanisms being used in UMTS [111]. Here, the specification defines four different traffic classes: conversational, streaming, interactive and background. The main difference between these classes is the delay sensitivity. The conversational class is supposed to be used for real-time conversations with very high requirements on delay and jitter. The streaming class provides services for applications like (real-time) video streaming. In this case, the delay requirements are not that hard compared to the conversational class, but delay and jitter must still be within acceptable limits. The interactive class is designed for applications like web browsing, where the traffic is manly characterized by a request-response pattern. Thus, delay variation is less important and data needs only to be delivered within a certain time. Finally, the background class offers best effort services without any delay guarantees.

Park et al. propose a vertical handover strategy based on the differentiation of real-time and non real-time traffic [65]. Each application is assigned to one of these two groups for controlling handovers between WLAN and CDMA systems. The decision is mainly focused on the delay sensitivity of the applications in each group. For real-time applications the goal is to minimize the handover delay, since they are supposed to be sensitive to increasing delays and especially jitter. In contrast, for non real-time services, a connection to the WLAN network is maintained as long as possible. The authors argue that for applications belonging to this class a high throughput is more important than low delays.

Another class-based approach for heterogeneous handovers between WLAN and CDMA 2000 is presented by Fan and Lu [112]. Here, three types of classes are distinguished. In addition to real-time and non-real-time services, they propose to handle applications with unknown service class separately. The decision criterions in this approach are the received signal strength as well as a QoS Matrix that includes common parameters like bandwidth, delay and error rate. Unfortunately, nothing is said about how the matrix is really determined. For each of the proposed classes, the handover process of an application is handled differently. For real-time applications the mobile device stays connected to a network as long as it provides sufficient performance to meet the QoS requirements. If the received signal strength falls below a predefined threshold and the candidate network may provide a higher QoS than the current network, the algorithm triggers a fast handover to the new network. For non-real-time applications, the authors propose to switch to a handover-pending state and to cache as much information as possible if the received signal strength falls below a given threshold. Afterwards, it waits for the time the cache can provide the application with data and rechecks the received signal strength again. If the signal strength drops further or the QoS level of the new network exceeds that of the old one, a handover is triggered. Otherwise, the mobile device will stay connected to the current network and repeats the process iteratively as long as a handover is executed or the signal strength increases and exceeds the threshold again. The intention of this mechanism is to reduce the number of unnecessary handovers. However, such an approach might not be applicable to all services in all scenarios. Finally, for applications with unknown service class, the mobile device switches to a handover pending status as well if the received signal strength falls below a certain threshold. In contrast to the previous case, the mobile device does not trigger the application to cache data, but reevaluates the signal strength after a certain time. Depending on whether the received signal strength drops further or increases again, a handover is executed or not.

Bejaoui and Nasser describe a scheme to distribute the available bandwidth of a mixed WLAN-UMTS scenario [65]. They propose to classify the importance of users and applications separately. Mobile users are rated with respect to the necessity of a handover. The highest priority is given to users that leave the coverage area of one WLAN access point and want to handover to a new WLAN access point. If no further resources are available at the candidate WLAN, those users will switch to the UMTS network. Intermediate priority is given to WLAN users that try to acquire additional resources from the network. Finally, the lowest priority is given to users being connected to the UMTS network that want to handover to the WLAN, since those handovers may only be desirable but not imperative. The type of service for the applications is classified according to the aforementioned scheme used in UMTS. Based on these three user classes and four application classes, the authors propose a resource allocation function (RAF) that defines the proportion of the bandwidth capacity for each specific combination of user and service class:

$$RAF_{i,k} = \frac{u_i}{a_k} \quad .$$

(2.1)

In this equation $u_i \in \{1,2,3\}$ describes the class of user i and $a_k \in \{1,2,3,4\}$ states the respective service class of the application. The handover strategy controls the number of users that are admitted to use the WLAN. In addition, the authors propose to prioritize the resource requests for mobile users in the same class having the same requirements for their application. This priority function depends on the remaining power level of their device, the security requirements of the application and received signal strengths of the networks.

In comparison to the trivial approaches, class-based strategies for network selection account for application and user requirements to a certain extent. The definition of different QoS levels makes it possible to pursue different strategies for choosing a suitable communication path for applications belonging to that specific level. Moreover, the implementation of class-based approaches is comparatively simple. Nevertheless, class-based decision strategies provide only a coarse-grained diversification of applications. Typically, only a limited number of classes and parameters are considered, as complex parameter sets would require a huge variety of classes. This means that class-based approaches do not scale well with the number of parameters to be considered and the number of levels to be distinguished. In addition, these approaches are less flexible since they cannot be easily extended and adapted. If the decision criterions change, it may be necessary to completely reorganize the structure of the preexisting service classes. Another drawback is that service level guarantees can hardly be assured in strongly heterogeneous environments since communication characteristics may change frequently. Thus it may be difficult to really meet the demands of all classes at any time.

2.5.3 Policy-based Approaches

Policy-based decision strategies enable a more precise definition of QoS requirements by using a set of rules that describes the desired system behavior. In the context of policy-based network management, a policy is defined by the IETF as a "set of rules to administer, manage and control access to network resources" [113]. Each rule of a policy set is made up of a set of conditions and a set of actions comparable to if-then-constructs [114]. Basically, a rule set may have many different shapes [115]. They can describe the system requirements at a very high level or even in a very detailed way. The complexity of rules may differ as well. Policy refinement techniques make it possible to transform high level policies into concrete configurations [116]. Therefore, the process of selecting the most suitable network for an application or device means iterating through the set of rules and evaluating which rules match the current input parameters.

The general architecture for policy based management developed by the IETF and the Distributed Management Task Force (DMTF) is shown in figure 2.11 [113, 117]. It is made up of four main components:

- ▶ a policy console,

- ▶ a policy repository,

► a policy decision point, and

► a policy enforcement point.

The policy console is the administrative interface that allows for the definition or change of policies and the management of the whole system. The policy repository stores all policy information including the rules as well as additional context information and data that may be needed to evaluate the policy rules. The policy decision point deduces conclusions from given policy conditions by evaluation the policy information stored in the repository. Finally, the policy enforcement point is responsible for putting the decisions into action.

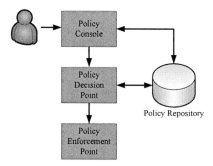

Figure 2.11: General model of a policy-based management system

Previous work discusses several examples on how to use policy-based architectures for network selection in heterogeneous environments. Murray et al. propose an approach for realizing call admission control and intersystem mobility with the help of policy-based management [118]. Here, the policy repository stores all necessary information on the current network characteristics as well as on user or QoS requirements. A full policy engine with the aforementioned components is needed in the network as well as at the mobile device. While the engine in the network cares about admission control, the actual network selection is performed at the mobile device. Both engines exchange information and make a common decision. Call admission control is realized with the help of a formula for determining the network health. For this, they use parameters like the video frame drop rate and the block error rate. The resulting factor is used to adapt the potential cell capacity. Moreover they propose a mix of voice, web and streaming services for each network that may be adapted by policy parameters. The network selection strategy uses three different types of policies: a handover selection policy, a return policy and an admission control policy. As the name suggests, the handover selection policy decides on whether the mobile device should use a different communication path. For this, parameters like the terminal capabilities, bandwidth requirements, session type, and user mobility are proposed. The task of the return policy is to decide on whether it might be advantageous to switch the communication path back to the previous network in case that the conditions are getting better again. Finally, the authentication policy should control the network authentication mechanisms and admission. However, the authors present only a vague concept on the actual realization of these policies. Moreover, there is no evaluation of the decision process analyzing the quality and performance of the approach.

Gutierrez and Milouchera present another approach for policy-based network selection developed from the European NETQOS project [119, 120]. Here, a hierarchical policy framework is proposed for selecting the most suitable access network. Thereby, policies of the user, the service provider and the network operator are distinguished. User policies describe the perceived QoS and costs desired by the user. Service providers may define preferences for access networks based on the application traffic. In addition, network operators are able to define policies for the scheduling of resources at the access routers. Besides, they mention bottom-up learning mechanisms for adapting high level policies of the service provider or network operator according to the user requirements. This approach aims on improving the system efficiency as well as adapting to the user's satisfaction. The proposed system architecture is comparable to that of the previous approach. It also comprises a central policy repository as well as a policy decision and policy enforcement points. The policies themselves are defined as if-then-else clauses. This framework is extended by Avallone et al. [121]. They introduce a context manager and an ontology repository to offer the possibility to describe policies and concepts with the help of ontologies. In contrast to the previous solution, the NETQOS approach focuses on an autonomous communication architecture where policies can be added or modified dynamically. Nevertheless, the published work presents only theoretical models and ideas, but few details on the realization. Moreover, they provide no evaluation of their decision strategy.

A further approach for policy-based network selection has been developed in the context of the FOCALE project [122]. Strassner et al. describe the use of autonomic networking techniques for implementing seamless mobility in heterogeneous networks. The FOCALE architecture is based on a closed loop control system. The system goals and the desired behavior are defined with the help of state machines on the basis of key performance and quality indicators. Multiple control loops are used to ensure that these goals are met and to adapt policies according to changes of the system context. Ontologies and data model on the basis of DEN-ng [117] are used to model knowledge, user expectations and network configurations. This way, decisions are mapped on handover commands and configurations for network interfaces. The central element of the FOCALE architecture is the Autonomic Manager that analyzes information on the network status und communication characteristics that has been collected. It decides on whether any actions have to be taken. Moreover, the authors propose the use of machine learning and reasoning techniques to adapt to user preferences and expectations as well as for balancing policies. In contrast to other policy-based approaches the FOCALE architecture does not deal with static policies, but is able to adapt its operation mode depending on the current context. The policies themselves are determined according to predefined business goals. The authors describe a possible example scenario, where three operation profiles can be selected by the user each implementing different goals. However, the concept proposed in this work remains very theoretically and no concrete details on a potential realization are given. Additionally, the authors do not say anything about an application-specific selection of communication paths.

In summary, policy-based approaches enable a fine-grained and detailed description of requirements and constraints for network selection. There are several ways for defining policies. In related work on network selection, they are often expressed as if-then-else clauses. In addition, ontologies or other context models like DEN-ng are used to integrated knowledge and context information into the policy framework. Another advantage of policies is the possibility to define them at different abstraction layers. Moreover, several mechanisms are proposed for mapping high layer policies to low layer policies or configurations vice versa. This makes it easy to express requirements and to model constraints at different system layers. But, most of the approaches that have been proposed do not show concrete realizations or even evaluation results of policy-based systems for network selection. In most cases, only very simple examples are given to illustrate a possible solution. One reason for this may be the fact that the complexity of policies clearly increases with the number of parameters that have to be considered. Thus, the flexibility of these approaches is reduced. With increasing number and complexity of the policies, it becomes complicated to extend and adapt the system. This is emphasized by the fact that in most approaches policies are only managed in a static way. Here, even the order of evaluating these policies may strongly affect the resulting decision. Another drawback of policy-based approaches is the lack of suitable strategies for balancing different policies against each other that may be equally likely or even conflicting. Only the FOCALE approach addresses this issue by using ontologies, data models as well as learning and reasoning techniques for adapting policies against the current system context. But even this concept remains only an idea and no possible realization is mentioned. Finally, it may be difficult to deal with incomplete or vague information in policy-based systems. Policies are often expressed as conditional statements, which makes it hard to deal with imprecise information and results.

2.5.4 Intelligent Control

Decision strategies on the basis of intelligent control techniques try to overcome the limitations of static rule sets and the need for precise input data. They are able to handle vague information by using reasoning mechanisms and concepts of artificial intelligence computing [123, 124]. The idea behind these approaches is to enable smarter decisions that are not solely based on precise information, parameters and rules. Moreover, the volatile communication characteristics and requirements in heterogeneous network environments can hardly be mapped on a static parameter range as well as a set of fixed rules or classes. The main advantage of using intelligent control techniques is the possibility to process incomplete or uncertain information. In several situations it is not possible to decide on whether the value of a specific parameter means that an access network is well suited. The interpretation of several performance characteristics clearly depends on the current system status and the present context regarding, for instance, user mobility, number and kind of concurrent applications as well as the local availability of alternative communication paths. The question whether a network meets the decision objectives, cannot be easily answered with "yes" or "no". Even if it fulfills the requirements only to a specific degree, it can be better to use this network than an alternative one, as it may have additional advantages. Further, there may be strong dependencies between some characteristics. This means that a single parameter can only be evaluated in the context of other input values. In addition, artificial computing techniques offer the possibility to use several techniques for knowledge representation and machine learning [124]. Thus, it is possible to learn from earlier decisions and to adapt parameters or rules to match more exactly with the given objectives.

In previous work in this area, two approaches gained special importance:

► Fuzzy Systems

► Neural Networks

Fuzzy systems allow for processing uncertain information with the help of rules that need to be defined by an expert. In contrast, neural networks are able to detect and classify similar input patterns. They are mainly used in combination with fuzzy approaches in, so called, neuro-fuzzy systems to adapt fuzzy rules to changing environments. In the following, both of these wide spread approaches will be introduced.

Fuzzy Systems

The foundations of fuzzy logic were introduced by Lotfi Asker Zadeh in 1965 [125–127]. The main intention was to be able to describe expert knowledge in problem solving with uncertain information by the use of intuitive rules. Fuzzy logic uses a set of if-then-statements which are expressed in a natural, linguistic way to map the input parameter space on an output parameter space. These parameter spaces are defined as, so called, fuzzy sets. In contrast to the mathematical definition of a classical crisp set, a fuzzy set has no clear boundary. Each single element may belong to the fuzzy set to a specific degree between 0 and 1, where 0 means it does not belong to the set and 1 means it fully belongs to it. The degree to which each element is a member of the fuzzy set is described with the help of membership

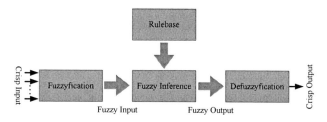

Figure 2.12: Fuzzy controller

functions. These functions assign to each element of the input space a degree of membership to the fuzzy set $deg_{member} \in [0 : 1]$. In principle, a membership function may have any arbitrary shape. However, common membership functions are based on, for instance, triangular, rectangular, or Gaussian distribution functions [128].

Generally, there are two important types of fuzzy inference systems: the Mamdani-type [129] and the Takagi-Sugeno-type [130]. According to [128], the Mamdani fuzzy controller is widely used. Thus, its functioning is exemplarily described in following. A fuzzy controller consists of the four building blocks that are shown in figure 2.12. At first, the fuzzyfication maps crisp input values onto fuzzy sets. The process of mapping the uncertain input parameters to reasonable consequences is called fuzzy inference. It uses a set of rules that define the system's behavior. Finally, the defuzzyfication maps the resulting fuzzy output of the inference process back to a crisp output.

Figure 2.13 illustrates the decision process using fuzzy reasoning. In the first step, the crisp input values of the fuzzy controller have to be mapped onto the fuzzy sets with the help of the corresponding membership functions. As already mentioned earlier, fuzzy reasoning is based on a set of rules that are expressed as conditional statements with linguistic terms. First, in the if-part of these statements, membership grades are assigned to all input parameters (1). If the if-part comprises several conditions, fuzzy logic operators can be applied to connect them. For combining different conditions, various basic operators like AND, OR, or NOT can be used. The decision logic evaluates all fuzzy rules in the knowledge base in parallel, starting with the if-part. In our example, we assume to have three different rules. In the first two rules, two input parameters are combined with an OR operator. Thus, a joint membership degree for the whole if-part is determined, that states to which degree a specific fuzzy rule is supported (2). Afterwards, the implication of each rule is determined. The result of this step is represented by a membership function that is shaped depending on the outcome of the rule's if-part and its weight (3). In our example, we assume the rules to have equal weights. Common implication techniques are the minimum inference and the

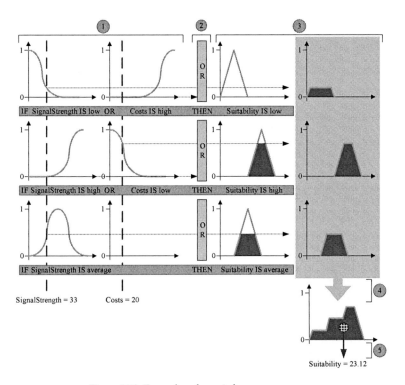

Figure 2.13: Exemplary fuzzy inference process

product inference. Minimum inference simply cuts off the resulting fuzzy set of the then-part to the degree of the if-part. Thus, the consequence in the then-part of the rule is true to the degree of the if-part. This is the approach that we illustrate here. In contrast, product inference scales the output fuzzy set with the resulting fuzzy degree of the if-part.

The concept of fuzzy rules offers the opportunity to determine the validity of a statement, but does not say anything about how several rules are combined to a single fuzzy set at the output. Thus, in the next step the outputs of all rules are combined to get the joint output fuzzy set (4). In our example we use the common approach of maximum aggregation for this [124, 128]. Finally, the resulting fuzzy set needs to be reconverted to a crisp output value with the help of defuzzyfication (5). Widely used techniques for this process are, for instance, the maximum method, mean of maximum or the centroid method.

In the literature, several approaches for network selection on the basis of fuzzy logic have been proposed [131–140]. Basically, all of these approaches are based on the same foundations. Thus, in the following only some of them will be described exemplarily. Simple fuzzy-based approaches like the ones proposed by Lin et al. or Majlesi and Khalaj only use very trivial input parameters as, for instance, the received signal strength (RSS) [137, 138]. Here, fuzzy membership functions are used to describe the quality of the radio signal. Basically they can be compared to the trivial ones.

Liao et al. use the power level, cost and bandwidth as input parameters for the decision process [132]. But, they only use very simple membership functions in their model. To give an example, the bandwidth is modeled as a linear function, where a bandwidth of 0 results in a membership degree of 0 and the maximum bandwidth in a degree of 1. Wilson et al. propose the use of a more complex parameter set [134]. They distinguish between user expectations, application requirements and network characteristics. The decision process is made up of three phases. In the pre-selection phase, all potential candidate networks are checked for their general suitability. This process should be based on criterions like usage restrictions or cost constraints. Available networks that do not fit the given requirements of users and applications will not be considered in the following steps of the decision process. Next, the suitability of each network is evaluated with the help of a fuzzy controller. The authors say that the type and amount of the metrics being used depends on the specific access network. Finally, in the last phase the system decides on which access network to use. Unfortunately, the evaluation of this approach shows only results for using the signal-to-noise ration and the data rate as inputs. Thus, it remains unclear how good the process will really perform. Moreover, the authors state that the fuzzy rules need to be simple and the rule base should have as few rules as possible.

Another approach for dynamic network selection on the basis of fuzzy logic is presented by Bechler et al. [33, 135]. The so called MoccaMuxer is intended to provide seamless handover between heterogeneous networks in vehicular environments. Here, the decision process is split into two phases as it is illustrated in figure 2.14. The proposed inputs to the process are, for instance, statistical information on packet counters, the current and maximum data rates, the utilization of input and output queues for each network as well as information on packet errors. First, this basic information, that is dependent on the respective networks, is passed to an Abstraction Controller. The Abstraction Controller maps this basic information on generic parameters like the relative data rate, the relative queue utilization as well as the relative error rate. Afterwards, these parameters are passed to the Decision Controller, where the fuzzy reasoning process is executed. The output of the Decision Controller is a rating that describes the suitability of each possible network. By comparing the ratings for all paths, the MoccaMuxer selects the most suitable network for data communication. A disadvantage of the MoccaMuxer is that it does not consider any user or application requirements. In addition, only quantitative evaluation results are shown. Thus, there is no statement on the quality and correctness of decisions being made by the MoccaMuxer.

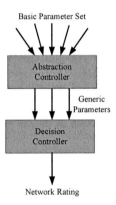

Figure 2.14: Mocca decision process

Neuro-Fuzzy Systems

In addition to pure fuzzy approaches, there are also proposals to use a combination of fuzzy controllers and neural networks for network selection [141–145]. Neural networks [124, 146] are a synthetic approach for modeling the biological processes in the human brain. They are able to process large amount of input data in parallel. Moreover, neural networks learn from previous input information to adapt their internal structure. A neural network consists of numerous similar basic entities called neurons. These neurons are made up quite simple

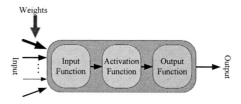

Figure 2.15: Model of a synthetic neuron

and act independently. Each neuron is characterized by a set of three functions that are illustrated in figure 2.15. The input function is a weighted sum of all input signals [124]. Thereby, the weighting of each signal describes its strength at the input of the neuron. The result of the input function is passed to the activation or transfer function. This one models the neuron's memory which is adapted based on earlier events. Thus, the results of the activation function may vary over time and describe a specific activation value. Finally, the resulting measure of the neuron's activity is mapped onto its output space with the help of the output function.

A neural network is typically organized into layers, where several of these single neurons are connected in series. Figure 2.16 illustrates this fact. First, there are an input and an output layer that is visible to the user. Additionally, there may also be further hidden layers. The performance and complexity of a neural network depends on the organization and number of these layers. On the one hand, using more hidden layers increases the system's flexibility and performance. However, each additional hidden layer makes the training of the network

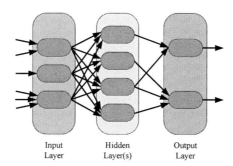

Figure 2.16: Neural network

even more complex. A central characteristic of neural networks is their ability to learn to solve even challenging problems with the help of training data. Thus, after the structure of a neural network has been designed, example data is used to train the network for its concrete task. Afterwards, it is able to generate an appropriate output for unknown input data based on the internal structure which is set up during the training phase. Different learning strategies for training a neural network can be distinguished: supervised learning, unsupervised learning and reinforcement learning [146, 147].

Although fuzzy logic and neural networks are completely different approaches, in combination they complement one another. Numerous approaches of using neuro-fuzzy systems are described in the literature [141–145]. One of them is proposed by Giupponi et al. that realize a Joint Radio Resource Management for WLAN, UMTS and GERAN [142, 143]. Here, the task of the neural network is to obtain new fuzzy rules and to adapt fuzzy membership functions based on the patterns that were recognized in the input data. Thus, the fuzzy decision process is dynamically adapted and optimized with the help of the neural network. A reinforcement learning algorithm is used to minimize the measured user dissatisfaction probability. According to the authors, there are two reasons for a user to be dissatisfied:

1. if the current bit rate offered by the system is lower than the one agreed upon and

2. if the user loses its wireless connection.

The reinforcement learning algorithm is triggered after each run of the fuzzy controller. Input parameters to the selection process are the signal strength that is experienced by the receiver and the availability of resources at each access network. In addition, the speed of the mobile devices is taken into account as well. A resource reservation mechanism is used to reserve capacities in the target network of a handover.

Another neuro-fuzzy approach for handovers between UMTS and WLAN is presented by Horrich et al. [141]. Compared to the previous approach, it uses a neural network with lower complexity for adapting fuzzy membership functions. The proposed decision objectives are signal strength, network load, and the speed of the mobile device. All input parameters are characterized by three membership functions: low, medium, and high. The neural network is designed to learn the membership functions for the input parameters UMTS throughput, WLAN throughput, and the average time between handovers. The network is trained with the help of supervised learning algorithms. Guo et al. use the neural network not for adapting the fuzzy membership functions, but for predicting the number of users that will share the channel after a handover decision [144].

Summary

In summary it can be stated that intelligent control mechanisms provide a very good basis for selecting the best network from a set of possible candidates. Fuzzy logic is able to work on uncertain and incomplete information. It is fault-tolerant with respect to the input parameters and the reasoning process provides good results even for controlling complex systems. Moreover, fuzzy logic allows for a fine-granular mapping of QoS requirements onto input parameters and rules. Nevertheless, fuzzy systems still need experts that define the rule base as well as the membership functions for input and output parameters. The complexity of the system increases significantly with the number of parameters that are considered for network selection. In related work, the proposed systems are often very limited and have only around three input parameters. In particular, if there are dependencies between rules and parameters or if the system is made up of multiple layers of fuzzy controllers, enhancements or changes may become very complex in challenging scenarios. A further drawback of pure fuzzy systems is that the rule base and membership functions are static. In a heterogeneous environment, it may be not be easy to find suitable functions for all kind of possible scenarios and access networks. Neuro-fuzzy systems try to overcome this issue by adapting membership functions dynamically. But, the neural networks being used need to be trained in some way. Thus, the quality of the training data or learning process has a clear impact on how well they perform for the task. Furthermore, complex neural networks are difficult to design and to handle. Their adaptation to the network selection process is a very challenging task. Further alternative techniques from the area of intelligent control mechanisms are Bayesian classification or pattern matching approaches [103, 148]. However, both methods do not work very well and did not gain importance in the literature.

2.5.5 Analytic Approaches

Finally, there is also work on selecting the best network with the help of analytic functions. Thus, the criterions and decision parameters are put into mathematical formulas. Afterwards, the possible communication paths are ranked on the basis of the final results. Basically there are proposals that use cost or utility functions as well as ones that rely on Multi-Criteria Decision Analysis techniques.

Cost and Utility Functions

Basically all selection strategies using cost or utility functions are based on a weighted sum of decision parameters:

$$S(i) = \sum_k w_k C_k(i) \quad . \tag{2.2}$$

The suitability S of each possible network i is the sum of the contributions C of all decision criterions weighted with the individual importance w. In general, the selection strategy chooses the network with the highest or lowest score depending on whether the function models the costs or the utility of a network. Typical parameters that can be found in related work are bandwidth, power consumption, signal strength and network costs [149–156].

Zhu and McNair focus on the decision parameters bandwidth, battery power and delay [149, 150]. For each access network, the cost function sums up the normalized QoS factors for all services and weights them with a specific factor. In addition, a so called network elimination factor is considered that reflects the fact that a network may not meet the requirements of a specific service. It is determined as follows:

$$E_{s,k}^i = \prod_k \frac{1}{I_{s,k}^i} \quad , \tag{2.3}$$

where

$$I_{s,k}^i = \begin{cases} 0 & \text{if minimum constraint cannot be met} \\ 1 & \text{if minimum constraint can be met} \end{cases} \tag{2.4}$$

The authors present an exemplary cost function based on the signal strength and bandwidth [150]. For each network i and service s, the costs are determined by:

$$C_s^i = \frac{1}{u(R_i - R_{th})} \cdot \frac{1}{u(B_i - B_{req})} \ln \frac{1}{B_i} \quad . \tag{2.5}$$

In this equation is R_i the current signal strength, R_{th} the signal strength threshold, B_i the available bandwidth and B_{req} the bandwidth requested by the application. The function u() is defined to be a step function modeling $I_{s,k}^i$. The proposed approach takes two options into account: the possibility to select a network for each session individually or a collective handoff for all active sessions. Unfortunately, the authors use only very simple QoS factors. Examples for implementing more complex objectives are very abstract [149]. Moreover, there is no integrated optimization according to the needs of an individual application and the overall requirements for all applications. A further problem of this approach is that the concurrency of different applications using the same access network is neglected.

Nasser et al. propose to use additional decision parameters like security and network stability, but they do not say how these parameters may be mapped on the cost function that is supposed to be used [151]. Their work presents only a very general formula of normalized criterions. Information on how the single criterions should be determined or implemented is missing. Finally, Ormod et al. present a network selection strategy for optimizing the consumer surplus of a mobile user [153, 154, 157]. The decision is based on the costs for using a specific network, the predicted completion time of a data transfer, and the predicted utility to the user. The authors propose an equation that aims at determining the monetary benefit for a user when using a specific network for data transmission:

$$CS = U_i(T_c) - C_i \qquad \text{when} \qquad T_c \leq T_{c_{max}} \tag{2.6}$$

with

$$T_c = \frac{F_i}{r} \tag{2.7}$$

Thereby, the utility CS for the user is a function of the duration of the data transfer T_c against the amount of money the user is willing to pay for getting the content at that time $U_i(T_c)$ and the actual costs C_i of the network. The duration of the data transfer is calculated from the size of the file to be transferred (F_i) divided by the data rate (r). The drawback of this approach is that it only works for non real-time data. Moreover, no further QoS characteristics are considered. Further, the author made several simplifying assumptions on, for instance, the mobility of users and the network environment that are supposed to be unrealistic in real environments.

Multi-Criteria Decision Analysis

In addition to these rather simple approaches that use cost or utility functions for selecting the best network, there are further approaches using techniques for Multi-Criteria Decision Analysis. Methods like Multiplicative Exponent Weighting (MEW), Simple Additive Weighting (SAW), Technique for Order Preference by Similarity to Ideal Solutions (TOPIS) and the Grey Relational Analysis (GRA) have been proposed in this context [158]. Another common technique to determine the specific importance of decision parameters is the Analytic Hierarchy Process (AHP). Following, some of these approaches will be presented in more detail.

Bari and Leung propose a two-phase decision process [159]. In the first phase non-compensatory Multi-Attribute Decision Making (MADM) algorithms are used to narrow the list of possible candidate networks down to those that are available and may suit to the user's basic requirements. The criterions for this phase are the authentication mechanisms, networking technologies and services that are supported by the device. Furthermore, the availability of a network at the current location and the question of whether the coverage area is large enough for communication are considered. In the second phase, the TOPIS algorithm is used for the actual decision. TOPIS is a compensatory MADM algorithm which assumes that the best solution for the given scenario is the one closest to the ideal solution and furthest to the worst solution of the given problem. In a first step, current values of the decision parameters have to be gathered and normalized. Moreover, these values have to be adopted with the relative weight of each parameter. In the next step, the decision algorithm determines the best and worst values for each parameter as well as their Euclidean distances. Based on this information it is possible to determine a network's level of preference.

$$\Psi = \frac{S_{worst}}{S_{best} + S_{worst}} \qquad (2.8)$$

S_{worst} and S_{best} are the Euclidian distances to the worst and the best case respectively. Finally, the network with the highest level is selected for data transmission. As the actual assignment of weights to the parameters is critical, QoS profiles are stored in the user's home network. These profiles define the overall service level and the QoS requirements of all possible services. Unfortunately, no concrete evaluation results are provided on this.

The Analytic Hierarchy Process (AHP) [160, 161] is a framework that assists complex decision processes by trying to split them up into a hierarchy of simpler sub-problems that may be solved independently. Figure 2.17 shows an exemplary AHP hierarchy for the problem of selecting the most suitable network. The root element of the hierarchy represents the problem that has to be solved. Afterwards, there may be one or more layers of decision objectives. Finally, the bottom layer includes all possible alternative solutions to the initial decision problem.

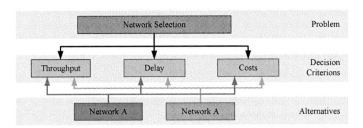

Figure 2.17: Exemplary AHP hierarchy

After gathering all necessary information for the decision process, elements in the same level of the decision hierarchy are compared in pairs for determining their relative importance to the parent elements in the level above. This ranking is done on a scale between 1 and 9, where 1 means both parameters are of equal importance and 9 means that one element is of extreme relative importance compared to the other element. Table 2.2 an exemplary result of this process for the AHP hierarchy shown in figure 2.17. Here, the relative importance of throughput compared to delay is 3. Accordingly, the reciprocal importance, which is 1/3, is assigned to the inverse pair. All values are arranged in the so-called AHP matrix.

In the next step, the eigenvector of this matrix is determined for getting the relative weights of each objective. In addition, a consistency ratio is calculated that indicates whether the chosen levels were meaningful or not. The weights of the decision elements with respect to the initial problem are determined by multiplying the weights of all sub-problems with

	Throughput	Delay	Costs
Throughput	1	3	$\frac{1}{3}$
Delay	$\frac{1}{3}$	1	$\frac{1}{2}$
Costs	3	2	1

Table 2.2: Exemplary AHP matrix

the respective weight of the parent element. Nevertheless, the Analytic Hierarchy Process only provides the weighting of decision factors and thus their individual contribution to the initial problem. It is still necessary to rate the available networks with respect to the decision criterions.

Guan et al. and Ahmed at al. propose concepts that use AHP in combination with cost functions for selecting the best network [162, 163]. This way, the weights that are determined with the help of AHP are used as factors for the separate terms in the cost function. The advantage compared to choosing these factors directly is, that AHP supports the user to come to decisions in a more rational way. He only has to define the relative importance of two decision factors, while the AHP process determines the global weights of the factors with respect to the decision problem and offers the possibility to check the result for consistency.

Another widely used approach is the combination of AHP with Grey Relational Analysis (GRA) [164]. GRA is used to quantify relations between two data sequences where one sequence states the optimal case and the other sequence the measured data. For this purpose, GRA calculates a Grey Relational Coefficient (GRC) indicating the similarity of both sequences. The larger this factor is, the closer is the measured sequence to the optimal one. In the first step, the data has to be normalized with respect to three possible cases: the-larger-the-better, the-smaller-the-better, and nominal-the-best. Afterwards, the optimal sequence has to be determined. The values of the optimal sequence define the bounds for the data sets. Finally, the GRC is calculated by:

$$\Psi = \sum_{j=1}^{n} \frac{\Delta_{min} + \Delta_{max}}{\Delta_i + \Delta_{max}} \quad , \tag{2.9}$$

where

$$\Delta_i = |x_0^*(j) - x_i^*(j)| \qquad \Delta_{max} = max_{(i,j)}(\Delta_i) \qquad \Delta_{min} = min_{(i,j)}(\Delta_i) . \tag{2.10}$$

Here, $x_0^*(j)$ is the j-th element of the normalized optimal sequence and $x_i^*(j)$ is the j-th element of the normalized sequence i.

This combined approach of AHP and GRA is used, for instance, by Song and Jamalipour [165, 166]. Here, AHP is used to determine the weights of QoS parameters while the selection of the best network is done with the help of GRA. The main parameters being considered are availability, throughput, timeliness, reliability, security, and cost. The GRA compares the current network conditions with the optimal ones. The resulting GRCs are weighted with the factors determined on basis of the AHP. Finally, the GRCs of the candidate networks are compared and the one with the highest coefficient is chosen for data transmission.

Summary

There is various work on realizing dynamic network selection in heterogeneous environments on the basis of cost functions and analytic models. These approaches work quite well if the decision is made on crisp and certain information. Moreover, the adaptation of cost or utility functions is very easy since only weighting factors have to be adapted or factors may be added or eliminated from the function. Nevertheless, the approaches that have been proposed are very simple and often only use few parameters. In addition, they lack on the support of using uncertain or soft criteria for the network selection. The procedures of more complex approaches like AHP or GRA are better structured and allow for a meaningful definition of decision elements and weights. Nevertheless, context information or soft conditions may only be considered in a pre-selection phase, where undesirable candidate networks are sorted out in advance. Moreover, the ranking of the networks is always done with respect to the ideal network conditions, but it remains unclear how the ideal conditions are determined. In heterogeneous environments with high mobility, even the ideal conditions may change frequently over time. Another drawback of these approaches is that they become complex and computational expensive with increasing number of candidate networks and decision elements. Thus, they do not scale very well.

2.5.6 Discussion

The review of related work in the previous sections shows a wide range of possible approaches and techniques trying to address the problem of selecting the best network in various different ways. Our overview does not claim to be exhaustive, but it shows the major directions that are discussed in the area. Table 2.3 summarizes the findings of this review with respect to the characteristics of the decision process that are needed to meet the objectives of our work.

We can state that *trivial* algorithms are very simple to implement, but their basic approach to ABC service is bounded to a very limited scope. In most cases this is the availability of a network. Thus, flexibility and QoS mapping are rated strongly negative. The combination

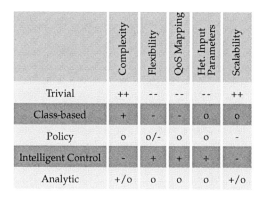

	Complexity	Flexibility	QoS Mapping	Het. Input Parameters	Scalability
Trivial	++	--	--	--	++
Class-based	+	-	-	o	o
Policy	o	o/-	o	o	-
Intelligent Control	-	+	+	+	-
Analytic	+/o	o	o	o	+/o

Table 2.3: Comparison of related work on network selection

of heterogeneous input parameters is also not considered by these solutions. The scalability of trivial approaches is very good as the decision process is basically the comparison of few metrics.

Class-based approaches do also feature a low complexity as long as only few classes are provided. However, their flexibility depends strongly on the number of different classes. Thus, a differentiated mapping of diverse QoS characteristics would result in an unmanageable variety of individual classes. In general, it is possible to combine heterogeneous input parameters to the decision process, but again only at the costs of an increasing number of classes. Thus, this issue is rated with 'o'. The scalability of class-based decision concepts is good with respect to increasing numbers of applications and networks, but very low in terms of integrating additional objectives. The combination of both aspects leads to an average rating.

The use of a *policy-based* approach for network selection comes with a higher system complexity, but increased flexibility at the same time. Nevertheless, there are still some limitations, as the design of policies and their processing order may be relevant to the final result. Thus, one has to consider these aspects when adapting the system. Policies are able to provide a finer consideration of QoS characteristics. But, they still have problems with incomplete and vague input information. Another issue is the fact that, in general, the defined policies are static. Further techniques are needed to provide adaptations and, for instance, a dynamic weighting of objectives. Those increase the complexity of the system. Finally, the scalability of the approach received an average rating, as the rule set may become bulky the more objectives need to be considered. Thus, due to the aforementioned dependencies of rules, an implementation of enhancements or additional objectives may become difficult.

Intelligent control techniques overcome some of the aforementioned problems. Depending on the design, the resulting systems may be highly complex, but feature a high flexibility in modeling decision objectives and adapting to certain scenarios. They allow for dealing even with uncertain information and provide reasoning mechanisms that are able to cope for a fine-granular mapping of QoS characteristics even in heterogeneous scenarios. But, they still rely on experts that design the decision process for specific scenarios. Moreover, dynamic modifications of the rule set using neural networks require the availability of suitable training data. Moreover, the resulting configuration will be optimized only to those scenarios that are covered during the training phase. Extensions to the system may be manageable in small systems, but can require significant changes in the whole design for complex setups. Thus, scalability is rated negatively.

Finally, *analytic* approaches provide an average to low complexity, depending on the actual set of functions that are used. But again, this comes with a lower flexibility in designing and enhancing the system. In dependence of the algorithm's complexity a reasonable consideration of QoS characteristics is possible in general. But, the handling of highly different input parameters is difficult and may require further processing steps. The integration of additional objectives is almost simple for basic cost or utility functions, but can require a higher amount of changes in more complex models.

In general, we can state that most previous work only realizes a very simple mapping of QoS characteristics. Thus, the accuracy and performance of such systems is quite limited. Those proposals that describe more complex approaches to the decision problem often do not present any proof-of-concepts or evaluation results. Their concepts remain theoretical ideas only. In many cases, the proposed solutions also lack on flexibility due to fixed profiles that have to be used or strong constraints for the input parameters. This fact comes with a rather poor modularity of existing approaches. Finally, a major drawback of existing approaches is their isolated view on either selecting the best path for an application or selecting the best network for the mobile device. In order to find the best configuration, both aspects have to be combined. The best network has to meet the requirements of each single application, but parameters like costs or power consumption need to be considered for the device as a whole. Moreover, existing approaches completely neglect aspects of concurrent applications that share a common communication path. Additionally, the potential of using context information for optimizing the decision process is considered insufficiently. This information can be used for predicting communication characteristics in the near future in order to delay data transmissions or to avoid unnecessary handovers. Another suitable option if a single network does not meet the requirements of the applications is the use of concurrent multipath transfer over different access networks.

2.6 Related Projects on Integrating Heterogeneous Networks

In the last years, the problem of integrating heterogeneous networks has been addressed by numerous research projects in very different ways. Especially the Information Society Technologies (IST) and Information and Communication Technologies (ICT) research initiatives within the European framework program put a focus on these issues. The proposals range from joint radio access and spectrum management via new technologies for converging today's infrastructures, up to future Internet and networking technologies [167]. In the following, we introduce projects that are related to our target of providing a framework for dynamic network selection in heterogeneous environments and evaluate their contributions with respect to our research targets.

2.6.1 Daidalos (II)

Daidalos[1] and its successor Daidalos II [168] are EU-funded Integrated Projects running from November 2003 to December 2008 within the Sixth EU Framework Program. Daidalos stands for "Designing advanced interfaces for the delivery and administration of location independent optimized personal services" and aims at developing a user-centric architecture for pervasive communications with seamless integration of heterogeneous networks based on IPv6 [169]. The seamless handover process in Daidalos is implemented at Layer 2 of the ISO/OSI reference model using the proposed IEEE 802.21 that was already mentioned above. A handover can be initiated either by the mobile device or by the network. The decision on a handover is made by independent interface selection modules in the network and on the mobile terminal respectively. Terminal mobility as well as multihoming of mobile devices is managed at the network layer with the help of Mobile IPv6 [57, 170]. In addition to the support of infrastructure networks, Daidalos also proposes mechanisms for the integration of broadcast technologies, mobile ad-hoc networks [171], or mobile networks, so-called NEMOs [60].

In summary, Daidalos provides an architectural framework that supports a variety of different technologies and networking concepts. However, in contrast to the requirements of our approach it focuses primarily on terminal rather than service mobility. Thus, the proposed mechanisms do not provide the required granularity of handling data flows as it is needed for our concept. In addition, there is the need for a strong infrastructure support. Although the design of the Daidalos framework provides a so-called Intelligent Interface Selection module [172], we were not able to find concrete information on the implementation of any network selection approach. Only mechanisms for managing context information and user requirements where proposed [173]. Finally, aspects like the concurrent use of multiple networks or disruption tolerance are not addressed in the project.

---
[1]http://www.ist-daidalos.org/

2.6.2 Ambient Networks (II)

Ambient Networks (AN) and Ambient Networks II [174] were large-scale integrated projects within the Sixth EU Framework Program running from January 2004 to December 2007. They focused on a long-term perspective for future communications systems, where heterogeneous networks may act cooperatively and share radio resources across different operators and communication techniques. The research activities focus on the ability to compose heterogeneous networks dynamically and in a transparent way. The main requirements being considered are a scalable and flexible architecture providing a common interface to heterogeneous networks as well as seamless interoperation between them. Ambient Networks are defined to be of any arbitrary technology or size, but offer generic interfaces to services, users or other networks. The primary objectives in the AN paradigm are self-management functionalities, context awareness as well as strategies for network composition and access selection. The core element of the AN architecture is the Ambient Control Space which can be described as a kind of middleware encapsulating all necessary management functions (see figure 2.18). The control functions are split up into several modular functional entities, each dealing with a specific task, but all acting in a cooperative manner. Besides, the Ambient Control Space implements three interfaces to upper layer services (ASI), network resources (ARI), and cooperating networks (ANI).

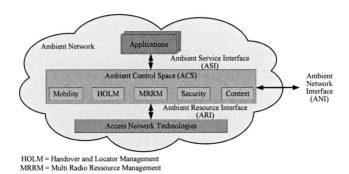

HOLM = Handover and Locator Management
MRRM = Multi Radio Ressource Management

Figure 2.18: Architecture of an Ambient Network [2]

The problem of access network selection is addressed within Ambient Networks in different ways. On the one hand, the network, a mobile device connects to, is selected within the Multi Radio Resource Management (MRRM), while the end-to-end path is managed within the Flow and Mobility Management [175]. For the former mechanism, a so-called Generic Link Layer module determines different performance criterions and maps them onto abstract evaluation criterions. Based on the set of detected access networks, predefined policies depending on, for instance user preferences and network functionalities, are used to eliminate those ones that do not meet the basic requirements. Next, the remaining networks are sorted according to their suitability with respect to the requested performance of each specific flow. A handover decision might be made at the mobile device, the network controller or in a cooperative way. Unfortunately, there is only a general description of these concepts in the literature. We were not able to find any details on implementations or evaluations of the proposals. In addition, from the published papers that refer to the Ambient Networks project, it appears as if different groups in the project had diverse ideas and proposal on how the aforementioned problems should be solved. The mobility management is based on an abstract handover toolbox that is intended to support various mobility protocols. In the literature, especially Mobile IP, the Host Identity Protocol (HIP) [54] and the Session Management Layer [2, 176] are mentioned. The protocol that is actually being used is selected in dependence of the capabilities of the communicating peers.

The architecture of Ambient Networks follows a highly modular and flexible design. However, the implementation requires drastic change of the concepts that are used in the Internet today. In addition, the interaction of the different components and functions in the architecture is quite complex. The concepts that were proposed for access selection allow for an allocation of network resources to individual applications, but their description remains vague in the literature that is available. We were not able to find information on concrete implementations or evaluations of the concepts that have been proposed here. In addition, aspects of sharing resources between concurrent applications have not been discussed. Any aspects of multipath transfer or the deferral of application requests in time are not explicitly mentioned. Finally, the project does not provide any evaluation of the proposed mechanisms or protocols above the network layer.

2.6.3 End-to-End Reconfigurability (Efficiency)

End-to-End Reconfigurability (E^2R) (January 2004 to December 2007) and its successor End-to-End Efficiency (E^3)[2] (January 2008 to December 2009) are large scale projects in the Sixth and Seventh EU Framework Program. Both were motivated by the target to integrate heterogeneous networks into a common efficient framework based on cognitive radios. These radios can be reconfigured dynamically and may adapt to changes in the environment.

E^2R and E^3 aim at implementing autonomous optimization and self-management functionalities into mobile devices and network elements for spectrum and radio resource utilization. This covers techniques and mechanisms for dynamic spectrum and resource allocation between different access technologies and network operators. A key feature is a close

---

[2]https://ict-e3.eu/

cooperation between the different network elements that exchange context information or policies and may negotiate resources. Dynamic network selection and vertical handover issues are handled by a Joint Radio Resource Management (JRRM) below network layer. A Cognitive Pilot Channel is introduced to exchange context information and policies between the network entities for enabling distributed decision making. Within the projects two access selection strategies were proposed. On the one hand, a quite simple analytic model based on the criterions throughput, delay and loss is proposed by Feng et al. [177]. On the other hand, Giupponi et al. [178–180] introduce a neuro-fuzzy approach using reinforcement learning techniques.

Most work in E^2R and E^3 focuses on issues at lower layers of the protocol stack. Higher layer issues and application-oriented requirements are not addressed by the projects. The proposed decision concept is quite complex and relies on the availability of suitable training data as well as rules defined by an expert. Thus, it can be expected that extensions of the decision objectives or the technologies being supported are more complex. The proposed concept does not consider multipath issues or the deference of application requests. Furthermore, effects of the resource allocations to concurrent applications are neglected as well.

2.6.4 Perimeter

Perimeter[3] is an EU FP 7 project that develops user-centric concepts for ABC services in the future Internet. It started in May 2008 and will run until April 2011. One key objective in the project is to choose the access networks based on the user's Quality of Experience. For this, it aims at combining different decision objectives. However, up to date there are only few publications on the concepts and mechanisms that will be used in the project. On the one hand, there are two different approaches on managing application-oriented vertical handovers. The first proposal is based on IP tunneling and requires a so-called Anchor Node in the Internet that acts as tunnel endpoint [181]. The second proposal is a cooperative approach based on an application-layer middleware and IEEE 802.21 [44]. On the other hand, Khan et al. proposed a network-centric approach for allocating network resources to applications using mechanisms from game theory [182]. Here, the authors propose to implement a so-called Common Radio Resource Management entity in each operator network that manages the allocation process. It receives bandwidth offers from the different networks of an operator as well as request from applications on the mobile device.

Although, the general idea of the Perimeter project goes along with the objective in our research work, it is not possible to evaluate the concepts due the limited amount of information that has been published so far. For now, the proposed concepts do not meet the objectives of our work. Moreover, the network-centric approach for bandwidth allocation is

---

[3]http://www.ict-perimeter.eu/

bound to specific network operators that implement this feature and may have to agree on a cooperative concept. For the user, this aspect limits the system's flexibility as it would not be possible to connect to arbitrary access networks.

2.6.5   Further Projects

There are numerous further projects dealing with similar aspects of providing ABC services for Internet access of mobile devices, but it will not be possible to discuss them all in detail here. First, there are several projects dealing with the design of mobile routers in the vehicular environment. Some representatives of this group are, for instance, MYCAREVENT [183], COMCAR [184], DRiVE [185] and OverDRiVE [186], or MAR [187]. The NETQOS project [120, 188] worked on a policy-based framework for providing end-to-end QoS guarantees in heterogeneous networks and investigated handover issues in this context. Additionally, there are also further projects on future IP networks as, for instance, Moby Dick [189], IPon-Air [190] or ScaleNet [191]. All of them propose solutions that relate to our research problem, but none of them meets all of our aforementioned requirements and objectives.

2.6.6   Discussion

Our review on related work concluded with the finding, that none of the aforementioned projects meets all of our objectives that we stated in the introduction of this thesis. Table 2.4 summarizes the characteristics of the projects that have been described in a qualitative way.

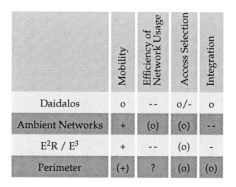

	Mobility	Efficiency of Network Usage	Access Selection	Integration
Daidalos	o	--	o/-	o
Ambient Networks	+	(o)	(o)	--
E^{2}R / E^3	+	--	(o)	-
Perimeter	(+)	?	(o)	(o)

Table 2.4: Comparison of related projects

Daidalos deals with mobility issues in terms of vertical handovers, but it does not provide an application-oriented mobility management. Furthermore, it does not address aspects on how to use the heterogeneous communication environment more efficiently by integrating, for instance, concurrent multipath transfer or disruption tolerance. The proposed concept for access selection might probably provide a good basis, but we were not able to find details on how the actual decision strategy should be implemented. Finally, the integration of the Daidalos approach into the existing Internet is rated with 'o', as it requires additional infrastructure components and relies on the deployment of IEEE 802.21 and MobileIPv6. Although both mechanisms are standardized, they have not been widely deployed today.

Ambient Networks addresses mobility management issues as well. In the project, path management concepts and a close interoperation between ambient networks are proposed. But, one can find only few concrete details on implementing them. Multipath transfer is mentioned, but has not been explicitly addressed, while disruption tolerance seems to be out of scope for this project. Again there are is only little information on a strategy for access selection. Several issues remain unclear and there is no real evaluation on how well the concept works. Any problems regarding to multiple applications that share a network concurrently were not discussed. Moreover, AN bases on a completely different networking concept compared to today's approaches.

E^2R *and* E^3 propose to handle mobility management below the network layer. However, like Daidalos, the project does not deal with concurrent multipath transfer or the deferral of application requests. The access selection strategies being presented in the context of the projects do only focus on lower layer aspects and have only been evaluated with respect to an optimization of scenarios with UMTS/GERAN and WLAN networks. As the final concept of access selection in those projects is not fully clear, we rated this criterion with '(o)'. Finally, the integration of E^2R and E^3 requires clear changes in the network infrastructure that need to be implemented by the network operators.

Perimeter aims at implementing application-oriented path management, but there are only few details on this topic. Moreover, the available information does not say anything about issues regarding the concepts for making efficient use of network resources. So far, two concepts for access selection are provided, but the descriptions remain general. One of these concepts requires proxies in the network, the other one is based on IEEE 802.21. Thus, the integration receives an average rating, although it is not clear whether any of these proposals will actually be used in the project.

2.7 Summary

In this chapter, we gave an overview on the background of our work and discussed basic technologies as well as related work. First, we introduced the range of different networking technologies and showed that there is a huge potential for communication available that is not efficiently used today. Afterwards, we presented the concept of "Always Best Connected" (ABC) as a user-centric approach that aims at making full use of the networking resources in heterogeneous communication environments and at providing each application with the required resources to maximize the quality that is experienced by the user. We described the ABC reference model and introduced the proposed components of an ABC service. Afterwards, we presented related work for managing the mobility of devices with a focus on vertical handovers, concurrent multipath transfer and disruption tolerance. Here, we concluded that a transport layer approach is well-suited to meet the objectives of our work. Moreover, we identified that there are still open issues in evaluating the effects of vertical handovers in heterogeneous scenarios as well in optimizing and evaluating mechanisms for concurrent multipath transfer. Following, we discussed different approaches for the dynamic selection of access networks and concluded that they still leave room for optimizations. Especially, the issues of multiple applications that have to share one network and may interfere with each other, multipath transfer, and the deferral of application requests have not been investigated in this context. Finally, we gave an overview on related projects that aim at integrating heterogeneous networks. All of them address the mobility of the mobile device, but only few worked on application-oriented handover. Moreover, several approaches excluded the actual design of an algorithm for network selection.

In the following chapters we introduce our proposal to dynamic network selection and present concepts and evaluations for a transport-layer path management as well as a highly flexible and modular decision concept.

Chapter 3

muXer – A Flexible Approach to Dynamic Network Selection

The key aspect to increase the perceived quality of mobile users that access the Internet or other communication services on the move, is an efficient and flexible approach to dynamic network selection. Generally, dynamic network selection describes the ability to choose one network for communications that fits best to the given requirements from a set of candidate networks. It includes the possibility to switch to another network if the networking conditions or the requirements change. Ideally, this process is transparent to the applications and to the user. Only the specific demands need to be configured, while the actual network selection process itself runs in the background. In chapter 2 we already discussed that implementing a dynamic network selection concept for Always Best Connected (ABC) Internet access requires a set of further functional components. Besides the actual network selection strategy, one needs to gather information about the current network characteristics as inputs to the decision process. Moreover, there must be some network management functionalities to put the result of the selection strategy into action.

We already discussed numerous approaches that relate to the aforementioned aspects and also evaluated other research projects working in this area with respect to various requirements. As a result, we found out that they leave a lot of potential untapped. At this point, we tie in with our work. To overcome the limitations of existing approaches, we designed a modular architecture for dynamic network selection that is called muXer. The name comes from the word "multiplexer", as our architecture acts as a kind of an inverse multiplexer. It aims at using the full communication capabilities that are available via a set of different networking technologies. The core element of this architecture is the application-oriented two-tier decision process based on an arbitration concept.

The remaining part of the chapter gives a general overview of the muXer architecture and introduces the different components and functionalities. At first, section 3.1 presents the major requirements and design issues for our muXer system. The general architecture of muXer is introduced in section 3.2. Following, we describe the three key aspects of our architecture in more detail. This starts in section 3.3 with a concept for collecting information on different networks and mapping them onto a common set of parameters. Section 3.4 presents the conceptual design of the decision module that actually runs the network selection process and is a central topic of our work. Finally, our approach to network management issues is described in section 3.5. At the very end, section 3.6 concludes this chapter with a summary.

3.1 Requirements and Design Issues

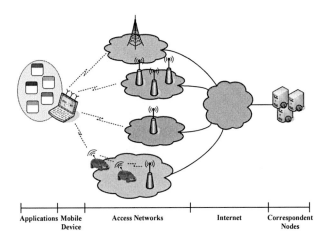

Figure 3.1: Target scenario

Figure 3.1 illustrates a generalized view on the target scenario that was already presented in the introduction of this thesis. On the left, it shows the mobile device running a set of applications. These applications want to access correspondent nodes on the Internet that are depicted on the right. The mobile device is equipped with a set of network interfaces providing Internet access via different communication technologies. These interfaces may be used concurrently. In addition, for each communication technology, a mobile device may choose from multiple candidate networks to which it can connect to. To give an example, if the mobile device is equipped with a WLAN interface and moves in the center of a city, there will probably be multiple WLAN hotspots available. However, typical interface cards only allow for connecting to one of these networks at a time.

The primary intention of an ABC service is to provide efficient mobile Internet access. Thereby, it relieves the user from the decision of which network to use. On the one hand, efficiency means to make full use of the available communication capabilities. On the other hand, the service has to care for meeting specific application and user demands. In section 1.1, we already introduced a set of requirements that have to be considered by our approach:

1. Efficient use of communication capabilities:

   The ABC service should make a maximum use of the communication capabilities. Therefore, it should not regard just those networks as possible candidates that are available at the moment, but also those ones that may become accessible in the near future.

2. Flexible and modular decision concept:

   The heterogeneous environment of different networks, applications, and requirements results in an imprecise definition of what an optimal decision really is. Thus, a flexible and modular decision concept is required to be able to adapt to various integration scenarios and communications situations.

3. Technology independence:

   The ABC service should be as independent as possible of technology specifics to support a wide range of networking technologies.

4. Transparency to network changes:

   From the perspective of users and applications, the process of network handovers as well as modifications of network configurations should be as transparent as possible. Ideally, such changes are noticeable by variations of the communication characteristics only and have no relevant effects on the actual operation of an application.

5. Adaptation to application and user requirements:

   There is a wide range of applications having very specific requirements on the underlying communication network being used. Users may define additional constraints as, for instance, the maximum costs or the importance of specific applications. The ABC service has to balance these inputs and needs to find a global solution that meets all of them as well as possible.

To meet these requirements, we based the design of our muXer architecture on a set of general concepts. They allow for an increased efficiency in using the available network capacities and, in their entirety, differentiate muXer from related work:

Flexibility in combining heterogeneous decision criterions and objectives

Requirements 2 and 3 target at the aspect that an efficient ABC service needs to be able to handle a wide range of input parameters stating distinct requirements and networking characteristics. This is getting even more complicated as the characteristics of different networking technologies may not be directly comparable to each other. They are measured differently or describe technology-specific features. Furthermore, the decision concept has to be able to combine this set of heterogeneous and highly different optimization objectives to an overall rating for the suitability of a particular network, where the specific relevance of certain objectives may depend on the respective application.

Thus, a basic design issue of our muXer architecture is a high modularity that allows for the integration of today's and future technologies. MuXer has to provide mechanisms for decoupling the technology-specific networking characteristics from the decision process with the aim to make networks comparable on a common basis. The same design paradigm needs to be applied to the network selection process itself. Here, it has to be possible to merge a variety of different objectives to a final result.

Application-oriented network selection

MuXer addresses the adaptation to the requirements of individual applications (requirement 5) by implementing an application-oriented network selection concept. Thus, application data flows are handled separately and the decision strategy can schedule particular applications to networks that match their specific requirements. This differentiates muXer from a wide range of approaches that do not account for any individual application requirements.

Hybrid decision making concept

A second aspect in requirement 5 is the adaptation to user-related requirements. A pure application-oriented network selection process will not meet this requirement, as several aspects, for instance the maximum costs, have to be evaluated for the entirety of all applications running on the device. Another problem that may arise is the situation where the selection process allocates multiple applications to the same network that fits best to each of these applications, but is not able to serve all of them concurrently with the requested QoS. With respect to requirement 1, in this case it would be better to reschedule some of the applications to other networks, although they may be rated slightly worse.

In muXer, these aspects are tackled by using a hybrid decision concept that accounts for both, application-specific requirements and higher-level optimization objectives. It implements a two-tier approach that avoids overload situations and aims at finding an allocation of network resources that fits best in the context of the entire device.

Seamless handover and network bundling

Requirements 3 and 4 suggest the need for vertical handover mechanisms that are transparent to the applications and do not depend on certain functionalities of specific networking technologies. They should provide the ability to switch between different networks without interrupting a session between sender and receiver. In combination with the aforementioned basic concepts, it must be possible to manage application data flows individually. Another aspect relating to network management is the problem that resource demands of an application may not be served by a single network, although the entirety of all available networks might provide enough remaining capacities. The use of these resources is advantageous with respect to requirement 1.

MuXer implements a mechanism for vertical handovers that is independent of specific networking technologies and complies with the aforementioned requirements. While handover mechanisms are common to ABC services in general, muXer accounts for an additional option to bundle heterogeneous network paths. Thus, remaining resources can be used more efficiently by the applications.

Proactive delaying of data transmissions

Besides network bundling, there is a further option to increase the efficiency of network usage with respect to requirement 1. In situations where the sum of all application requests exceeds the available network capabilities, it might be advantageous to defer the data transmission of certain applications proactively. Therefore, one ensures that the remaining applications work properly. E-mail or a file download in the background are possible examples of applications that might be inherently tolerant to such long delays or disruptions without significantly reducing the quality of user experience. Moreover, the communication environment of mobile devices may change over time due to the user's mobility. Thus, if there is no suitable network available at the moment, which is able to serve the application, it might be an option to wait for upcoming communication opportunities that are expected to appear shortly. The muXer architecture and decision concept have to address these aspects and need to provide the necessary functionalities to support a proactive delaying of data transmissions.

3.2 The muXer Architecture

Based on the aforementioned design issues we developed a flexible architecture for efficient and dynamic network selection. A first general question in designing this architecture is the location of the entity that controls the selection process. In section 2.3.2 we already discussed two different concepts that can be used:

1. network-controlled or

2. device-controlled selection.

The former case brings advantages for the network operator or the ABC service provider as it has the final control on which access network is used by a mobile devices. But, it reduces the usability of the ABC service for the users themselves. They are bound to the mechanisms and functionalities that are supported by their providers. We assume that a user may have different contracts with multiple operators or may want to be able to connect to arbitrary networks to make an efficient use of the communication capabilities for accessing the Internet. Thus, we decided on adopting a device-controlled network selection process for muXer. This approach is more focused on the individual demands of applications and users and provides a good basis to meet our design requirements. Moreover, it is independent of specific providers or networks. Nevertheless, one might still account for provider specifications by integrating respective objectives into the decision process. A disadvantage of this solution is that the processing capabilities of a mobile device are limited. Thus, efficient strategies for decision making are required.

Figure 3.2 illustrates the architecture of muXer. The right side of the figure shows the application data paths. The network selection mechanisms are separated from them. The integration point of muXer is located at the transport layer or at the bundle layer respectively. While muXer extends the transport layer with mechanisms for seamless handover and multipath transfer, the bundle layer acts as an ISO/OSI session layer and is intended to provide disruption tolerance to users and applications.

At the application layer, muXer has three major interfaces. First, users are able to define policies on their preferences in using communication networks. These policies represent general constraints for the network selection process that may, for instance, limit the overall costs or state priorities on applications being used. Second, applications provide their specific requirements on the underlying network. This information is required to optimize the network selection process with respect to the needs of the individual applications. Finally, muXer is designed to make use of external data sources providing, for instance, context information like the position of the mobile device or other additional data about networks and/or providers. Further, muXer relies on local performance measures of the networks and networking technologies to state their performance. Those can be obtained at various layers of the network protocol stack.

The muXer itself is made up of five main components. The *Link Monitor* observes the status of possible communication paths and determines the current network characteristics. Especially parameters regarding the networks' availability, communication performance and security mechanisms are of interest for the decision process. The whole process of link monitoring runs asynchronously and independently from the actual decision process. Thus, the

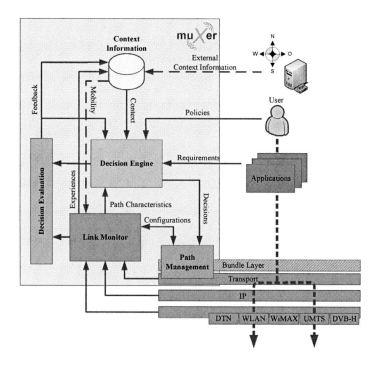

Figure 3.2: The muXer architecture

measures for each candidate network are updated continuously. Nevertheless, several networking technologies feature different metrics and characteristics that may not be directly
comparable. One example for this is the signal strength that is measured by different metrics
and in different granularities such as simple link levels or the received signal power in dBm.
Therefore, the *Link Monitor* has to map technology-specific measures onto generic parameters that can be used for a technology-independent rating. Thus, it provides a universal
interface to the *Decision Engine* and hides technology-specific characteristics of the underlying communication networks. In addition, it is also responsible for estimating the future
trend of specific parameters, for instance, based on previous measurements, context information and the mobility of the mobile device. This additional data is stored in the *Context
Information Storage* which also includes information on services and service costs of specific
network providers. In addition, location-specific data like the position of WLAN hotspots
can be used to predict whether any access networks will become available in the near future.

The most crucial part of the architecture is the *Decision Engine*, where the selection strategies are implemented. An application registers at the *Decision Engine* with its specific requirements concerning, for instance, the need for certain network characteristics. In combination with user-defined policies like the maximum costs or the application priority, these
requirements are mapped onto available or upcoming communication opportunities. Further details on this process are described later on in chapter 5. The results of the *Decision
Engine* are passed to the *Path Management*, which is responsible for handling the different
network connections and to enforce the decisions being made. In the scope of this work, we
only control the first hop towards the Internet, since today's Internet architecture typically
does not allow for explicitly selecting a path from source to destination. Nevertheless, there
may be additional options in Mobile Ad-hoc Networks (MANETs) or Delay Tolerant Networks (DTNs) to make decisions on the next hop to be used at each individual node along
the route to the destination. However, these aspects cannot be considered here.

Finally, the *Decision Evaluation* module introduces self-optimization capabilities to the
muXer architecture. Its intention is to verify continuously whether the decisions that have
been made do really map onto the expected system behavior. In the case that it discovers any
optimization potentials or outdated context information, the module is able to adapt decision parameters or to update context data. However, the realization and detailed evaluation
of this part is not covered by this work and thus left for future research.

The following sections describe the major components of muXer and present details on
their specific design and implementation.

3.3   Link Monitor

Before it is possible to make any decisions on the allocation of network resources to applications, it is necessary to collect information about available networks and their current
characteristics. This is the task of the *Link Monitor*. It has to gather data about available
networks (or even about ones that will become available in the near future) and to prepare
them as inputs for the decision process. A specific challenge in this context is the fact that
different network technologies or even hardware interfaces from different manufacturers
measure certain aspects, such as the signal quality, with different metrics and granularities.
Thus, a second major task of the *Link Monitor* is to map these technology- or manufacturer-
specific measures onto a set of generic ones which makes different networks comparable
and provides an abstract interface to other muXer components.

Figure 3.3 illustrates the conceptual design of the muXer *Link Monitor*. It consists of a set
of *Monitor Agents* that collect information about certain networks. According to the target
scenario described in section 3.1, there is generally a one-to-many relation from interfaces
to networks. Thereby, the list of potential networks differentiates not only between separate network providers, but also between diverse networking paradigms as, for instance,

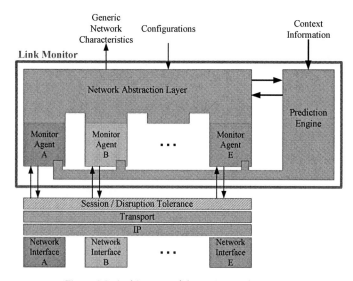

Figure 3.3: Architecture of the muXer Link Monitor

infrastructure, ad-hoc or store-carry-forward networks. The *Monitor Agents* have to account for these aspects and need to provide individual sets of parameters for each network. The information gathered by the *Monitor Agents* is mapped onto abstract metrics and passed to the *Network Abstraction Layer (NAL)*. The *NAL* brings the outputs of the different *Monitor Agents* together and implements a generic interface to the decision process and other muXer components. This makes it possible to integrate further networks and technologies easily. Finally, the third important component in the *Link Monitor* is the *Prediction Engine*. Its task is to forecast events like network disconnections, relevant changes in the networking characteristics and networks that may get available shortly. In doing so, the *Prediction Engine* requires input from context information about, for instance, the current location and movement or hotspot locations. If for some parameters the *Prediction Engine* is reliant on technology-specific characteristics, it has to interact with the *Monitor Agents* and may require technology-specific hooks there.

3.3.1 Monitoring and Mapping

To rate and compare different access networks, it is important to gather multiple performance measures that can be mapped onto respective application requirements. Information sources for these measures can be found across the protocol layers of the ISO/OSI reference model at different abstraction levels and granularities. Just to give an example: In networks with contention-based mechanisms for Medium Access Control (MAC), the link layer data rate indicates only an upper bound of the achievable throughput, while the throughput experienced by the application can be clearly lower. Thus, cross-layer interaction for gathering information on network characteristics is an inevitable requirement for muXer.

To measure specific network characteristics we can make use of multiple strategies. On the one hand, it is possible to send active probes into the network. This may require some additional support by the infrastructure components, but allows for estimating the network's performance even if it is not used by any application. A second option is the monitoring of network traffic, which is characterized by the inverse qualities to the former option. It does not require any additional external support, but only works if the monitored network is in use. Finally, we can make use of information that is provided by a specific network interface or even by specific services of a networking technology. Examples for this can be the signal quality or the bit error rate. However, for other parameters, such low layer information may only indicate an upper bound for the performance that is actually achievable. One example for this is the possible throughput as mentioned above. In addition, lower layer measures often only provide information on the first hop along the path from the mobile device to the correspondent node. Although this is sufficient for our target scenario, it becomes relevant for the alternative communication scenarios that were discussed in section 2.2.

However, monitoring of network characteristics is just one part of the whole task. A further issue is to make heterogeneous communication technologies comparable by using a common set of performance measures. For some of these measures there are generic and almost well-defined metrics. For instance, throughput, delay and packet loss are usually measured in bit/s, seconds and percent respectively. Thus, they have a common basis for comparing measurements of different networks. Nevertheless, there is still the need to define a common basis on how these metrics are determined. To give an example, for the throughput one needs a common understanding about the layer at which the measurements are obtained as the link layer data rate that is provided by a network may clearly differ from the application layer throughput. Also for measuring delay, one has to define whether the value relates to transferring one single bit or a larger packet. But, there are other examples that are even more complicated. One of them is the signal strength. Here, there is no such common objective and well-defined measure. WLAN drivers, for instance, measure the signal strength in different metrics (dbm, RSSI, or percent) depending on the manufacturer. In addition, the gathered information needs to be interpreted with respect to the specific hardware characteristics. While WLAN drivers often provide almost fine-granular information about the signal strength, UMTS modems may only state one level out of five to describe the signal strength. One option to make these results comparable is the definition of a hardware-specific function that maps the measured values into a fixed interval, where the semantic of the output values is well-defined. In the example of the signal strength, this could be:

$$f_i : signalstrength \rightarrow x \in [0, 1],$$

where 0 means that the network is not available and 1 indicates the best possible signal level. The concrete implementation depends on numerous parameters as the actual measures provided by the interface card, the sensitivity of the receiver and so forth. Another parameter that is challenging to map is the security level of a network. Here, different communication technologies use diverse techniques to provide, for instance, authentication and confidentiality. In some cases like IEEE 802.11 there may be multiple approaches that can be differentiated according to their robustness. In such a case it might be necessary to define security classes each of which provides certain guarantees. Afterwards, a set of policies can be used to map the technology-specific security functionalities onto one of these classes.

In related work, several approaches have been proposed addressing either one or both of the aspects monitoring and mapping. To stick to the example of the throughput, bottleneck bandwidths might be probed for instance by using packet pair techniques [192, 193]. Another option is proposed by Nicholson et al. [194], where the mobile device connects to certain reference servers on the Internet and probes the capacity of an access network by running a pre-defined tests. Other options are the use of transport layer parameters. However, this may require the combination of parameters across different applications using the same network and may only work as long as data is actively transmitted. A few attempts have been undertaken to find suitable solutions supporting a wide range of heterogeneous technologies. Sachs et al. proposed a Generic Link Layer (GLL) [195] in the context of the Ambient Networks project that is introduced in section 2.6.2. Here, the main idea is to represent the proposed metrics of link data rate, delay as well as bit and packet error rate in a relative way. For each resource, the GLL determines the minimum amount required by the application, the share that is occupied but might be feed up and the maximum amount. Based on this information, networks are rated in the decision process. A limitation of this approach is that it relies on a low number of parameters that relate mainly to typical QoS aspects, but neglects further aspects like the network costs, security levels or estimations of a network's future availability. Standardization approaches like the Media Independent Information Service defined in IEEE 802.21 [196] do not fully meet the requirements as they provide only a set of generic link layer metrics. Although none of these examples addresses all of the aspects and requirements defined in the context of muXer, they indicate the general feasibility of the *Link Monitor* concept.

3.3.2 Prediction

The aforementioned aspects only address the monitoring of networks that are available at the moment. However, in a mobile scenario, the communication situation may change continuously as a result of movement. If the *Link Monitor* is able to forecast any events like a connection and a disconnection to access networks or any clear changes of certain link characteristics, this information can be used within the decision process to improve the efficiency of Internet access. The expected future state might be considered for the decisions in the current situation. Within the *Link Monitor*, the *Prediction Engine* is responsible for estimating such future states and to enrich the generic parameter set with the respective information. Hereby, the predictions may just indicate trends of certain parameters or actually estimate certain events based on measured characteristics or context information. The first option can be implemented based on a short-term history of the measured network characteristics. Thus, it is possible to state whether, for instance, the number of packet losses is expected to increase or to decrease. Another example could be an indicator that states whether the device tends to leave the network's coverage area or not. The second option may interpret such short-term tendencies or may use long-term data to actually forecast certain events as, for instance, the disconnection of networks. In doing so it may rely on past experiences from previous traversals of the same geographical region. Nicholson and Noble propose a concept of mobility and connectivity forecasts using Markov models [197]. Based on this concept, the authors realized a strategy to forecast the device's mobility as well as the expected bandwidth. Such an approach makes use of the assumption that the mobile user will mostly move at the same paths in his day-to-day life. Thus, the system can be trained on this data to achieve quite high prediction accuracies, but it will fail in unknown scenarios. In addition to measured data that is stored in the device's history, external context information can be used for prediction as well. Sources for such context information can be, for instance, coverage maps or hotspot locations provided by network operators [198] as well as databases like JiWire [5]. But, this requires the availability of information on the devices' location and movement.

After predicting a possible chance that a certain network gets available, there is still the question of how to rate the characteristics of a network that is expected to be available in the near future. This can be solved either by using past experiences or by using context information, for instance, from external directories. In the former case, the mobile device may collect and aggregate information about networks being seen in the past. The latter option relies on context information that provides first hints on the possible performance of the access network that can be expected. Such an approach might be implemented in a cooperative way. Any devices that currently have access to the network in question may report on their experiences [199] and feed this information into a database where other users can make use of it.

3.3.3 Implementation

In the previous section, we discussed the main issues in implementing the muXer *Link Monitor* and presented related work in the different areas that indicates the general feasibility of our concepts, although there are still open research issues. A special challenge for the design of the *Link Monitor* is the fact that the implementation of the required modules is strongly dependent the specific hardware that is used.

However, to indicate the general feasibility of the concept, we implemented a basic prototype of the *Link Monitor*. For this, we realized two *Monitor Agents* for WLAN und UMTS that monitor a set of basic networking conditions. The gathered parameters are processed and combined to sets of network parameters. For the WLAN Agent we make use of features of the MadWifi Linux driver [200] and the Kismet IEEE 802.11 sniffer [201]. Link layer characteristics of the UMTS network are collected by querying the UMTS modem with the help of AT-commands. Moreover, our implementation uses a GPS receiver to log mobility information on the mobile node. To simplify the deployment of such a system, it would be desirable to integrate the *Monitor Agents* directly into the network interface drivers as they encapsulate all technology specific functionalities. We did not choose this option for our prototype, as the modifications would dependent on the specific hardware being used and, at least for the UMTS modem, there is no public documentation of the manufacturer-specific functionalities. For debugging purposes the *Link Monitor* is able to store and replay traces of obtained measurements. The implementation is realized as a separate process. Thus, it does not necessarily need to run on the same host than the *Decision Engine* itself. This simplifies the integration into alternative target scenarios as they were discussed in section 2.2. Here, a mobile router may provide Internet access to multiple devices or a swarm of devices may share their communication capabilities with each other. Therefore, network monitoring and the actual decision process may run on different devices.

Additionally, we implemented a Prediction Engine that uses context and mobility information to identify possible networks that may be accessible in the near future. Those potential candidate networks are transparently added to the list of candidate networks using the same data structure.

3.4 Decision Engine

The *Decision Engine* is the core module of the muXer architecture. It is responsible for the actual network selection process and balances different input measures to find one or multiple appropriate networks according to application and user requirements. In the following, we discuss the general design issues and concepts used for the *Decision Engine*. The decision process itself is discussed separately in chapter 5.

3.4.1 Design Issues

The task of the *Decision Engine* is to process sets of input parameters describing network characteristics as well as certain QoS requirements. Based on this, it has to find a suitable resource allocation that uses the available communication capabilities efficiently and meets the given requirements. Figure 3.4 illustrates the variety of different inputs. First, there are user preferences as, for instance, the amount of money he is willing to pay or a relative importance of applications. Other user-related inputs may be based on current user inter-actions. Thus, applications that interact with the user at the moment may require higher reactivity than background applications. Furthermore, a set of application requirements describe the demands of the applications to work properly. On the other hand, there are multiple measures describing the available resources. Technology and path characteristics describe the capabilities of the access networks. Monetary costs for using certain networks as well as the energy that is consumed by activating a specific network interface are further inputs to the decision process. Finally, the input data may be enriched by additional context information.

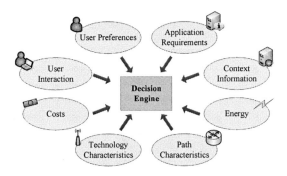

Figure 3.4: Inputs to the decision process

In section 2.5 we discussed multiple approaches for dynamic network selection strate-gies used in the context of ABC scenarios. Here, we found out that existing approaches commonly suffer from a degree of flexibility in combining highly heterogeneous charac-teristics and optimization goals. But, this is a central requirement for an efficient decision strategy as we stated before. In addition, the *Decision Engine* must provide a modular struc-ture to be able to adapt to future communication systems and new optimization goals. A further limitation of existing approaches is that they mostly focus either on an application- or device-oriented network selection strategy. The former one focuses solely on individual applications and their specific requirements, while the latter approach decides on which access network to use for all applications running on the device. In muXer we aim at combining both approaches to account for cross-application interferences as well as individual requirements.

3.4.2 An Arbitration Concept for Decision Making

To overcome the limitations mentioned before, we make use of an arbitration concept coming from the domain of mobile robot navigation for our *Decision Engine*. The Distributed Architecture for Mobile Navigation (DAMN) [202] was designed for controlling autonomous mobile robots. In such autonomous driving scenarios, real-time responsiveness and dealing with uncertain information are inherent aspects that have to be managed. To address these issues, Rosenblatt proposes a framework for centralized arbitration that is characterized by a combination of deliberative and reactive decision elements. Figure 3.5 illustrates the general arbitration concept. It is made up of two major components:

▶ a centralized arbiter and

▶ a set of independent decision modules.

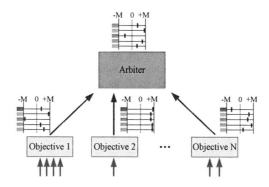

Figure 3.5: The concept of arbitration

The decision modules implement different desired system behaviors. Each of these modules is responsible for one specific system objective. In DAMN, these objectives relate to possible behaviors of the mobile robot. The modules rate independently and asynchronously for or against the suitability of these objectives with respect to the value of a specific control parameter, as for instance speed and direction. Their internal realization can be arbitrarily complex and may be tailored exactly to the needs of the specific goal. Just the semantics of their ratings are well defined to allow for an evaluation and comparison of the output coming from different decision modules. Therefore, the ratings of all modules needs to be of the interval $[-M, +M]$ where

$+$**M**   implies a strong support for a decision alternative,

0   indicates a neutral position, and

$-$**M**   expresses a strong decline of a decision alternative.

The size of the interval can be chosen almost arbitrarily, as the semantics of the votes are more important than their actual values. It affects only the granularity of the ratings that can be modeled. The votes of all decision modules are evaluated by an arbiter. An arbiter is responsible for deciding on the value of one specific system control parameter. It implements a higher-level reasoning by combining and weighting all votes of the decision modules. Afterwards it has to decide on the final value of that control parameter from the set of candidate values. The aim is to meet the different objectives as well as possible. In the simplest case, an arbiter may select that alternative with the maximum weighted overall vote. However, in general it may also consider a set of additional policies like, for instance, exclusion criterions or dynamic weighting. This avoids any drawbacks of methods that jointly evaluate different goals and simply average specific ratings, which leads to decisions being suboptimal to any of the individual goals.

Characteristics and Advantages of Arbitration in the muXer Context

Several design aspects of this arbitration concept correspond to the aforementioned requirements of the muXer architecture in general and the network selection process in particular. It was inherently designed to provide a very high level of dynamics and flexibility. The arbitration concept is based on a set of independent and asynchronous decision modules. Each of these modules focuses only on one specific objective. Thus, its internal realization can be tailored to that specific task and the module requires only that set of input parameters that is really relevant for its own focus. This feature of the concept simplifies the system design and results in a high modularity. As the decision modules act independently from each other, they may be exchanged, added or weighted on-the-fly, without affecting other modules. They simply have to be connected to the centralized arbiter that has to consider the votes of these new modules in future arbitration cycles. Further on, the decision modules can operate asynchronously from each other, providing a higher degree of real-time responsiveness. The update interval of each decision module can be tuned exactly to the needs of the respective objective that it implements.

The general arbitration concept does not make any restrictions to input or output parameters. This is a clear advantage to other techniques like, for instance, utility functions or fuzzy logic that always have some specific requirements or boundary conditions on these values. Examples for this are fuzzy membership functions or arithmetic and normalized representations of decision criterions. The decision modules can use arbitrarily complex input parameters in any possible shape that fit best to the specific objectives. Additionally, the internal design of the optimization objectives can be highly heterogeneous as well.

Another advantage of the arbitration concept is that it is intentionally designed to cope with uncertain and unforeseen scenarios. This is one of its main strength as the system does not need an expert for designing rules reflecting the whole expected behavior. Instead, independent behaviors are modeled, each focusing only on one single system objective. Afterwards, the arbiter is responsible for taking actions based on the votes it gets from the different modules. This design makes it possible to find unconventional, but viable solutions to the given decision problem. Therefore, the arbitration concept avoids the drawbacks of, for instance, policy-based systems that occur if conflicting policies have to be handled. On the other hand, it makes the system behavior clearly less predictable. Depending on the implementation of the objectives, it may not even act in a deterministic way. On the other hand, such a behavior can help to reduce the probability of problems that may appear if multiple devices at one location run the same decision algorithm, as it may avoid that several devices make the same decisions at the same time and thus probably interfere with each other.

To sum up, the major advantages in using the arbitration concept for network selection in contrast to previously proposed approaches is a clear gain in handling heterogeneous input parameters and optimization goals. This is an inevitable feature of a selection strategy that is not focusing on a specific set of technologies or networks. In addition, it provides a high level of flexibility and expandability making it easy to include additional optimization goals. Moreover, the concept does not simply average the results of the single decision modules. It allows for case-based adaptations and may handle specific outliers in the results of the decision modules explicitly instead of just setting them off against the other results. Finally, it enables a dynamic weighting of decision factors depending on certain scenarios. The balancing of the different goals within the arbiter may result in creative solutions, but improves the system capability to handle unforeseen scenarios.

3.4.3   The muXer Decision Process

Figure 3.6 shows the general design of the *Decision Engine* used in muXer. In contrast to existing work, the decision process is split-up into two phases:

▶ an application-oriented arbitration, followed by

▶ a global resource allocation phase.

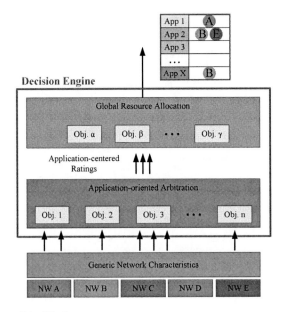

Obj. = Objective

Figure 3.6: Architecture of the Decision Engine

The first phase of the decision process evaluates candidate networks with respect to the specific requirements of individual applications. Afterwards, these results are used in the second phase, where the application-centered ratings are combined and cross-checked against the network capabilities as well as further global optimization criterions. The advantage of this two-tier approach is that the resulting decisions meet the individual requirements of the applications without neglecting aspects of applications using a network concurrently as well as any global objectives like the costs a user is willing to pay. A pure application-oriented approach would only result in locally optimal results with respect to one specific application. But, problems like the limited capabilities of a network in serving multiple concurrent applications would remain unconsidered. Compared to an integrated approach, the separate realization of both tiers has the advantage that they may run asynchronously and are not required to be located on the same device. The latter aspects simplify the integration into alternative target scenarios as they were presented in section 2.2. The following sections introduce the general concept of both phases.

Application-oriented Arbitration

The first tier of the decision process implements an application-oriented arbitration process. This is realized with the help of a set of arbiters, each evaluating the specific suitability of one candidate network provided by the *Link Monitor* for the respective application the arbiter is focusing on. In doing so, it makes use of a set of decision modules. Each of these modules implements one specific objective and rates the candidate networks according to the application's needs. The final output of this tier is a set of ratings representing an isolated view on the current communication scenario for each application.

Global Resource Allocation

The second stage combines the application-centered ratings by analyzing, whether the joint requirements of a set of applications preferring the same network really comply with the network's total QoS offer. If that is not the case, it is necessary to assign a subset of these applications to a different network. In addition, global reasoning criterions for minimizing the overall monetary costs and energy demand of data transmission are considered. This way, it is assured that available networks are used to their full capacity without breaking the user-defined requirements.

Output

The final output of the *Decision Engine* is a mapping of applications to networks. Hereby, the *Decision Engine* assigns one of three possible actions to each individual application:

▶ use one network,

▶ use multiple networks in parallel, or

▶ wait for an upcoming transmission opportunity.

The first option is straightforward: The resulting decision assigns a specific network to the application which will be used for communication. This option is common practice for ABC scenarios. In contrast, the latter two options go beyond existing ABC approaches. When using multiple networks concurrently, the application data flow is split across them to increase the QoS offered to the application[1]. This option can help to meet the requirements of demanding applications in situations with limited networking capabilities. Another advantage is the possibility to use spare capacities of networks more efficiently. Finally, the third decision alternative deals with the possibility to defer data transmissions for a specific time period. In several scenarios, an immediate data transmission is not mandatory. Thus,

---

[1]see section 2.4.2

application data may not be delivered now if only expensive networks are available, but, for instance, may be transmitted in 10 minutes when a different access network is expected to appear.

3.5   Path Management

The *Path Management* module is responsible for putting the outcome of the *Decision Engine* into action. It bundles all required functionalities and implements suitable interfaces and protocol optimizations. For this, it has to handle three main aspects:

▶ seamless vertical handovers (VHOs),

▶ concurrent multipath transfer (CMT), and

▶ disruptions or long delays.

Figure 3.7 shows the internal architecture of the *Path Management* module. It consists of two major components: a *Network Broker* and a *Registry*. Each application that requires Internet access registers at the muXer. Thereby, it is added to the *Path Management Registry* that maintains additional information, as for instance the process ID, an identifier for the respective transport layer or session layer service access point, and the current network being used. This information is required by the *Network Broker* that receives the decisions from the *Decision Engine* and checks whether any actions have to be taken. If that is the case, it initiates, for instance, a handover process or sets up a network bundle. For this, it communicates with a set of agents that care about the implementation of the requested actions. Moreover, it forwards changed interface configurations to the *Link Monitor* that implements the technology-specific methods to switch to a different network and cares about further issues, such as authentication and obtaining an IP address in the respective network.

3.5.1   Handover and Multipath Transfer

In section 2.4, we discussed various approaches for mobility management at different protocol layers of the ISO/OSI model. Each of them comes with its specific advantages and disadvantages. The lower the layer used for mobility management, the less protocols or applications have to be adapted in order to benefit from the ABC service. But, lower layer integrations tend to get more specific to technologies or may require special functionalities from the network operator. The other way round, the higher the mobility management is located in the stack, the more modifications of applications or common network protocols might be necessary. However, this comes with the advantages that data flows can be managed fine granularly, protocol mechanisms might be adapted to changes in the network characteristics, and the reliance on technologies or additional services is minimized.

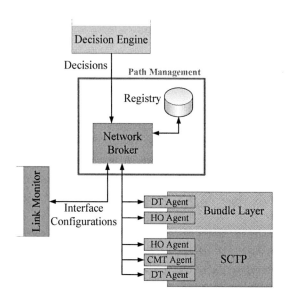

Figure 3.7: The muXer Path Management component

As stated in section 3.1 the muXer architecture requires a separation and individual handling of application flows to be able to realize an application oriented network selection. An additional requirement is the highest possible independence of specific networking technologies. To achieve a maximum flexibility, the reliance on specific infrastructure components or network operators should be minimized. Finally, as the target scenario in figure 3.1 at the beginning of this chapter showed, muXer operates in a highly heterogeneous communication environment, where the characteristics of different access networks may differ clearly. Thus, the change of access networks at lower layers may result in performance degradation as, for instance, upper layer protocol mechanisms like flow and congestion control mechanisms misjudge the change of networking parameters.

For these reasons, we implemented the muXer path management functionalities for handovers and network bundling at the transport layer. Both are based on the Stream Control Transmission Protocol (SCTP) [12] that provides multihoming support innately and thus is able to handle multiple IP addresses for one single connection. A transport layer approach meets the aforementioned requirements best and keeps the remaining architecture of the Internet untouched. It inherently optimizes routes between the mobile device and the correspondent node and avoids overhead that is caused, for instance, by triangular routing [203]. Moreover, it is independent of any network provider and does not rely on additional infrastructure components that mask changes of the device's access networks. In addition, it offers the option to integrate additional protocol optimizations increasing the overall performance in the event of handovers between highly heterogeneous networks. However, a disadvantage of the transport layer approach is that it requires additional location services and link layer support, for instance, to define a dedicated interface for outgoing data to a single-homed host for instance. Furthermore, it is only transparent to the application if this does not use IP addresses within its own communication messages [203]. The mechanisms for network bundling are implemented at the transport layer as well. Both aspects will be analyzed more closely in chapter 4.

3.5.2   Disruption Tolerance

A transport layer approach may also be used to handle network disruptions. We already presented the advantages and opportunities in increasing the communications performance in challenging networking scenarios in section 2.4.3. However, tolerance to network disruptions is often a specific feature that has to be supported by the application to some extent. A lot of applications will timeout or do not work correctly if they are not able to exchange data within a certain period of time. Such effects cannot be handled by any transport layer mechanisms. Moreover, muXer aims at supporting not only communication via infrastructure networks assuming that there is always at least one network to use, but also via challenged networks with unstable networking characteristics and probably no end-to-end paths [7].

This is a reasonable assumption as a national or even a transnational seamless connectivity with mobile Internet access at high bandwidths cannot be expected. In section 2.1 we pointed out that this is not even the case for the GSM system in Germany.

To manage such disconnections and long delays, the application needs to have a certain notion of this behavior and has to be designed to cope with these aspects. Based on this, a session layer protocol may transparently manage such periods of disconnection for the applications. Thus, the muXer *Path Management* module is designed to provide such a session layer support on the basis of the DTN bundle protocol [93]. The bundle protocol implements a generic approach to disruption tolerance that splits application data up into bundles that are handled individually. For this, it follows a store-carry forward paradigm, where bundles are stored at a node until they can be forwarded towards the destination.

Closer investigations on the consequences of different DTN variants like store-carry-forward networks [204] or simply disruption tolerant access to infrastructure networks [87] are out of the scope of this thesis. Therefore, we only implemented a proof-of-concept showing that an integration in the IBR-DTN implementation [205] of the Bundle Protocol is possible in general. Further questions on gathering and describing path characteristics of different DTN variants as well as routing issues are left for future research.

3.5.3 Support of Legacy Applications

In designing the muXer path management concept, we decided to base the respective mechanisms on the Stream Control Transmission Protocol (SCTP). This raises the question on how legacy applications can be supported by muXer. Currently, TCP and UDP are by far the dominating transport protocols being used on the Internet. SCTP provides reliable and ordered data delivery and also unordered delivery and an optional partial-reliable data service. Thus, it is possible to map both protocols, TCP and UDP, on SCTP using the respective services.

Basically, there are two options to implement a support of such legacy applications as illustrated in figure 3.8. First, as being illustrated in (a), one can use a legacy wrapper that alters the TCP socket into an SCTP socket as show in the upper part of the figure. This is done, for instance, by intercepting the respective library calls. The advantage of this solution is that the wrapper can be implemented transparently to the application and used even for applications where no modifications of the source code are possible. In addition, no further infrastructure components are needed for this approach. On the other hand, it is not only required at the client side, but also at the correspondent node to make the server SCTP capable as well. An alternative option would be the use of a Performance Enhancing Proxy (PEP) [46]. To support legacy applications at the mobile device, a local proxy is required that converts standard transport layer Internet protocols into SCTP. For full legacy support, a second proxy is required on the Internet that performs the backward conversion. This second

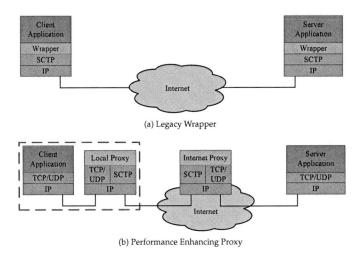

(a) Legacy Wrapper

(b) Performance Enhancing Proxy

Figure 3.8: Concepts for legacy applications

proxy might also be used in conjunction with the legacy wrapper. The proxy concept brings the advantage that it may be able to support further optimizations of application protocols for challenged networking scenarios as proposed by Ott et al. [87]. However the second proxy comes at the cost of losing the independence of special infrastructure components. Moreover, it increases the dependence on a certain network or service operator that runs the proxy. Nevertheless, this second option might probably be the most promising option for an early deployment of the muXer functionalities.

3.5.4 Location Management

Another important issue is the question of how to locate a multihomed device that runs an ABC service from the Internet. As the access networks that are used by the device may change frequently by mobility and local decisions of the network selection strategies, a corresponded node on the Internet may not know about how to connect to the mobile device or requires at least frequent updates. Besides, as the mobile device uses multiple networks concurrently, the correspondent node may not be able to choose the best destination address. Figure 3.9 illustrates this problem.

In general, there are multiple approaches to implement location management for multihomed devices. Some examples are presented by Riegel and Tuexen [50] as well as Koh et al. [206]. For instance, it might be possible to use Mobile IP (MIP) [56, 57]. The mobile node

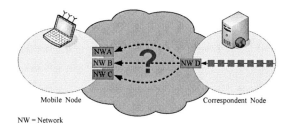

Figure 3.9: Location management issue

may either update its co-located care-of address (MIPv4) or its care-of address (MIPv6) or it may be extended in such a way that it is capable of handling multiple interfaces. Afterwards, the home agent concept can be used to locate the mobile device, while the actual data transfer and handovers are managed by SCTP. Further options can be the use of a Reliable Server Pooling (RSerPool) [207] or even adaptations to SIP [39] or DNS [208] with dynamic updates [209]. However, in the context of the muXer target scenario the characteristics of the networks being used can differ clearly. Thus, it may not be advantageous, if a correspondent node chooses an arbitrary interface for connecting to the mobile device. The information on which network or bundle of networks to use may be provided during the initial connection setup or already in advance. In the former case the mobile device needs to register a dedicated network interface for connection setup at the location service. The correspondent node uses this interface for connecting to the mobile node. Afterwards, it may trigger, for instance, a handover to a different interface. The latter case may require more context information about the device's communication capabilities to be transferred to the location service or to the correspondent node itself. Thus, the mobile device provides all relevant information that allows either the location service or the correspondent node to make a qualified decision on which interface is selected.

Actually, there are several proposals to use one of the aforementioned approaches for location management in heterogeneous networking environments [49, 53, 210, 211]. However, the question of which of them is best and might be extended to requirements in the context of muXer is far beyond the basic scenario mentioned at the beginning and thus, is out of scope of this thesis.

3.6 Summary

In this chapter we proposed the muXer architecture for dynamic network selection in heterogeneous communication environments. By the design of our architecture we aim at overcoming the limitations of existing approaches. MuXer provides a very high level of flexibility and modularity. In addition, we consider disrupted and bundled paths as candidates for data transmission instead of focusing only on single path transfers along available networks. The core module within muXer is the *Decision Engine* that runs the actual network selection process. This process is made up of two phases. At first, it determines an application-centered rating of the candidate networks by using arbitration. This stage is followed by a cross-application refinement process that allocates the respective network resources to the applications or decides on deferring an application request. In doing so, muXer tries to find a global optimum for all applications running on the mobile device. Moreover, we proposed our approach of a *Link Monitor* that collects information on the available networks and provides a generic set of performance measures for the decision process. Finally, we presented our approach to mobility management at the transport layer using the Stream Control Transmission Protocol. The *Path Management* module is able to handle a set of application data flows and may initiate handovers or set up network bundles. Data flows might be deferred for a certain time, either with the help of transport layer functionalities or by making use of the bundle protocol at the session layer. By managing these issues at the transport layer, we can reduce the dependencies on specific providers or network operators.

In the following, we will turn to two specific aspects within the muXer architecture as illustrated in figure 3.10. First, in chapter 4 we evaluate the capabilities of transport layer handover and concurrent multipath transfer in heterogeneous networking scenarios. The main focus of our work is an efficient decision strategy that inherently supports multipath transfer and delaying of data transmissions as additional decision options. The resulting hybrid decision concept for muXer is presented in chapter 5.

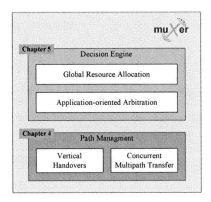

Figure 3.10: Key building blocks for this thesis

Chapter 4

Transport-Layer Issues

The transport layer has the crucial task to provide communication services to the application processes. In the Internet protocol stack, it is located directly between the application layer and the network layer [212]. The transport layer sets up a logical channel that allows for exchanging messages between applications without any particular knowledge on the network infrastructure. Today, the Internet is dominated by two transport protocols: the User Datagram Protocol (UDP) and the Transmission Control Protocol (TCP) [213]. More than 90 % of the Internet traffic is allotted to TCP, while almost the rest results from UDP traffic. UDP provides an unreliable and connection-less service without any service guarantees. In contrast, TCP provides a connection-oriented service with flow control mechanisms and certain guarantees on the data delivery. In section 3.5.1, we identified the transport layer as the most promising option to implement our path management functionalities. Nevertheless, both protocols were not inherently designed for dynamic scenarios with changing access networks as we consider them in muXer. They do neither inherently support vertical handovers or concurrent multipath transfer as required in muXer, nor do they provide at least any mechanisms for supporting such functionalities. Implementing these features into either TCP or UDP would require significant modifications at both peers: the sender and the receiver.

In 2000 the Internet Engineering Task Force standardized a further transport protocol, the Stream Control Transmission Protocol (SCTP) [12, 214]. It aims at overcoming some limitations of TCP and provides additional features like multihoming and multistreaming capabilities. Although SCTP does not provide handover or concurrent multipath transfer mechanisms as well, its concept still provides a set of basic functionalities that allows for an integration of these mechanisms with fewer changes in the standard protocol. For this reason, we chose SCTP as a basis for implementing our transport layer mechanisms. However, the high popularity and wide distribution of TCP requires solutions to support legacy application as well, as it cannot be expected that SCTP replaces TCP in the near future.

In the following, we introduce our research on implementing vertical handover mechanisms and concurrent multipath transfer in heterogeneous scenarios on the basis of SCTP. Our particular interest is focused on a proof of the general concept and the performance of these mechanisms with respect to our target scenario stated in section 3.1. The results build the basis for the actual design of the network selection strategy. First, this chapter starts with an introduction to SCTP and its novel features in section 4.1. Afterwards, in section 4.2 we introduce our prototypical implementation of the *Path Management* module in the muXer architecture including the support of legacy applications. This goes along with an introduction of the protocol mechanisms for vertical handovers. We presented these aspects already in [11]. In section 4.3 we turn to the problem of concurrent multipath transfer and propose some modifications to existing research work in this area. Approaches for freezing the transport layer connection in times of disconnections have been researched extensively in the past. Thus, we do not address these issues within the scope of our work. Finally, another major aspect in this chapter is the evaluation of the proposed mechanisms in heterogeneous communication environments to derive conclusions about the feasibility and efficiency of our concept for dynamic network selection.

4.1   The Stream Control Transmission Protocol

Initially, the Stream Control Transmission Protocol (SCTP) [215] was designed as a transport protocol for signaling traffic, as for instance SS7, over IP networks in telephone systems. In 2000 the first protocol definition was passed by the IETF in RFC 2960 [214]. Later, the standard was revised in RFC 4960 [12]. As for now, implementations of SCTP are available for various operating systems [216, 217]. The aim in designing SCTP was to overcome known issues and limitations of TCP. SCTP introduces the concept of an *association* that broadens the common notion of a TCP connection, as it is illustrated in figure 4.1. In contrast to TCP, for each communicating peer, an SCTP association allows for binding multiple IP addresses[1]. This feature is called *multihoming* and was designed to make SCTP more robust against network layer faults at one of the peers. A network path between the communicating peers is defined by a pair of IP addresses that are bound to the association at each peer. If these paths are independent, a peer remains reachable even if one of the subnets it is connected to will fail. SCTP uses only one of the possible paths for data transmission. On each peer, one of the associated addresses is defined to be the primary address. The pair of these addresses is called the *primary path* that is used for data transmission. The remaining addresses are only used in terms of failures or for retransmissions. Each peer is able to change its primary address dynamically within an existing association. The capabilities of SCTP's multihoming

---

[1]Without loss of generality, we assume in the following that the Internet Protocol (IP) is used as the network layer protocol.

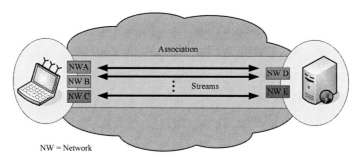

NW = Network

Figure 4.1: The concept of an SCTP association

feature are limited by two major issues. On the one hand, if one interface breaks down, this will lead to the failure of a subset of paths depending on the number of interfaces of the other endpoint. On the other hand, to select specific source addresses for outgoing packets, network layer support is always needed. SCTP can only define the outgoing transport layer address, but has no possibility to dictate the outgoing interface. This is the task of the network layer protocols that chose the interface based on the entries in the routing table.

A second feature of an SCTP association is its *multistreaming* capability. In general, a stream is a kind of a logical unidirectional communication channel between the SCTP endpoints. In contrast to TCP, a stream does not refer to a sequence of bytes, but to a sequence of user messages. Messages that are sent along the same stream are delivered in-order unless they are not explicitly marked for unordered delivery. On the other hand, the correct sequence of messages sent along different streams is not necessarily guaranteed. SCTP allows for establishing multiple independent streams within a single association. This concept was intentionally designed to reduce the head-of-line blocking problem known from TCP [218]. TCP delivers messages always in order to upper layer protocols. Thus, if one message is lost any later messages are delayed at the receiver, even if they may potentially be independent.

Besides the aforementioned aspects, SCTP provides a set of further features:

► a reliable or partial-reliable[84] service, and

► a four-way handshake to achieve a higher robustness against denial of service attacks like SYN flooding [219].

A further difference between SCTP and TCP or UDP becomes obvious when looking at the packet format shown in figure 4.2. Each SCTP packet is made up of a common header and one or more additional chunks. These chunks may contain either payload data or control information, as for instance, for association setup and shutdown or to acknowledge

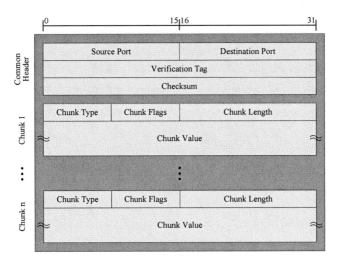

Figure 4.2: The SCTP packet format

data. The common header includes the source and destination port, a verification tag that allows for validating the sender of a packet and a checksum for the whole packet. Each chunk starts with a header of three fields that indicate its type, a set of flags whose interpretation depends on the actual type of the chunk and a parameter stating the size of the chunk. Finally, the *Chunk Value* is the actual information that is carried within this chunk. This concept facilitates future enhancements of the protocol functionality by introducing new chunk types. Except for some special control chunk types, several chunks may be bundled into a single SCTP packet as long as the MTU restrictions are met. For a full description of the packet format and the different chunk variants we refer to RFC 4960 [12]. In the following we will present some of SCTP's mechanisms in more detail.

4.1.1 Path Management and Failure Detection

SCTP's multihoming capabilities allow for defining multiple paths between both communicating peers within one association. During the setup of the association, both peers negotiate the addresses that are used and thus define the possible communication paths. One of these paths is actively used for data transmission. To check whether the remaining addresses of a peer are still reachable, they are continuously monitored. Thus, each peer periodically sends *heartbeats* to every destination address of the remote peer which acknowledges them upon reception. The heartbeat mechanism is intended to detect path failures for backup addresses in advance and thus to increase the reliability of the protocol in the case that the primary path needs to be changed. This comes at the cost of an additional overhead along paths that are not being used for data transfer at the moment. However, the overhead is quite small since only two small packets are exchanged within an interval of on average $RTO + 30s$, where RTO states the current value for retransmission timeouts [12]. Futhermore, *heartbeats* are used to measure the round-trip time (RTT) to the remote address. Upper layers can change the heartbeat interval or disable the whole mechanism if reliability is of less importance to the application scenario.

While the heartbeats are used to check the availability of backup paths, a failure of the primary path is detected, if the number of retransmission on this path exceeds a certain limit. This way, the path is assumed to be inactive and SCTP performs a failover to an alternative destination address if one is available. Additionally, SCTP maintains a further error counter for the whole association. If the number of successive retransmission retries along any path exceeds the limit for the association, the remote peer is assumed to be no longer available[2].

Actually, the detection of path failures takes quite long time since SCTP was designed for wired networks and the suggested parameters are chosen very conservatively. According to [220], it takes on average around 63 s to detect a failover if the SCTP default parameters are used [12]. In the context of muXer, we are faced with wireless networks, where path failures are much more common and thus a faster detection might be necessary. One option to address this issue is the use of more aggressive parameters. But, such modifications have cross-effects on the congestion control mechanism. However, in the literature different approaches to improve SCTP's behavior relating to failures and in-depth evaluations of its performance even in mobile and wireless scenarios have already been proposed [221–225]. In the muXer architecture, we do not have to rely on failover mechanisms that are integrated in SCTP, as the decision of which network to use is made in the *Decision Engine*.

4.1.2 User Data Transfer

In contrast to TCP, SCTP provides a message-oriented service, similar as UDP does and preserves message boundaries. User data is encapsulated in DATA chunks that are carried in the SCTP packet potentially together with other data or control chunks. Yet, SCTP implements a reliable transport service as well. Thus, user data that is received at the remote peer is always acknowledged. For this, SCTP inherently implements selective acknowledgements (SACKs) that compare to the optional mechanisms proposed for TCP in RFC 2018 [226]. A description of the packet format of DATA and SACK chunks can be found in appendix A. In addition, SCTP follows the concept of delayed acknowledgements [227]. Thus, the receiver may only send an acknowledgement for every second packet received, but at

---

[2]In RFC 4960 the authors propose to set the maximum number of retransmission attempts per path to 5 and per association to 10 [12].

least within a certain interval after the last chunk with unacknowledged data was received [12]. Only the receipt of out-of-order or duplicate chunks requires an immediate acknowledgement. The SACK may cumulatively acknowledge multiple DATA chunks. This is done based on the Transmission Sequence Number (TSN) that is assigned to each DATA chunk by the sender. Besides, it may contain any *Gap Ack Blocks* if the receiving peer misses any DATA chunks that need to be retransmitted. They may either be lost or still on their way to the receiver. The sending peer that is informed about any gaps decides on the action it takes. SCTP inherently supports Fast Retransmit and Fast Recovery [227]. Thus, retransmissions of data chunks are triggered at the sending peer either by the receipt of three successive SACKs, reporting a certain DATA chunk to be missing or by the expiration of the retransmission timer for the specific destination address. The handling of retransmission timers in SCTP compares to the procedures in TCP. In addition to SCTP's reliable transport service, RFC 3758 [84] proposes a partial-reliability extension where the user has the opportunity to state the level of reliability that is actually required on a per-message basis. This feature is advantageous to time-critical applications and data. Using the partial reliability feature, SCTP is able to cancel the delivery of a data chunk if its lifetime has expired and will not trigger any further retransmissions. Thus, SCTP is, for instance, able to provide an ordered and unreliable service as an extension to the service provided by UDP.

4.1.3   Flow and Congestion Control

The approaches to SCTP's flow and congestion control mechanisms are adopted from those being used in TCP [227, 228]. These mechanisms are well-proven and cause SCTP to adapt its sending rate in a TCP-friendly way. Major differences between SCTP and TCP result from SCTP's multihoming capabilities. While the flow control is managed for the whole association as in TCP, congestion control is handled individually for each destination address. This is necessary as the different addresses may belong to different paths with potentially different communication characteristics. However, there is no further separation between different streams that may be set up within an association. For each destination address of the remote peer, SCTP maintains a separate triple of the following parameters:

► the size of the congestion window (cwnd),

► the slow-start threshold (ssthresh), and

► the partial number of bytes beeing acknowledged (partial_bytes_acked).

The former two parameters have the same meaning as in TCP. But, SCTP employs an additional parameter called *partial_bytes_acked* that is used for adjusting the congestion window during the congestion avoidance phase. Although these parameters are maintained separately for each destination address, the congestion control mechanisms are still designed with respect to using only one path for data transmission.

SCTP's slow start mechanism is identical to the one used in TCP. During the slow start phase, the congestion window increases exponentially if data chunks are acknowledged at the receiver. At the point, where the size of the congestion window exceeds the slow-start threshold, the sender enters the congestion avoidance phase, where the size of the congestion window increases linearly as long as no packet losses are detected. In general, a sender uses the slow start mechanism if the congestion window is smaller than the slow-start threshold. This is also the case, if any data is send to a specific destination address for the first time or after long idle periods. In the latter case SCTP reduces the congestion window for the destination addresses that are not being used with the period of a retransmission timeout. Thus, we can expect that SCTP will go into slow start after a handover.

SCTP assumes packet losses to be caused by congestion in the network. However, comparing to the approach that is proposed for TCP in RFC 2581 [227], SCTP implements Fast Recovery if any data chunks are reported to be lost by SACKs. For this, a SACK may carry one or more so called Gap Ack Blocks. If three successive SACKs state a data chunk to be lost, it is marked for fast retransmit even if the retransmission timer is not yet expired. If a packet loss is detected by a timeout of the retransmission timer, the sender will enter the slow-start phase and reduce its congestion window to one MTU. For further details of the whole mechanisms we refer to RFC 4960 [12].

4.1.4 Dynamic Address Reconfiguration

The basic SCTP protocol features multihoming with the only intention to provide a higher tolerance against the failure of one of the destination addresses that are bound to the association. The only way to bind a set of IP addresses to an association between two peers is during the initialization phase [12]. Afterwards, there is no mechanism that allows for changing these sets of addresses during the lifetime of the association. Especially for wireless networks and in the context of our target scenario this is a strong limitation. New networks may become available over time and links to other networks may break down as a consequence of the user's mobility. Another possible scenario is that a user inserts a new network interface card into his mobile device. This interface cannot be used for an active SCTP association unless the association is shutdown and reestablished again. However, such a behavior is not acceptable as strong effects on the communication performance and an increased handover period can be expected. Thus, it makes SCTP's multihoming capabilities almost useless for dynamic network selection approaches in heterogeneous environments.

A solution that eliminates this problem is proposed by the *Dynamic Address Reconfiguration* enhancement to SCTP that has been standardized by the IETF in RFC 5061 [229]. It overcomes the aforementioned limitations by defining mechanisms to add and remove IP addresses dynamically and to inform the remote peer about any changes. Futhermore, it provides a feature that enables the receiving peer to request the sender to use a different primary address to send data to.

This feature is very interesting in the context of our scenario. A mobile node may detect link changes earlier and thus can advice a sender to switch the primary path before the communication link breaks down. Additionally, it may be used by providers, for instance, to implement load balancing between different access networks. If one network gets close to the capacity limit, users may be handed over to a different access network with spare capacities.

To implement these features, RFC 5061 [229] introduces a new control chunk that is called *Address Configuration Change* (ASCONF). Each request that is sent in an ASCONF chunk has to be acknowledged with an ASCONF-ACK chunk. The ASCONF chunk includes a sequence number and an address parameter that indicates the respective association the ASCONF belongs to by the means of one of the IP addresses that are bound to it. Besides, it contains one or more ASCONF parameters each representing a certain change request. Three types of these requests are defined:

▶ add an IP address to the association,

▶ delete an IP address from the association, and

▶ change the primary address.

Each request includes the respective address the change request relates to and a request correlation ID that is used by the sender of the request to assign an incoming ACK to the request it belongs to. The ASCONF-ACK acknowledges the reception of an ASCONF chunk and may include error reports for one or more requests.

The combination of SCTP and the *Dynamic Address Reconfiguration* enhancement is also referred to as mobile SCTP. Two Internet drafts have been proposed to this subject by Riegel and Tüxen [50] as well as Koh et al. [206]. Both follow similar concepts and describe the general procedure of using SCTP and *Dynamic Address Reconfiguration* in handover scenarios and propose solutions to the problem of location management. However, the Internet drafts are expired by now.

4.2   Path Management and Vertical Handovers

In the muXer architecture, the *Path Management* module is responsible for implementing the actual multiplexing of application data streams onto different access networks. It receives the decisions from the *Decision Engine* and triggers a handover or initiates a multipath transfer if required.

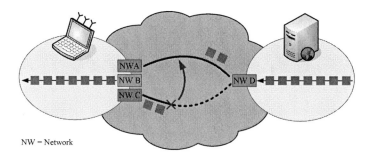

NW = Network

Figure 4.3: The general idea of vertical handovers

The first major path management aspect in muXer is the support of vertical handovers. This feature provides the basis for being able to select an access network dynamically, with respect to the current networking characteristics. Figure 4.3 illustrates the general idea. In our target scenario, we require a mechanism that allows for handling these handover separately for each application in a transparent way. SCTP does inherently support most of the features that are required for implementing such application-oriented vertical handovers. To allow for dynamic handovers, we employ the *Dynamic Address Reconfiguration* enhancement to SCTP that was described in section 4.1.4. However, as most of today's applications use TCP and UDP as transport protocols, we need to provide a support for these legacy applications as it was explained in section 3.5.3. In the following, we introduce the prototypical implementation of our path management concept and describe the procedure of a handover.

4.2.1 Implementation of the muXer Path Management Module

Based on the concepts mentioned in section 3.5, we implemented the required *Path Management* functionalities. Our prototype is made up of two components: first, a *Network Broker* that manages the different applications which require network access and executes any decisions coming from the *Decision Engine* and second, an *SCTP Agent* that interacts with the SCTP Linux kernel module. To support legacy applications that either use SCTP but are not aware of the additional muXer functionalities or that even use a different transport protocol, as for instance TCP, we implemented a *Legacy Wrapper*. The interaction of these modules is illustrated in figure 4.4.

The *Network Broker* maintains a list of applications that are identified by their process ID and the socket file descriptor. It is responsible for triggering changes of the connection settings. The *SCTP Agent* represents the interface to the transport layer functionality. In our proof-of-concept, its implementation is designed to be independent of the specific

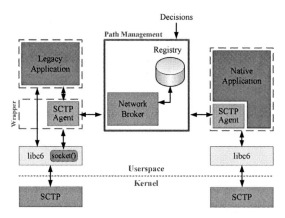

Figure 4.4: Path Management implementation

SCTP kernel implementation. Thereby it is located in the userspace and uses only the SCTP socket API defined by Stewart et al. in [230]. Although, for production use, the functionality should be integrated into the SCTP Linux kernel module itself, this approach increases the flexibility for the evaluation and makes it possible to support different versions of the SCTP kernel module which is still work in progress. The communication between the *SCTP Agent* and the *Network Broker* is message-based. The protocol implements six different messages. First there are two different messages called ADD_REG and DEL_REG to manages the (de-)registration of applications at the *Network Broker*. The GET_ADDR message is used by the application to request new address information from the *Network Broker*. Next, the ADD_PA and DEL_PA messages indicate that the address that comes with the messages has to be added or removed from the association with the help of *Dynamic Address Reconfiguration*. Finally, the SET_PRIM message is required to change the primary path of an association and thus to perform the handover.

In the first step, an application has to register itself at the *Network Broker*. Whenever the *Network Broker* is informed by the *Decision Engine* about new decisions, it triggers any application that is affected, by sending a SIGUSR2 signal. Hereupon, the application's *SCTP Agent* requests a new address information from the *Network Broker*. The concept of using a signal handler allows for an efficient integration of our approach that minimized the overhead for the *SCTP Agent*. The actual modification of the parameters of the transport layer connections is implemented on the basis of socket API calls. The *SCTP Agent* uses the functions setsockopt() and sctp_bindx() from the socket API to modify the parameters of the transport layer connections. If an application does no longer require network access, it deregisters itself from the *Network Broker*.

Furthermore, we implemented a transparent *Legacy Wrapper* that allows for providing compiled applications that are unaware of the *SCTP Agent* with the respective functionalities. This is done by implementing a shared library that is preloaded and intercepts some of the original library function calls with modified ones. Thus, whenever the legacy application calls the `socket()` function, the wrapper first initializes a signal handler and registers itself with the *Network Broker*. Afterwards, it calls the original `socket()` function, but ensures that the protocol family is set to SCTP. Now, the wrapper behaves to the *Network Broker* like a common native application until the socket is closed again, which removes the signal handler as well. The wrapper can easily be used together with binary applications by just setting the `LD_PRELOAD` environment variable.

4.2.2 Handover Procedure

In the following we describe the procedure of a handover and the interaction of the different components in more detail. Figure 4.5 illustrates the process of setting up an association, initiating a handover after some time and shutting down the association as it is implemented in our prototype.

Whenever an application is started, its *SCTP Agent* has to register at the *Path Management* module first, by sending an `ADD_REG` message to the *Path Management* module. The *Path Management* module adds the application to its internal registry and remembers the applications process ID and the socket file handler. Now, the *SCTP Agent* sends a `GET_ADDR` request to the *Path Management* module and asks for the local IP addresses that need to be bound to its association and the primary path that has to be used. The *Path Management* module replies with a `SET_PRIM` message containing the local address of the primary path that has to be used for data transfer. If this address is not yet bound to the association, the *SCTP Agent* adds the address and sets the primary path accordingly. At this time, the association is established and the connected peers can start to communicate. If the mobile node moves, communication characteristics may change. Thus, the *Decision Engine* may come to the decision that the application should use a different network. The *Path Management* module notices this change in the configuration of the application and triggers the respective *SCTP Agent* by sending a `SIGUSR2`. Upon this event, the *SCTP Agent* requests the new primary path from the *Path Management* module using the same procedure as before. Afterwards, SCTP's dynamic address reconfiguration mechanism is used to inform the remote host about the new destination address to be used. This is done by sending an Address Configuration Change control (ASCONF) chunk that is acknowledged by the remote peer as described in section 4.1.4. Hereupon, the handover is completed and the new path is used for data transfer. At the time the application is finished with data transfer, it shuts down the association. Finally, the application deregisters itself from the *Network Broker* by sending a `DEL_REG` message.

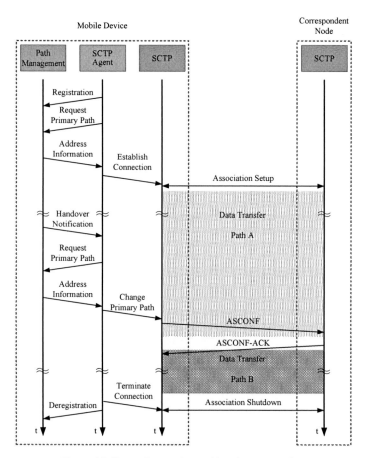

Figure 4.5: Protocol operation and handover procedure

4.3   Concurrent Multipath Transfer in Heterogeneous Environments

The general idea behind multipath transfer is to bundle several paths between the sender and the receiver to use them concurrently for data transfer. The data stream is demultiplexed across multiple, ideally independent, paths, while the receiver multiplexes the incoming packets to the original stream as it is illustrated in figure 4.6. Thus, the communicating peers experience a higher capacity of the logical transmission channel.

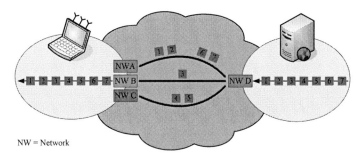

NW = Network

Figure 4.6: The general idea of concurrent multipath transfer

In section 2.4.2 we discussed several approaches of concurrent multipath transfer (CMT) that have been proposed in related research work. However, most of the proposals either assume that the paths to be bundled have equal characteristics in terms of the bandwidth, end-to-end delay, and/or the loss rate or they make assumptions on the protocol instances at the peers as for instance an unlimited receiver buffer. The former assumptions do not hold in the context of muXer, as we expect a heterogeneous network environment with clearly different communication characteristics. The latter one is unrealistic in real deployments. Thus, the focus of our research was the evaluation of the potentials and limitations of CMT in heterogeneous scenarios. For this, we implemented a CMT mechanism in SCTP and evaluated its performance with respect to the differences between the bundled paths in various scenarios.

In the following, we start with a discussion about the challenges in designing a CMT mechanism for heterogeneous networking environments. Afterwards, we present our implementation that is called muXer CMT (XCMT). It combines several enhancements to cope with challenging scenarios.

4.3.1   Challenges and Requirements

The primary objective of using CMT mechanisms is the aggregation of the bandwidth that is provided by multiple underlying network paths. In the context of muXer, we assume that the bottlenecks of the end-to-end paths are the different Internet connections of the mobile devices. Thus, the aggregation of multiple networks brings real advantages in terms of the available bandwidth and they do not share a common bottleneck. This is a reasonable assumption in real-world scenarios. Although WLAN networks provide high bandwidths in general, they are often only connected to the Internet via ADSL links. These feature a lower capacity that the WLAN technology itself. A CMT approach aims at balancing the load on these access networks in a way that the available capacities are used to full capacity. In the case, where the bundled paths provide similar characteristics, the solution to this problem is almost straightforward and the overhead for splitting and merging the stream is quite low. However, in muXer we expect the different paths to show clearly different communication characteristics. Thus, reordering of data packets at the receiver becomes a problem if an ordered delivery to any upper-layer protocols or the application itself is requested. Figure 4.7 illustrates this issue. Basically, the effect of reordering increases the higher the asymmetries between the bundled paths are. If data packets arrive at the receiver out-or-order, they have to be buffered until a full, ordered sequence of packets can be delivered to the application (figure 4.7 (a)). However, the size of a receiver buffer is generally limited to a certain size. Thus, if this buffer is full, all further packets arriving at the receiver will be discarded (figure 4.7 (b)) until the missing packet arrives (figure 4.7 (c)). This issue results in additional retransmissions of packets that already have been successfully delivered to the destination, but could not be stored in the receiver buffer. Furthermore, the buffering of packets increases the end-to-end delay and the jitter that is experienced by the applications and, frequently, bursts of packets may be delivered to the application.

To sum up, a smart and dynamic adaptation of the amount of data send along either path is an essential feature for implementing a CMT mechanism with high performance. The required functionalities can be classified into three groups:

► the scheduling of data along the different paths,

► the monitoring of path characteristics, and

► the mechanisms for reliable data delivery.

The first group builds the heart of the CMT approach and implements the core functionalities. It includes the scheduling mechanisms for allocating application data to the respective paths in an efficient way that minimizes any reordering issues, but maximizes the usable bandwidth. A further aspect of this group is the strategy for choosing a path for data retransmissions. The second group includes all mechanisms to estimate the characteristics of

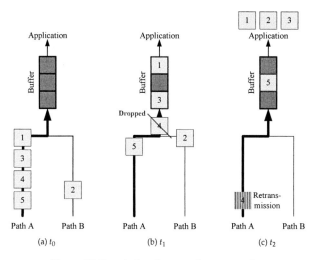

Figure 4.7: Reordering due to path asymmetries

a certain path. Obviously, one requires certain measures as input for the scheduling process to provide the basis for deciding on how data is split-up. However, the concrete parameters that need to be obtained depend on the requirements of the scheduling process being used. Finally, the modifications that relate to the last group highly depend on the transport protocol that is actually extended by CMT mechanisms or newly implemented. They cover functions for controlling the data flow and for ensuring the correct delivery of data at the receiver. To give an example, functions that belong to this group can be congestion control mechanisms or an appropriate sequencing of data packets at the receiver.

4.3.2 The Idealized Scheduler

To analyze the problem of scheduling data along the different paths more closely, we start with an idealized abstraction of the scheduling concept [231]. The aim of our idealized scheduler is to make best possible use of the available capacities.

In figure 4.8 we show a scenario of two network paths A and B with different bandwidths bw_A and bw_B that are bundled to one logical channel. In the first step, we make the assumption that both paths have equal delays $d_A = d_B$. Further, without loss of generality, we assume that the ratio of the amount of data that might be sent along path A is an integer multiple of the amount of date that might be sent along path B to simplify our analysis.

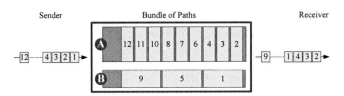

Figure 4.8: Ordered delivery of data for $bw_A > bw_B$ and $d_A = d_B$

In the case that there is no reordering at the receiver, the time $t_A = \frac{N \cdot ps}{bw_A} - d_A$ to transmit N packets along path A is the same than time t_B that it takes to transmit one packet along path B.

$$\frac{N \cdot ps}{bw_A} + d_A = \frac{ps}{bw_B} + d_b \tag{4.1}$$

For our example, this means that the scheduler sends the first packet along the path with the lower bandwidth, while subsequent $N = \frac{bw_A}{bw_B}$ packets are sent along the faster path. As we can see from the figure, even in the idealized case, this procedure results in an unordered delivery of packets at the receiver. The reordering can only be reduced if the sender knows about the information that is sent in a subsequent packet in advance, in order to expedite the sending of the respective packet along the slower path. For some applications, for instance the streaming of recorded videos, such an approach is conceivable. But, there will be multiple exceptions where those assumptions do not hold. Thus, a certain level of overhead caused by reordering cannot be avoided, either at the sender or the receiver.

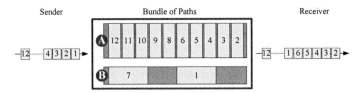

Figure 4.9: Ordered delivery of data for $bw_A > bw_B$ and $d_A < d_B$

In the next step, we extend our model of the optimal scheduler by allowing for additional differences in the delay characteristics of the paths. Thus, data arrives with an additional time-shift at the receiver as one can see in figure 4.9. Here, we assume that the delay of path A is lower than the delay of path B. Our modification results in a further increase of the ratio of data that is sent along both paths. Thus, the additional delay reduces the share of the worse path of the bundle. Based on equation 4.1 the ratio amounts to

$$N = \frac{bw_A}{bw_B} + \frac{bw_A}{ps} \cdot (d_B - d_A).$$
(4.2)

As in the previous case, a further reduction of reordering at the receiver will only be possible, if the sender is able to expedited subsequent packets of the data stream.

As a result of our study of an optimal scheduler, we can make the point that a scheduling strategy that aims at making best use of the capabilities of the bundled paths and at minimizing the reordering at the receiver has to account for three major parameters:

1. the bandwidths of the bundled paths,

2. the difference in the delays of the paths, and

3. the amount of data that is sent along them.

Moreover, the effect packet reordering at the receiver cannot be fully avoided. Even in the idealized scenario of the optimal scheduler a certain level of reordering is experienced that depends on the difference in the path characteristics. This reordering of packets results in an additional overhead and limits the potential benefit of bundling different paths in challenging and heterogeneous communication environments. In general, these findings are not limited to scenarios with two parallel paths. It is also possible to create larger bundles. Such a scenario increases the complexity of the scheduling problem and comes with a higher chance of experiencing reordering at the receiver.

Comparison to Scheduling Approaches in Related Work

In section 2.4.2, we analyzed related work and identified multiple approaches for scheduling data along multiple paths concurrently. In the following, we compare theses approaches to our previous conclusions.

Congestion window driven scheduling: The congestion window (cwnd) driven scheduler is based on the assumption that a path's cwnd reflects its bandwidth delay product:

$$cwnd \approx bw \cdot d.$$
(4.3)

It assigns data according to the ratio of the cwnds of the bundled paths. This approach differs from the conclusions drawn from the optimal scheduler, which accounts for the delay difference between both paths. The approach works sufficiently well in scenarios where the bundled paths have almost equal end-to-end delays or bandwidth-delay products. But, it can be expected that it will result in an increased level of reordering in other heterogeneous scenarios as we can expect them in the context of muXer.

Bandwidth driven scheduling: Bandwidth driven scheduling approaches assign data to the paths in proportion to the ratio of their bandwidths. This approach does not consider any possible difference in the delays. According to our previous results, we can expect a high level of packet reordering at the receiver with increasing differences in the path delays.

Scheduling based on outstanding data: Zhang et al. propose a scheduling approach that is based on the ratio between the amount of outstanding data O_i for path i that has not yet been acknowledged and the size of path's congestion window $cwnd_i$ [74]. It chooses that path with the highest $score_i$, where

$$score_i = \frac{O_i}{cwnd_i} \qquad (4.4)$$

Such a procedure avoids a scheduling behavior where bursts of data are sent along one path before the scheduler switches to another one. However, the approach still suffers from the same limitations as the schedulers mentioned before.

Scheduling based on the ratio of packet size and bandwidth: The approach of this proposal is to overcome the limitations of the previous schedulers by adapting the size of packets that are sent along either one of the paths. The adaptation is done according to the share that a path has on the total available bandwidth. In the end, this results in a homogenization of the transmission times $t = \frac{ps_i}{bw_i}$ that are needed to send a certain amount of data ps_i along each path i. This approach may reduce reordering efficiently if the transmission times are primarily dominated by bandwidth constraints and not by the end-to-end delay. Otherwise, it will suffer from similar limitations than the approaches above. Furthermore, the adaptation of the packet size will require protocols support at other protocol layers, for instance, the network layer.

Scheduling based on the estimated reception time: Finally, the *Faster Path First* principle targets at the same direction as the previous approach. In contrast, it does not adapt the size of packets send on each path, but schedules a packet always to that path with the lowest estimated time of reception. But again, strong delay differences between the bundled paths are neglected in the calculation of this value.

In summary, we can conclude that previous work in the area of concurrent multipath transfer mainly focused on scheduling strategies that assume the bundled paths to have almost comparable characteristics or require at least that the overall transmission time of data packets is primarily dominated by bandwidth constraints. Thus, the results of previous research work do not map reasonably well onto the scenarios considered in muXer and require additional optimizations. This goes along with a lack of evaluations on the performance potentials and limitations of CMT in mobile and wireless communication environments.

4.3.3 muXer CMT (XCMT)

Heterogeneous communication environments, as we consider them in the context of muXer, require an optimized approach to concurrent multipath transfer that is able to manage even with strong heterogeneities in the characteristics of the bundled paths. Thus, we developed XCMT, the muXer CMT extension to SCTP. XCMT provides the general functionality to integrate CMT into our muXer concept and to evaluate the potentials and limitations of CMT in heterogeneous scenarios. In the following we will present the functionalities of XCMT that base on related work, but aims at increasing the performance in terms of the bandwidth that can be effectively used and, thus, the reduction of reordering at the receiver. Implementation details on the integration of XCMT into the Linux kernel SCTP module can be found in the appendix B.

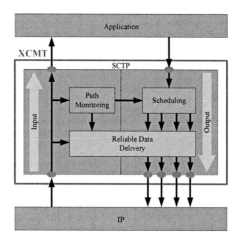

Figure 4.10: Architecture of XCMT

XCMT is based on SCTP. It combines several enhancements that have been proposed for TCP and SCTP and provides adaptations that are intended to increase the communication performance in challenging multipath scenarios with heterogeneous network characteristics. Figure 4.10 illustrates the architecture of XCMT. To make SCTP capable of using multiple paths concurrently, we had to implement and modify three parts of the protocol:

1. the scheduling approach to assign data to the paths,

2. the management of the individual paths with respect to the actual data delivery, and

3. the monitoring of path characteristics that are required to provide the necessary information for the scheduling algorithm.

In the following, we present the functionalities of each of these three main components in more detail.

Scheduling

The *Scheduling* component has the task to allocate application data to the different paths that belong to the bundle of networks. In XCMT, we adopt the principle of the Faster Path First (FPF) scheduler. For each path i in the bundle, FPF estimates the time t_{r_i} a packet is received at the destination if it would be sent along this respective path. Afterwards, the packet is scheduled to that path ϕ where it is expected to be received first ($t_{r_\phi} \leq t_{r_i} | \forall i$). We modified the FPF approach in a way that the end-to-end delay of a path and a correction summand δ are considered for calculating the reception time. The latter one is used for adjusting the scheduler in the case of a considerable amount of packet is received out-of-order at the remote peer. This ends up in the following equation:

$$tr_i = \frac{O_i + B_i + C}{bw_i} + d_i + \delta_i \tag{4.5}$$

In this equation, O_i gives the amount of outstanding data that has been sent along path i, but which is not yet acknowledged. The parameter B_i is the amount of buffered data that has been scheduled to path i and has not yet been sent. Finally, C is the size of the current packet that has to be scheduled, while bw_i and d_i represent the path's bandwidth and delay respectively. With these modifications, the scheduling approach comes close to the concept of the aforementioned concept of the optimal scheduler.

The granularity of the scheduler is limited to data chunks, but not to particular amounts of bytes. The scheduler will not fragment any data chunks, but decides on message level which path is to be used. Thus, it will not be able to avoid the occurrence of reordering at the receiver completely. Another potential source for is the estimation of the outstanding data, as retransmissions may become necessary. The measured path characteristics as, for instance, bandwidth and delay are subject to certain inaccuracies as well. They are only de-termined periodically within certain intervals and are typically smoothed. Thus, the values being used for scheduling change more slowly than the actual characteristics. All of these issues result in estimation errors for the expected reception time of a packet. For this reason, we integrated a mechanism for adjusting the scheduler with respect to such inaccuracies into XCMT.

To determine the current variation of the scheduler from the actual characteristics, XCMT makes use of the gap reports. They are included in SACKs and indicate missing data chunks. The information on these missing chunks is used to determine the correction factor δ_i of a path. At this point, we make the assumption that the gaps at the receiver do mainly result from reordering due to path asymmetries, while packet losses in terms of transmission er-rors or congestion have a minor impact. Thus, we can estimate the scheduler inaccuracies by measuring the amount of data that was sent along path i but has not yet been acknowledged although other data chunks that were sent on a different path have already arrived at the receiver. Hereinafter, this measure is referred to as R_i. The value is determined each time a SACK arrives at the sender. If R_i exceeds a predefined threshold R_{max}, we increase a counter C:

$$R_i > R_{max} \Rightarrow C = C + 1 \quad . \tag{4.6}$$

To avoid a behavior that is too sensitive to any fluctuations, the correction factor δ_i is only adapted, if R_i exceeds R_{max} for at least N times. In that case, we increase δ_i by one MTU.

$$C > N \Rightarrow \delta_i = \delta_i + \frac{MTU}{bw_i} \tag{4.7}$$

This approach of increasing δ_i in small increments has been proven to perform well by evaluations.

The aforementioned scheduling approach is based on a set of parameters that are required to determine the reception time along each path. However, at the beginning of a data transmission these parameters are not known. First, data has to be transmitted along each path to obtain measurement samples. Thus, during the *initialization phase* data chunks are assigned to path ϕ that is allowed to send data according to its congestion window and has the minimum amount of data in flight. This approach was chosen by evaluation from different alternatives and performed well in heterogeneous scenarios.

$$\left((O_\phi + B_\phi) < cwnd_\phi \quad \wedge \quad (O_\phi + B_\phi) \leq (O_i + B_i) \right) \mid \forall i \tag{4.8}$$

A further special case in the context of scheduling is the *handling of retransmissions*. This issue is critical as data chunks that have to be retransmitted are preferred to new data and thus increase the overall transmission time. It is well known that unnecessary retransmissions result in a lower size of the congestion window. Although SCTP implements the mechanism of Fast Retransmission, subsequent losses of the same data chunk will force SCTP into slow start and thus reduce the performance.

In related work, a variety of different strategies for handling retransmissions in the context of CMT are proposed [77, 79, 225]:

► handle retransmissions in the same way as new data chunks

► use a different path than the one the packet was sent before

► use the same path than the one before

► send fast retransmissions along the same path and other ones along a different path

- ▶ use the path with the highest congestion window

- ▶ use the path with the highest slow start threshold

- ▶ use the path with the lowest loss rate

In XCMT, we adopt the last approach that depends on the lowest loss rate. This option outperformed the other ones according to evaluations in the literature, as well as own experiments. However, a second aspect is the time that it takes to deliver the packet to the destination. Thus, we combine both aspects and schedule retransmissions to the path ϕ with the highest probability that the data is actually delivered at the receiver within time t:

$$P_{deliver_i}(t) = 1 - P_{loss_i}(t) \tag{4.9}$$

$$P_{deliver_\phi}(t) \geq P_{deliver_i}\forall i \tag{4.10}$$

Evaluations by Iyengar et al. showed that retransmission policies that account for the loss rate of a path are likely to perform better than any other strategies that do not consider losses [77]. However, while the information on the loss rate in that paper was provided by an oracle, we implement an additional monitoring mechanism to estimate the loss rate for each path in the bundle. Details on this mechanism will be presented later with the path monitoring issues in XCMT.

Reliable Data Delivery

The implementation of functionalities for providing a reliable delivery of data is a technical aspect, which strongly relates to the transport protocol that is used as a basis for CMT. The required features are almost the same across different CMT approaches and have been evaluated well in the literature.

As SCTP comes with an inherent support of multihoming, it provides a good basis for integrating CMT mechanisms. However, it was not designed in the way that multiple paths are used concurrently for data transfer, but only one path at a time. Thus, several changes are required to implement congestion control features and mechanism for handling data chunks that are reported to be lost. For CMT, those features need to act independently for each individual path. Although several parameters as, for instance, the congestion window, the slow start threshold, the round trip time estimate, and the retransmission timeout are already maintained by SCTP per destination address, we have to implement additional per-path delivery mechanisms to make a concurrent use of multiple paths possible.

For this, we extended SCTP with a multi-buffer architecture that maintains a separate send buffer for each particular path. This architecture goes along with the introduction of implicit Path Sequence Numbers (PSNs) [78, 81]. They are required to keep track of which data chunks have been sent along the respective path, but have not yet been acknowledged. This procedure does not require any modifications of the packet format as the information is only used locally at the sender.

Standard SCTP adjusts its congestion window on the arrival of a SACK, which acknowledges a Transport Sequence Number (TSN) that increases the so-called Cumulative TSN Ack Point of the association. This parameter is used by SCTP to keep track on the data chunks that have been delivered to the receiver in the correct order. Any SACKs that arrive out-of-order are discarded by the protocol. However, this case will be a common issue for any CMT approaches. As data chunks are sent in-order but along different paths, one can expect that they arrive unordered at the receiver. Therefore, each path has to maintain its own Cumulative Path Sequence Number (PSN) Ack Point that carries the TSN of the last data chunk being delivered in-order along the respective path. The value is updated each time a SACK contains a cumulative acknowledgement for a data chunk that was sent along the path. Thus, the Cumulative PSN Ack Point allows for an individual adjustment of each path's congestion window. Furthermore, each time a data chunk is retransmitted along a different path than the one used before, the responsibility for its delivery is transferred completely to the new path and does not limit any congestion window adjustments of the original path.

Another necessary modification relates to the Fast Retransmission mechanism. SCTP triggers Fast Retransmissions if three consecutive SACKs report the TSN of a data chunk to be missing. However, using heterogeneous paths concurrently will inherently result in a higher reordering at the receiver. SACKs for data chunks that are sent along the faster path will report the chunks that are sent along the slower path to be missing. Thus, unnecessary retransmissions are triggered. To overcome this issue, XCMT makes use of an approach proposed by Perotto et al. [81]. It increments the counter for the number of times that a chunk c is reported to be missing, only if an incoming SACK meets all of the following three requirements:

1. The SACK reports the TSN of the respective chunk c to be missing.

2. It acknowledges one or more data chunks with a higher TSN than TSN_c for the first time.

3. At least one of these data chunks was sent along the same path than c.

Instead of using the Cumulative TSN Ack Point to increase the counter of missing reports, XCMT uses the Cumulative PSN Ack Point mentioned above. This procedure ensures that the Fast Retransmission algorithm is triggered individually for each path if any data chunks are received out of order.

A final problem of SCTP's data delivery management in the context of CMT is the choice of a suitable strategy for sending and interpreting SACKs. One option is to send SACKs always to the same destination address from which the last data chunk was received. This behavior compares to that of standard SCTP, but comes with the problem of reordering of SACKs at the sender. First, SCTP expects a SACK that carries a lower Cumulative TSN Ack Point than the one maintained at the sender to be received out of order and thus discards the SACK. Second, if the Cumulative TSN Ack Point of a SACK does no longer include a TSN that was previously acknowledged by a Gap Ack Block, the respective TSN is assumed to be missing [12]. Both rules are problematic in CMT scenarios. On the one hand, the comparison of the Cumulative TSN Ack Point is not sufficient to detect SACKs that are really obsolete. On the other hand, the second policy may result in spurious assumptions on the loss of a certain data chunk. To overcome this problem, Zhang et al. propose a policy that states that all acknowledgements are sent over the same path [74]. This way, the order of SACKs is preserved. However, such an approach makes the protocol susceptible to failures of the chosen path and reduces the flexibility in terms of dynamic configurations. Thus, for XCMT we modified the second condition of the original policy for sending SACKs. Instead, we use a stricter condition to avoid deceptive interpretations of SACKs:

1. A SACK with a Cumulative TSN Ack Point lower than the maximum Cumulative TSN Ack Point is discarded.

2. A SACK that reports the same Cumulative TSN Ack Point as the one maintained at the sender, but acknowledges a TSN that is higher than the TSNs that have been reported so far is assumed to be received out of order and thus discarded.

This policy is more restrictive than the approach in standard SCTP as it assumes that a receiver will typically not revoke an implicit acknowledgement by Gap Ack Blocks. However, it fits best to the requirements and the design goals of XCMT.

Path Monitoring

Finally, the last part of our modifications relate to the monitoring of the different network characteristics that are required for the mechanisms in XCMT. These are:

► the bandwidth,

► the end-to-end delay, and

► the loss rate of a path.

The *bandwidth* of a path is needed by the scheduler to estimate the time a data chunk is received at the destination (see equation 4.5). For determining the bandwidth, XCMT adopts a simplified bandwidth estimation technique that is used in TCP Westwood+ [81, 82]. The

Westwood approach has the advantage that it has been shown to provide good estimates of the bandwidth and does not generate additional communication overhead to gather bandwidth samples, as for instance a Sender-Based Packet Pair technique does [81, 193]. The general concept of the bandwidth estimation technique is to measure bandwidth samples within distinct and non-overlapping time intervals. The interval on which the bandwidth is averaged is the maximum of the current RTT and a predefined upper limit. In XCMT, we set this limit to 30 ms as an empirical value that is determined by evaluation. Thus, a bandwidth sample $\bar{b}_i^k$ for path i and time interval k is determined as the ratio of the amount of data D_i^k that has been acknowledged within the time interval k and the size of the time interval:

$$\bar{b}_i^k = \frac{D_i^k}{\max\left(RTT_i^k, 30ms\right)} \tag{4.11}$$

The actual bandwidth estimate B_i^k is calculated as s smoothed average of the new bandwidth sample and old bandwidth estimates with a weighting factor of $\alpha = \frac{1}{8}$:

$$B_i^k = (1 - \alpha) \cdot B_i^{k-1} + \alpha \cdot \bar{b}_i^k \tag{4.12}$$

One of the major drawbacks of this approach is the fact that bandwidth estimates can only be obtained if a path is actively used and any data chunks have been acknowledged. Thus, the XCMT scheduler must follow a different approach during the initialization phase as it has been mentioned above in the section on our scheduling approach.

The estimation of the *end-to-end delay* is based on the RTT measurements that are inherently done by SCTP. In XCMT it is approximated to be half of the measured RTT_i of path i. This is a common assumption that is inaccurate, but avoids the need for any additional mechanisms to actively measure the end-to-end delay by, for instance, using probe packets. Nevertheless, there is still one problem due to delayed acknowledgements that are implemented in SCTP. Thus, two data chunks may be sent along different paths to the receiver, but may be acknowledged with a single SACK on the second path. Thus, in the case that both paths show clear differences in their delays, the RTT estimate for the first path will be incorrect. The significance of this prediction error increases with the delay difference of the paths. Thus, to minimize this error XCMT updates the RTT estimate only for the destination address from which the SACK has been received. To avoid the problem that all SACKs are sent along the same path and thus the RTT of the other path is not updated at all, one might modify the SACK sending policy in a way that the receiver acknowledges at least two packets that are directed at the same destination transport address.

The final parameter that needs to be obtained is the path's *loss rate*. Allman et al. propose an approach to estimate network loss rates with TCP that ends up with good estimation results [232]. The general concepts of congestion and flow control in SCTP are almost equal to those of TCP. Thus, we integrated this mechanism into XCMT. In accordance with the approach to bandwidth estimation, we measure a loss rate within the same time intervals.

The estimated number of retransmissions is calculated on the basis of two parameters: $N_{spurious}$ and N_{total}. $N_{spurious}$ is a counter for the number of duplicates that are reported by the receiver. It is updated each time a SACK arrives by the number of duplicates that is reported:

$$N_{spurious} = N_{spurious} + N_{dups}(SACK). \tag{4.13}$$

N_{total} is incremented by 1 each time a data chunk is retransmitted either by the Fast Retransmission algorithm or by a retransmission timeout. In the end, $N_{retrans}$ amounts to

$$N_{retrans} = N_{total} + N_{spurious} \tag{4.14}$$

In the end, the algorithm determines a new loss rate sample according to the following equation:

$$\bar{l}_i^k = \frac{N_{retrans}}{N_{send}} \tag{4.15}$$

Here, $N_{retrans}$ states the estimated number of retransmissions by losses and N_{send} is the total number of packets sent within the time interval. Finally, to determine the path loss rate L_i^k, the new sample is weighted with the previous one by:

$$L_i^k = (1 - \beta) \cdot L_i^{k-1} + \beta \cdot \bar{l}_i^k, \tag{4.16}$$

where β is set to $\frac{1}{8}$ as an empirical value. Afterwards all counters are reset and the process begins anew.

4.4 Evaluation

To analyze the performance potentials and limitations of vertical handovers and concurrent multipath transfer using SCTP, we evaluated our approaches in a wide range of possible scenarios. We implemented a measurement suite that is used to obtain results about the throughput and the end-to-end delay that is experienced by an application. In the following, we first describe our evaluation concepts and the metrics that are obtained. Next, in section 4.4.3 we analyze the performance of handovers in scenarios with homogeneous and with heterogeneous access networks. Afterwards, we evaluate the benefit and limitations of concurrent multipath in heterogeneous communication environments in section 4.4.4.

4.4.1   Methodology

For our evaluation, we set up a testbed of four hosts as it is shown in figure 4.11. Two of these hosts act as the sender and the receiver of application data respectively. Each of them has been equipped with two Fast Ethernet network interfaces to model a multihoming scenario. The hosts are connected to each other via two independent paths that are labeled A and B. On each of these paths, there is another host that is configured as a router. The routers run a network emulator that allows for manipulating networking characteristics, as for instance the bandwidth, delay, jitter, or packet loss. In our testbed, we employ the NIST Net [233, 234] network emulator. NIST Net implements a Linux kernel module that intercepts IP packets of the data stream to be manipulated and injects them to normal routing afterwards. To the sender and the receiver, the emulator itself is transparent. The router does only decrement the TTL field in the IP-header by one. To manipulate data streams, one has to define rules including the source and destination address information of the respective stream and the requested network characteristics.

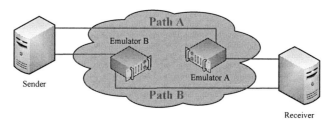

Figure 4.11: Measurement testbed

The approach of employing network emulation techniques has two major advantages compared to using real wireless network technologies or network simulators for the evaluation. On the one hand, we have the full control over the characteristics and the results are not affected by any external radio interferences that result in a distortion of the measured values. Moreover, we are able to configure arbitrary scenarios in our testbed. In contrast to network simulations, we are still able to use "real" implementations of protocols and applications instead of having to use special implementations for the simulation environment.

To obtain reliable results, we implemented a measurement application suite including tools for sending and receiving data packets as well as for determining statistics on the measured raw data. Figure 4.12 shows the concept of this tool suite. The data transfer is controlled by two applications: the *Meomat Client* running at the sender and the *Meomat Server* running at the receiver. The client acts a data sender and triggers events like handovers or

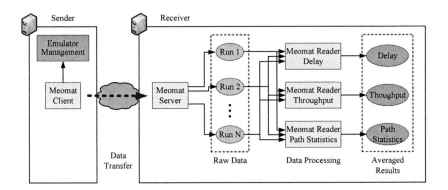

Figure 4.12: The Measure-o-Mat evaluation suite

changes of the path characteristics. It has an interface to the emulator management for manipulating the configured network characteristics. The *Meomat Server* receives the messages
and stores the raw data with additional information about the reception time of a message
and the path along which it was received. To get more dependable results, we perform multiple measurement runs with the same configuration. Afterwards the raw data is processed
by three further tools that determine averaged results for all measurement runs. Especially,
we focus in our evaluation on three parameters: The experienced end-to-end delay at the
application, the application throughput and the share of packets that are sent along every
path in the bundle. We measure the delay with the help of timestamps that are created at
the client and carried with the payload of the data message. To be able to determine the
delay from the time a packet is sent at the client and received at the server, we synchronized
the local clocks with the help of the Network Time Protocol (NTP) [235]. The precision of
this synchronization was determined by the NTP daemon to be lower than 1 ms [236]. The
throughput is determined by measuring the amount of data that was received within certain
time intervals. Finally, the *Meomat Reader Path Statistics* determines the number of packets
that arrived via each of the bundled paths. This information is primarily used for the evaluation of the CMT scheduler. Further details on the implementation of this measurement
suite are described in appendix C.

4.4.2 Scenarios

For our evaluation scenarios, we emulated the delay and bandwidth characteristics of typical access network technologies that are commonly used for mobile Internet. In section 2.1,
we already introduced the basic characteristics of different technologies. Here, we decided
to modeled two access links of cellular networks, which are *UMTS* and *HSDPA* as well as

WLAN links at two different link-layer data rates, namely 2 Mbit/s ($WLAN_2$) and 11 Mbit/s ($WLAN_{11}$). The parameterization of the different scenarios is based on both, parameters that are obtained in related work [237–239], and by our own measurements that have been obtained for all scenarios except for $WLAN_{USHA}$. Although we verified the parameters to compare to real characteristics, they are not universally valid, but model one specific scenario. In other scenarios, a user might experience different performance characteristics. In addition, we implemented the $WLAN_{USHA}$ and the *FastEthernet* link models to compare our handover approach with the TCP/IP-based handover mechanism that is proposed by Chen et al. [61]. Thus, these link characteristics are chosen to compare to the evaluation scenario used there. Table 4.1 summarizes the characteristics of the different access links that are used in our evaluation. For the *FastEthernet* scenario, we do not limited the bandwidth of the path in our testbed. Thus, this parameter is specified with a value of 100 Mbit/s.

Parameter	GPRS	UMTS	HSDPA	$WLAN_2$	$WLAN_{11}$	$WLAN_{USHA}$	Fast Ethernet
Bandwidth [Mbit/s]	0.04	0.260	0.825	1	5.5	5.5	100
Delay [ms]	400	125	50	3.75	1.25	7.25	1.75

Table 4.1: Link characteristics in the evaluation scenarios

4.4.3 Handover Performance

To evaluate the performance of handovers we modeled two paths with specific network characteristics. During each measurement run, the sender transfers 10 000 data packets to the destination along either one of the emulated paths. Each packet carries 1024 bytes of user data. After sending the 5000th packet, the sending application triggers a handover to the other path. For all scenarios, we analyze the achieved throughput to examine possible effects of the handover on the congestion control mechanisms of SCTP. We also measure the end-to-end packet delay and with a special focus on the characteristics during the handover event.

In the following, we will distinguish between two general handover scenarios: a horizontal and a vertical handover. In the former case, both paths have the same characteristics. Thus, the results that are obtained in these scenarios give us information about the actual effect of changing the primary path on the communication performance. In the latter case we analyze the performance of SCTP handover scenarios with heterogeneous path characteristics.

Horizontal Handover

In the first step, we want to analyze the general effect of a handover on the data transmission of the communicating peers. Thus, we modeled a horizontal handover scenario with two homogeneous $WLAN_{USHA}$ links that share the same network characteristics. According to the aforementioned handover procedure, one of the peers initiates the handover by switching the primary path to a different destination address. This event is triggered when 5000 of 10 000 packets were transmitted.

Figure 4.13 shows the measured throughput and end-to-end application delay for a payload of 1024 bytes. It can be seen that the end-to-end delay between the applications stabilizes quickly as the link becomes saturated. Figure 4.13 (b) presents the end-to-end delay against the running number of the packets that have been transmitted. Here, one can see that the end-to-end delay stabilizes at around 104 ms, although the network induced RTT

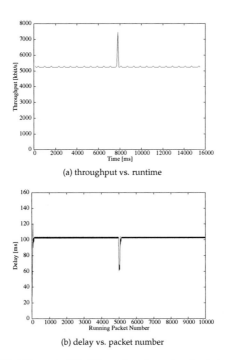

(a) throughput vs. runtime

(b) delay vs. packet number

Figure 4.13: $WLAN_{USHA}$ to $WLAN_{USHA}$ handover (payload size 1024 bytes) is only 14.5 ms. As our measurement suite is designed to send data at the highest possible rate, we conclude that most of the difference to the measured delay results from buffering on lower layers of the transmitting host. At the moment when the handover is initiated, one can observe that the measured end-to-end delay suddenly drops down. After about 50 packets, the delay stabilizes again at the level that was experienced before the handover. At the same time, the throughput increases significantly for a period of 100 ms (figure 4.13 (a)). Thus, for a short period of time it appears that the measured throughput exceeds the actual bandwidth of the path between both peers. We attribute this effect to the saturation of the former path. The delay in the short time after the handover compares to the period at the beginning of the transmission. During this time, SCTP is in slow start. Later, it increases its congestion window in a linear way. The same procedure applies after the primary path is switched to the new destination transport address. All new packets are transmitted via the new path. As long as this path is not saturated, packets are delivered with a shorter total delay between the communicating applications. At the same time, there are still some packets that are sent along the former path. Thus, new packets that are sent along the new path arrive earlier at the receiver than those sent along the former path before. This results in packet reordering at the receiver. It becomes visible in the peak of the measured throughput because a burst of data chunks is delivered to the application at the time the missing packets arrive at the receiver. In the delay graph in figure 4.13 (b), this effect does not appears as a distinct delay spike around packet number 5000. However, if we look into the data we can see that the first packets that are sent along the new path have a clearly higher delay that the following ones. While the measured delay for packet 5001 was still 101.12 ms, which compares to the delay before the handover event. In contrast, it was possible to deliver packet 5040 within 51.33 ms. Thus, although one cannot see a clear peak in the graph, there is still an effect of packet reordering after the handover. But, the characteristics of the unsaturated paths compared to the saturated one before the handover, cover partly the impacts on the measured delay.

To emphasize our findings, we repeated the homogeneous handover scenario with a lower payload size of 128 bytes. For this measurement we increased the number of transmitted packets to 40 000 to have enough time to observe any effects. The results are shown in figure 4.14. Due to the reduced packet size, the application throughput is about 1 Mbit/s lower compared to the previous scenario. This relates to the higher protocol overhead compared to the delivered payload in this scenario. The experienced end-to-end delay decreases to about 39 ms. This effect results from the fact that there is a clearly lower utilization of the link in this scenario. Thus, the need for buffering data at lower protocol layers is reduced. Another difference between both scenarios becomes visible at the time of the handover. While we observed a throughput peak in the scenario with a payload of 1024 bytes, now the throughput falls off at the time of the handover. This drop is followed by a small peak before

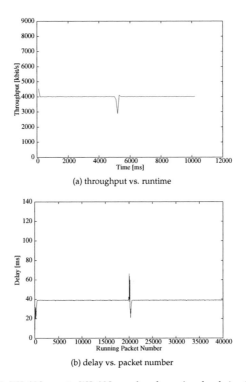

(a) throughput vs. runtime

(b) delay vs. packet number

Figure 4.14: $WLAN_{USHA}$ to $WLAN_{USHA}$ handover (payload size 128 bytes)

throughput stabilizes at the saturation level. Figure 4.14 (b) shows that the delay increases first, before it drops shortly after and stabilizes again. These effects prove our previous results and make the effects of path saturation in the previous scenario clear.

In summary, we found out that a handover is likely to cause reordering at the receiver. The evaluation results show that this may bring advantages in some scenarios, as packets are delivered along both paths for a short period of time. However, in general, the handover forces SCTP to go into slow start for the new destination transport address. The period of time during which the experienced throughput and delay are affected by the handover is less than 100 ms.

Vertical Handover

In the remaining part of our evaluation, we analyze the effects that are induced by a handover from a high capacity to a low capacity link. First, we modeled a handover from a $WLAN_{USHA}$ to a $HSDPA$ link. In this scenario, we compare again the results for the two different payload sizes that were also used in the horizontal handover scenario.

First, figure 4.15 shows the averaged results for 100 measurement runs with 10 000 packets and a payload size of 1024 bytes. The handover was triggered after sending the 9000th packet. One can see that the characteristics of the throughput graph in figure 4.15 (a) compare to the effects that were observed in the homogeneous scenario. Shortly after the handover, the measurements show a small throughput spike while packets a sent along both paths. Afterwards, the throughput quickly levels off at the bandwidth limit of the new path. In contrast to the homogeneous scenario, the delay measurement in figure 4.15 (b) shows

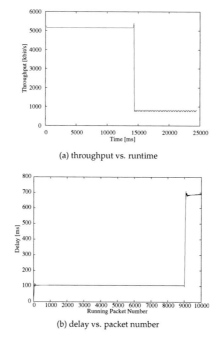

(a) throughput vs. runtime

(b) delay vs. packet number

Figure 4.15: $WLAN_{USHA}$ to $HSDPA$ handover (payload size 1024 bytes)

now a significant increase of the delay at the time of the handover. Instead, there is only a short glitch, first downwards than upwards, before the experienced end-to-end delay stabilizes at a level of 690 ms.

Again, we repeated the measurement with a payload size of 128 bytes and a number of 40 000 packets per run. The handover was triggered after sending 32 000 packets. The results of our delay measurement that are presented in figure 4.16 (b) show a spike of approximately 50 ms after the handover has been proceeded. Afterwards, the delay levels off at about 200 ms. Looking at the throughput measurements shown in figure 4.16 (a), one can observe a small drop immediately after the handover. However, SCTP adapts very fast to the bandwidth capacity of the new path.

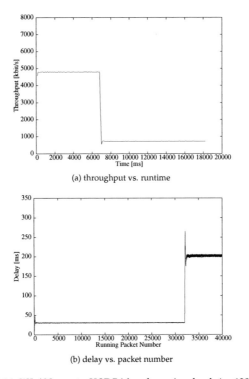

(a) throughput vs. runtime

(b) delay vs. packet number

Figure 4.16: $WLAN_{USHA}$ to $HSDPA$ handover (payload size 128 bytes)

In a final scenario, we analyzed the effect of increasing the difference between the paths
being involved in the handover process. Thus, we modeled a handover from a $WLAN_{USHA}$
link to a $GPRS$ link. We only focus on the scenario with a small payload size of 128 bytes
as this scenario features a lower saturation of the link. The measured throughput and delay
performance is shown in figure 4.17. The handover is triggered after sending 38 000 of 40 000
packets. Again, we find similar characteristics as those that were observed before. The
throughput that is presented in figure 4.17 (a) adapts fast to the changed conditions. The
delay measurement shows the same characteristic than in the previous scenario presented
in figure 4.16.

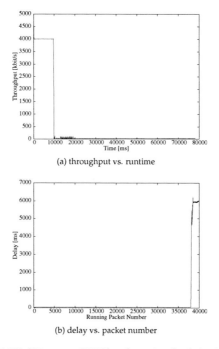

(a) throughput vs. runtime

(b) delay vs. packet number

Figure 4.17: $WLAN_{USHA}$ to $GPRS$ handover (payload size 128 bytes)

To sum up, we evaluated the characteristics of handover in heterogeneous communication scenarios and at different payload sizes. We found out that SCTP adapts quickly to the
sudden decrease of the available bandwidth capacity resulting from a handover to a path
with lower capacity. Thus, it provides a robust basis for implementing vertical handovers
with a seamless transition of data flows at the transport layer.

Comparison to Network Layer Handover and TCP

In the next step of our evaluation, we compare our SCTP-based approach to USHA that is presented by Chen et al. in [61]. USHA implements a network layer approach and the authors analyze the handover performance of TCP in this context. Thus, we reproduced the handover scenario between *FastEthernet* and *WLAN$_{USHA}$* in our testbed as it was described in the paper. During each measurement run, we sent 50 000 packets and 1024 bytes payload. The handover is triggered after 40 000 packets which is about 3.8 s after the measurement run started.

Figure 4.18 illustrates the results that have been obtained using SCTP. In general, the results are similar to the scenarios that were analyzed above. The throughput measurement in figure 4.18 (a) shows that SCTP achieves a maximum throughput of around 92.5 Mbit/s when using the *Fast Ethernet* link. Again, it performs very well at the moment the handover

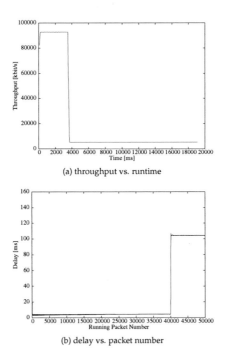

(a) throughput vs. runtime

(b) delay vs. packet number

Figure 4.18: *Fast Ethernet* to *WLAN$_{USHA}$* handover (SCTP)

is triggered and the available bandwidth decrease from 100 Mbit/s to 5.5 Mbit/s. The results do not show a drop in the experienced throughput after the handover. The expected peak in the delay measurements also turns out to be comparably low. The reason for this is the fact that we do not limit the bandwidth for the *FastEthernet* scenario. Thus the impact of path saturation is considerably lower, but also effects of buffering packets in the network emulator are reduced.

In contrast, figure 4.19 presents the results that have been obtained by reproducing the USHA scenario [61]. The measurement has been done with the same parameter settings as in the SCTP measurement. Instead of SCTP, we now use TCP with Binary Increase Congestion control as the transport protocol. This is the default implementation for recent Linux kernels. One can see in figure 4.19 (a) that the general throughput that is achieved by TCP compares to the results that have been obtained by using SCTP. However, one obvious difference between the results for TCP and SCTP appears in the graph shortly after the handover

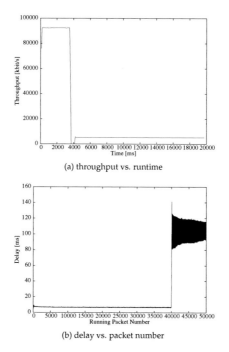

(a) throughput vs. runtime

(b) delay vs. packet number

Figure 4.19: *FastEthernet* to $WLAN_{USHA}$ handover (TCP)

is triggered. Using TCP, the handover event results in an interruption of the delivery of data packets that takes about 500 ms. Nevertheless, the duration of this interruptions that we experienced in our measurements is still considerably lower than the one that was measured in the original evaluation [61]. Here, the authors state an interruption that takes about five seconds. The difference between both setups is the fact that we modeled the actual handover event slightly different from the approach that was used by Chen et al. as we described it in section 2.4.1. While they use a virtual tunnel between the communicating peers and implement handovers by switching the tunnel interface, we reconfigure the network emulator at the moment of the handover. Thus, it is possible that the effect in the original evaluation is not solely caused by the bandwidth reduction, but is in fact a result of switching the virtual tunnel interface. This procedure may cause a heavy packet loss and force TCP into persist mode.

When looking at the delay graph in figure 4.19 (b), we can see that in the USHA scenario the experienced delay oscillates after the handover and thus suffers from high jitter of about 40 ms. Our SCTP based approach does not show a similar behavior, but is much more stable.

From our results we can conclude that the SCTP-based approach for implementing vertical handovers appears to feature a higher robustness against abrupt changes from a high bandwidth path to a low bandwidth one. TCP does even react with an interruption of around 500 ms and heavy jitter to the handover event.

Discussion of the Results

Our evaluation of the handover performance shows, that SCTP is much more robust against challenging communication environments compared to TCP. This fact makes SCTP a better choice for our purpose of implementing dynamic network selection in heterogeneous environments. Further, we observed that SCTP recovers much faster from the effects of any loss and delay spikes that are induced by a handover. The handover from a high capacity to a low capacity link leads to a sharp change of the available bandwidth. Nevertheless, SCTP adapts quickly to the changed conditions. In contrast to TCP, the data transfer is not interrupted. Moreover, the comparison to the network layer handover approach with TCP (USHA) shows that the performance of a transport layer handover is most probably superior to any network layer approaches based on tunneling and virtual network interfaces. Our reproduction of the USHA evaluation showed that the loss of successive packets owing to switching the virtual network interface results in a stall of data transmission. Although we were only able to evaluate a limited collection of scenarios, we found out that the characteristics of the experienced throughput and delay are almost comparable across the different scenarios. Thus, we can expect that our results may also apply in more general scenarios of handovers between communication paths with different characteristics.

4.4.4   Concurrent Multipath Transfer

In the second part of our evaluation, we focus on the potentials and limitations of concurrent multipath transfer (CMT) in heterogeneous communication environments. Our aim is to analyze how well CMT performs in heterogeneous scenarios and thus to conclude in which scenarios it brings a benefit to our muXer concept. Again, we start our evaluation with an analysis of homogeneous scenarios, where the bundled paths share the same characteristics. In the second step, we analyze the performance of bundles with heterogeneous communication paths.

Homogeneous Bundle

Our first scenario models a bundle of two $WLAN_{11}$ links. Figure 4.20 presents the measured throughput and delay for this scenario. We transmitted 10 000 packets with a payload of 1024 bytes between both peers. In figure 4.20 (a) we compare the throughput that has been achieved for XCMT as well as a congestion-window (cwnd) scheduler as it is described in

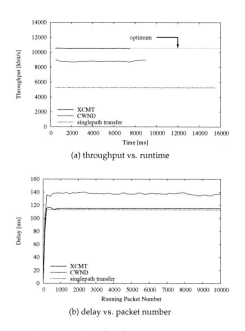

(a) throughput vs. runtime

(b) delay vs. packet number

Figure 4.20: Bundle of two $WLAN_{11}$ links

section 4.3.2. As a reference, we also show the results for a single path transfer over one $WLAN_{11}$ link. Furthermore, the graph shows an optimum throughput for the multipath transfer that is twice the average throughput of a singlepath transfer, which is used as a reference for stating the performance of the CMT mechanisms. As one can see from the obtained results, XCMT achieves a throughput that is equal to our optimum value. On average XCMT was able to deliver 10.5 Mbit/s. In comparison, the use of only one $WLAN_{11}$ path resulted in an average throughput of 5.25 Mbit/s. In contrast, the cwnd-based scheduler performs clearly worse. It achieves an averaged throughput of only 8.8 Mbit/s and the transmission of the 10 000 packets takes about 1.5 s longer than using XCMT. Looking at the share of packets that is sent along each path, we find that XCMT spreads the data chunks equally across the bundled paths, while the cwnd-based scheduler prefers one path to which it scheduled 59.68 % of the packets, while the other path carried only 40.32 %. The delay measurement in figure 4.20 (b) shows that the end-to-end delay of XCMT is only marginable higher than the delay that is experienced if only one path is used for communication. Again, the cwnd-based scheduler performs worse and suffers from an additional delay of about 20 ms.

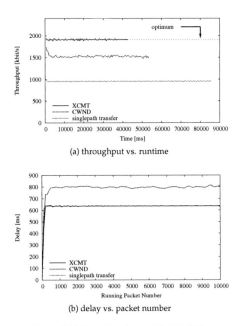

(a) throughput vs. runtime

(b) delay vs. packet number

Figure 4.21: Bundle of two $WLAN_2$ links

Figure 4.21 illustrates the results for two bundled $WLAN_2$ links. In general, we get the same results as in the previous scenario. XCMT is able to make full use of the capacity provided by the network bundle and achieves an average throughput of 1910 kbit/s. In contrast, CWND achieves only an average throughput of 1528.79 kbit/s. Also the results for the end-to-end delay in figure 4.21 (b) emphasize the previous findings as XCMT shows a similar delay as the singlepath transfer, while CWND features a higher delay.

As a third example, figure 4.22 shows the results that have been obtained by bundling two emulated $HSDPA$ links. Also in this scenario, we can see that XCMT performs as well as the optimum, while the throughput of the cwnd-based scheduler is again clearly behind the XCMT approach, even in a homogeneous scenario. The difference in the throughput of both approaches amounts to 309.26 kbit/s. The delay measurements in figure 4.22 (b) show similar results as well. Also in the $HSDPA$ scenario, the experienced end-to-end delay of XCMT compares to that of a singlepath transmission. Again, the use of the cwnd-based scheduler induces a delay that is significantly higher than that of XCMT. This results from the insufficient use of the available capacities and a higher amount of reordering at the receiver.

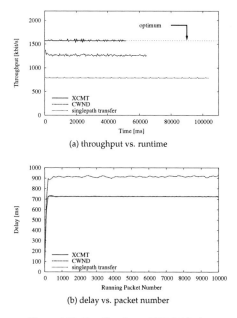

(a) throughput vs. runtime

(b) delay vs. packet number

Figure 4.22: Bundle of two $HSDPA$ links

To sum up, XCMT performs optimal in the homogenous scenarios with a packet size of 1024 bytes. This fact is emphasized by the comparison of the average throughputs that are achieved with the optimal throughput that is assumed to be the sum of the throughputs of two singlepath transfer. As figure 4.23 reveals, XCMT achieves the maximum possible throughput in all cases and thus provides a benefit of 100 % compared to a singlepath transfer. The cwnd-based scheduler performs clearly worse and ends up with an utilization of the available capacity, which is about 20 % lower than that of XCMT. The major reason for this is a higher level of reordering at the receiver.

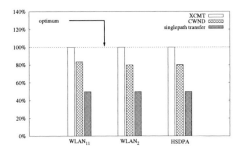

Figure 4.23: Throughput comparison

Heterogeneous Bundle

After evaluating the performance of XCMT in homogeneous scenarios, we now turn to scenarios that bundle heterogeneous communication links to increase the overall communication performance. First, we start our analysis with a bundle of a $WLAN_{11}$ and a $WLAN_2$ link. This scenario is characterized by a high difference in the bandwidth of the bundled paths, while the difference in their delay characteristics is low, i.e., 2.5 ms. As before, in each measurement run we sent 10 000 data chunks, each carrying a payload of 1024 bytes.

Figure 4.24 shows the results of the end-to-end delay and throughput measurements that have been obtained in our testbed. In figure 4.24 (a) we compare the throughput that has been achieved by XCMT and a cwnd-based scheduler against the time it takes to deliver all packets. The graph also shows the performance for single path transfers using either one of the bundled links, labeled as $WLAN_{11}$ and $WLAN_2$. Finally, we plot the sum of the average throughputs that have been achieved by the singlepath transfers into the graph to obtain a reference for the optimal performance that might actually be possible if both paths are used concurrently.

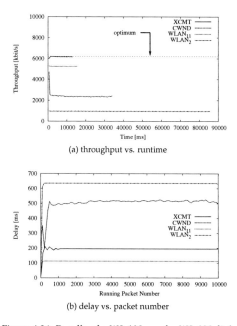

(a) throughput vs. runtime

(b) delay vs. packet number

Figure 4.24: Bundle of a $WLAN_{11}$ and a $WLAN_2$ link

The results show that XCMT comes close to the optimum. It achieves an average through-put of 6.17 Mbit/s. This is actually about 95 % of the cumulative link capacities and 99.3 % of their measured average throughput. The result indicates that XCMT is able to use the avail-able capacity very efficiently. In contrast, the cwnd-based scheduler performs clearly worse. Its throughput stabilizes at around 2.35 Mbit/s. This is higher than the throughput in the case the application would solely use the low-bandwidth path, but it is clearly lower than the capacity of the high-bandwidth path. When we analyze the way the cwnd-based sched-uler allocates packets to the different paths, we can see that it sends 60.3 % of all packets along the low-bandwidth path, while only 39.7 % of the packets arrive at the destination via the high-bandwidth path. By comparison, XCMT schedules 85.22 % of its packets onto the path that models $WLAN_{11}$ while 14.78 % of the packets are allocated to the $WLAN_2$ path. It appears as if the cwnd-based scheduler underestimates the capacity of the high-bandwidth link and thus, does not make full use of it. These findings are visible in the results of the delay measurement as well. Figure 4.24 (b) shows that the end-to-end delay, which is ex-perienced by the application in the case of using XCMT, is nearly twice than that of using only the path via the emulated $WLAN_{11}$ link. However, this is still drastically lower than the delay measured for the CWND scheduler. At the beginning of the transmission, we can see some fluctuations of the measured delay. These are effects of an increased level of packet reordering at the receiver during the initialization phase of the scheduler. Afterwards, the delay stabilizes around 195 ms. As the cwnd-based scheduler tends to schedule a higher portion of packets along the low-bandwidth path, its delay is closer to the values measured for the $WLAN_2$ link. It stabilizes around 500 ms.

As a second scenario for CMT in heterogeneous environments, we chose a bundle of $WLAN_2$ and $HSDPA$. In contrast to the previous scenario, here the bandwidths of both paths are almost comparable, but the delays differ clearly. The throughput graph in figure 4.25 (a) shows the same aspects as before. Again, the throughput of XCMT gets close to the sum of the singlepath throughputs. On average, XCMT delivers 1.72 Mbit/s, while the optimum amounts to 1.74 Mbit/s. For XCMT, we observe a clear fluctuation of the measured throughput at the beginning of the transmission. As before, this is an effect of the increased reordering during the scheduler's initialization phase. The cwnd-based scheduler performs

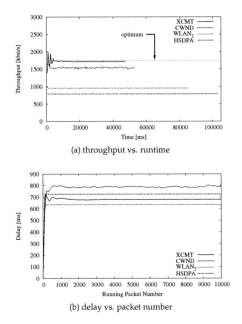

(a) throughput vs. runtime

(b) delay vs. packet number

Figure 4.25: Bundle of a $WLAN_2$ and a $HSDPA$ link

clearly better than in the scenario before. It achieves an average throughput of 1.54 Mbit/s, which is 88.5 % of the optimal throughput. This result indicates that the cwnd-based scheduler features a significantly higher sensitivity to differences in the bandwidth characteristics of the bundled paths than in their delay differences. The analysis of the end-to-end delay in figure 4.25 (b) shows that the cwnd-based approach has the highest delay of all options. The delay is even above the values that have been obtained for the singlepath transfers. It is likely that this results from a higher level of reordering at the receiver. The delay that was measured for XCMT stabilizes between that of the $WLAN_2$ and the $HSDPA$ link.

In the last scenario, we evaluate the performance of XCMT and the cwnd-based scheduling approach in the case of high bandwidth and high delay differences between the bundled paths. In this case, we model a $WLAN_{11}$ link and an $UMTS$ link that are used concurrently by our application. The results are illustrated in figure 4.26. XCMT achieves an average throughput of 5.2 Mbit/s. This is almost identical to the value that has been obtained for a singlepath transfer using the $WLAN_{11}$ link. Nevertheless, it is still lower than the optimal throughput of both paths that amounts to 5.5 Mbit/s based on the sum of the throughputs

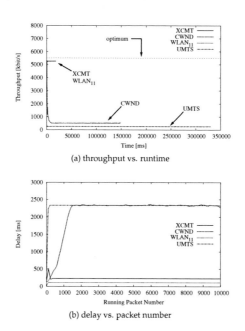

(a) throughput vs. runtime

(b) delay vs. packet number

Figure 4.26: Bundle of a $WLAN_{11}$ and an $UMTS$ link

that are achieved for singlepath transfers using the $WLAN_{11}$ and the $UMTS$ link respectively. This behavior is favored by the fact that the capacity gain of the second path is fairly low. Moreover, the characteristics differ clearly, which results in an extremely high level of reordering at the receiver. Both issues are reflected in the ratio of the packets that are sent along either path. XCMT uses almost only the $WLAN_{11}$ link. Actually 99.90 % of all packets are scheduled along this path. Thus, there is practical no benefit of CMT in this case. At least, XCMT performs better than the cwnd-based approach. Here, the low-bandwidth path again pulls down the performance of the data transmission. The scheduler tends to send more packets along the $UMTS$ link and thus suffers from an increased level of reordering and a higher delay as it can be seen in figure 4.26 (b). The delay of XCMT shows the same characteristics as before. During the initialization phase, we measure a higher delay that stabilizes at a level of about 227 ms.

As a summary, we can conclude from our evaluation of concurrent multipath transfer in heterogeneous scenarios that XCMT is able to manage well with challenging scenarios and provides a substantial benefit for increasing the communication performance, as the comparison of the throughputs in figure 4.27 shows. The average throughput of XCMT ranges between 99.2 % and 94.4 % of the expected optimum. In the first two scenarios it provides a benefit of 17.3 % and 79.9 % compared to a singlepath transfer along the fastest path in the bundle. In contrast, the cwnd-based scheduler does not perform well in heterogeneous scenarios. It suffers especially from strong differences in the bandwidth characteristics of the paths and tends to schedule more packets to the low-bandwidth path. This, in turn, affects the level of reordering at the receiver and thus results in a further degradation of the performance. Our throughput comparison shows that in two out of three scenarios, the average throughput of the cwnd-based scheduler is even lower than the one that can be achieved in using only the fastest path.

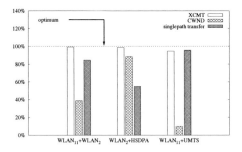

Figure 4.27: Throughput comparison

However, the results of our evaluation do not only show the benefits of CMT, but also its limitations in scenarios where the characteristics of both paths are strongly different. From the results that we obtained in the different scenarios, we can conclude that XCMTs performance depends on these differences as well. Especially the last scenario indicates the limitations of CMT in terms of increasing the communication performance quite plainly. Here, XCMT achieved the same throughput than the singlepath transfer over the fastest path, but suffered from a higher end-to-end delay.

Impact of Path Asymmetries

A furhter analysis in our evaluation addresses the benefit of using multiple paths concurrently for data transmission dependent on the bandwidth differences between both paths. For this, we defined a set of scenarios with two bundled paths. One path in the bundle has always a bandwidth of 1 Mbit/s, while the bandwidth of the other path is increased from 1 Mbit/s to 27 Mbit/s in steps of 1 Mbit/s. We chose these values corresponding to the possible range of bandwidths that may be experienced in an IEEE 802.11g network. The delay is assumed to be 7.25 ms (according to the $WLAN_{USHA}$ scenario) for both paths and the payload size was chosen to be 1024 bytes. For each scenario, we performed 15 measurement runs and averaged the results that have been obtained.

First, figure 4.28 (a) shows the ratio of the measured throughput and the maximum possible throughput in this scenario against the different bandwidth ratios. The maximum possible throughput is determined by measuring the throughput of SCTP for each of the two different paths and adding up both results. One can see from the results that the efficiency of XCMT remains stable for some time, until it decreases starting at a bandwidth ratio of 12 and finally reaches a value of 92.3 % in the scenario where the bandwidth of one path is 27-times higher than the bandwidth of the other path. This points out that the overhead of concurrent multipath mechanisms increases with higher path asymmetries. The CWND scheduler performs clearly worse and shows an exponentially decreasing utilization. While it is able to achieve a utilization of 86 % for a ratio of 1, this value decreases to 6.41 % for a ratio of 27. This behavior is due to the fact that the path with the lower bandwidth has a higher impact on the overall performance. When analyzing the share of data packets being sent along either of the two paths, one can see that the CWND scheduler is still delivering about 40 % of the packets along the path with the lower bandwidth. Thus, excessive packet reordering at the receiver is inevitable.

Figure 4.28 (b) puts these results in a context with the capacity of the faster path and thus determines the benefit of XCMT in the scenarios that have been modeled. The results show that the contribution of the low-bandwidth path decreases clearly with an increasing bandwidth ratio. One the one hand, this relates to the fact that the high-bandwidth path dominates the bundle more and more, while the contribution of the lower path is ever-decreasing.

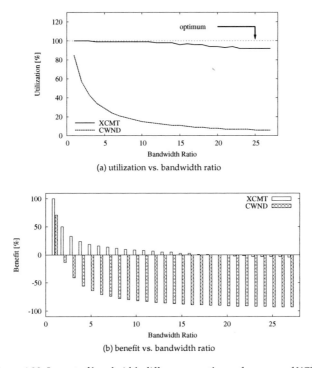

(a) utilization vs. bandwidth ratio

(b) benefit vs. bandwidth ratio

Figure 4.28: Impact of bandwidth differences on the performance of XCMT

Additionally, the level of reordering at the receiver rises with increasing differences between the paths in the bundle. From a bandwidth ratio of 19, the benefit of XCMT becomes negative. This means that the performance that has been achieved by multipath transfer falls off below the modeled bandwidth of the path. Thus, at such a point, it would be better to abstain from concurrent multipath transfer and to simply switch to the faster path. Nevertheless, the benefit that is achieved by XCMT stabilizes at an almost constant level. Thus, it adapts to the challenging scenario and sends almost all data along the high-bandwidth path. The CWND scheduler shows a negative benefit already at a bandwidth ratio of 2. The benefit is decreasing even further with higher ratios up to a value of -93.35 %.

These findings cannot be mapped directly onto arbitrary scenarios, as we analyzed only a small subset of possible configurations. But, the actual benefit of concurrent multipath transfer also depends on further parameters. In some scenarios even a low benefit may be

sufficient to serve an application with its desired QoS demands. However, the results still
show that the benefit of concurrent multipath transfer has limitations. It is not possible to
bundle arbitrarily different paths to achieve a benefit. Instead, the additional overhead and
the path asymmetries may result in performance degradations.

Impact of Path Changes

Finally, we evaluated the impact of path changes on the bundling mechanisms using XCMT
and the CWND scheduler. For this, we modeled a handover from a homogeneous bundle
of two $WLAN_{11}$ links to a heterogeneous bundle of a $WLAN_{11}$ link and a $WLAN_5$ link.
The handover is triggered after sending packet number 5000 of 10 000. The results of this
scenario are depicted in figure 4.29.

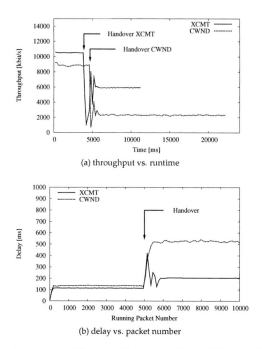

(a) throughput vs. runtime

(b) delay vs. packet number

Figure 4.29: Handover from a $WLAN_{11}$-$WLAN_{11}$ bundle to a $WLAN_{11}$-$WLAN_5$ bundle

The results of the throughput measurements are shown in figure 4.29 (a). The handover event occurs at a different time during the data transmission of both schedulers. This effect results from the fact that the handover was triggered after sending a fixed number of packets, while XCMT and the CWND scheduler achieve different throughputs and thus are able to transmit different amounts of data during a certain time period. The graphs for both schedulers show a clear drop of the throughput after the handover event. The throughput of XCMT reduces from 10.5 Mbit/s to 1.1 Mbit/s. The CWND scheduler is only able to transfer 696 kbit/s at that time. However, the throughput of XCMT recovers after about 500 ms. First, one can see fluctuations during a transmission time of 4600 ms and 5200 ms. They result from reordering at the receiver as well as from the initialization phase of XCMT, where the characteristics of the new path are determined. These findings are in accordance with the delay measurements shown in figure 4.29 (b). The fact that the new path over the $WLAN_2$ link is not saturated at the beginning, is another factor that has impact on the reordering. Afterwards, the throughput of XCMT stabilizes at about 6 Mbit/s. The CWND scheduler requires a similar time as XCMT to recover from the handover and to reach a similar throughput. But, it stabilizes at a significantly lower level and reaches only a final throughput of 2.3 Mbit/s. Both results correspond to our previous findings.

The results of the delay measurements (figure 4.29 (b)) show the behavior that can be expected from the previous scenarios during the times before and after the handover. But, during the handover phase, one can see a difference between XCMT and the CWND scheduler. The end-to-end delay measured for the CWND scheduler increases constantly to about 520 ms. In contrast, the values that have been gathered for XCMT show clear fluctuations. As already mentioned before, they result from reordering at the receiver and the fact that XCMT must obtain information on the characteristics of the new path, before it is able to spread data across the different paths in an efficient way.

Discussion of the Results

Our evaluation of concurrent multipath in homogeneous and heterogeneous communication scenarios showed that XCMT performs well in a variety of scenarios with different communication characteristics. We were able to show that it achieves a good utilization of the capacity that is provided by a bundle in the context of different bandwidth and delay characteristics. It was able to adapt to scenarios with highly different characteristics and does not suffer from significant performance degradations as those that were observed for the cwnd-based scheduler. As a further result, we found out that the overhead of the additional mechanisms in XCMT for allocating data onto the different paths and for recovering the order of data chunks at the receiver increases the higher the difference between the paths are. It cannot be expected that it is possible to eliminate this overhead, as indicated by our analysis of the optimal scheduler in section 4.3.2. In the context of our initial problem of dynamic network selection this means that a network scheduler has to factor this overhead into its scheduling decision. However, the parameterization of this procedure requires in-depth studies of the protocols in real world scenarios.

4.5 Summary

In this chapter, we introduced our concepts for the *Path Management* module in the muXer architecture. Therefore, we focused on two aspects: vertical handover and concurrent multipath transfer in heterogeneous communication environments. We identified that the transport layer is well suited for integrating these functionalities into the communication protocol stack. Our approach to both issues is based on the Stream Control Transmission Protocol (SCTP). In the first step, we presented our implementation of the handover mechanism using SCTP's extension for dynamic address reconfiguration. Additionally, we also implemented a legacy wrapper that allows for supporting applications that are not aware of the muXer functionalities or may natively use other transport protocols as, for instance, TCP. The evaluation of the SCTP-based handover mechanism showed that our prototype performs well in various scenarios with different characteristics. We were able to show that our method brings clear performance advantages in a comparison with a network-layer handover approach and TCP.

In the second part of this chapter, we dealt with the challenges of concurrent multipath transfer in heterogeneous environments. We started with an analysis of the theoretical concept of an idealized scheduler and compared our findings to scheduling approaches that have been proposed in related research work. Afterwards, we introduced muXer CMT (XCMT), our approach for integrating CMT functionalities into the muXer architecture. XCMT combines multiple enhancements to cope with heterogeneous paths. A performance evaluation of XCMT in homogeneous and heterogeneous scenarios showed that it performs well in a wide range of typical scenarios. However, we also encountered the limitations of concurrent multipath transfer. In scenarios with high differences in the characteristics of the bundled paths, XCMT performs even slightly worse than a singlepath transfer along the best path.

In the end, we can conclude that our transport-layer approach for *Path Management* performs well in heterogeneous scenarios and, thus, provides a very good basis for implementing dynamic network selection. Nevertheless, it is not possible to take advantages of an arbitrary bundling of network paths, as the overhead, which is mainly induced by reordering of data packets at the receiver, increases the higher the characteristics of the bundled paths differ from each other. Thus, the *Decision Engine* needs to provide a possibility to account for such aspects. However, a general quantification of the overhead will require extensive real-world experiments. Of course, our prototype implementations leave room for improvements. On the one hand, the CMT protocol might be enhanced further by, for instance, tuning the path monitoring mechanism. Another possible improvement might the handling of retransmissions in the way that the data sender employs information about the evolution of the receive buffer window at the remote peer. Thus, it is possible to draw any conclusion about the level of reordering and to adapt the scheduler accordingly. Another enhancement could be a soft handover mechanism as it was proposed by Budzisz et al. [240]. Here, the handover mechanism is combined with CMT for a certain time before the original path is switched off. Such enhancements may increase the performance of our *Path Management* concept in heterogeneous scenarios even further, resulting in a higher benefit for the dynamic network selection approach.

Chapter 5

An Arbitration Concept for Dynamic Network Selection

Mobile devices feature ever increasing capabilities and are equipped with multiple wireless network interfaces. In combination with an always growing density of different wireless access networks that can be used at affordable rates, these are key aspects for the growing popularity of mobile Internet in the past. However, the user's mobility, fluctuating network characteristics as well as the variety of network providers and technologies with different features and capabilities make efficient and seamless mobile communications still a challenging task to the user. In the end, he is still the one that has to decide which network to use. Some devices implement simple strategies like "prefer WLAN to UMTS", but these approaches are not able to make use of the potentials that are given by the heterogeneous communications ecosystem.

The approach of dynamic network selection targets at turning this heterogeneity and complexity of the communication environment into a benefit to the user by adapting transparently to changes in the communication environment. In chapter 3 we already presented our muXer architecture with its particular modules. Now, in this chapter we turn to one main part of our research and describe the actual process for making decisions which network to use.

In section 3.2 we pointed out that muXer aims at implementing a device-controlled approach to network selection that allows for an individual handling of concurrent applications. Thus, the objectives of our selection process focus on the basic conditions defined by the user and the requirements of the applications being used. Network operators or service providers may have the opportunity to contribute to the decision-making process, but the final decision is being made on the mobile device and may be controlled by the user.

There are two major challenges that have to be met by a holistic approach to dynamic network selection. First, there is a huge variety of input parameters to the decision process that describe the requirements of users and applications. A decision strategy for dynamic network selection must be able to cope with a wide range of possible decision objectives that either focus on the individual application or on the entirety of all applications running on the device. Second, these objectives will typically not follow the same line and may even be directly opposed to each other. As an example for one of these conflicts, it may not always be possible to provide a maximum level of communication performance and a minimum level of monetary costs at the same time. Thus, a network selection process that aims at covering this high level of heterogeneity requires a flexible design concept, which allows for a dynamic adaptation of decision objectives. It needs to be able to find reasonable tradeoffs and probably unconventional solutions even in challenging scenarios.

To get an idea of the different inputs that describe the requirements to the decision process, we start this chapter in section 5.1 with an overview of the variety of possible QoS categories. Actually, there is a wide range of technical and non-technical requirements that might either be stated as precise requirements or relate to subjective perceptions of the user that works with the applications running on his device. We also discuss the correlation of these categories and the resulting consequences for the network selection process. In section 5.2, we address tradeoffs that have to be made in the decision process in order to deal with conflicting objectives. This is an important issue to the decision process, as the actual definition of what is "best" relates to the subjective weighting of these objectives. Afterwards, we come to the central aspects of this thesis. In section 5.3 we put our general decision concept into concrete terms. It is made up of two tiers: an application-oriented arbitration phase, followed by a global resource allocation phase. Our approach to the first tier is presented in section 5.4. Here, we introduce the formal concept of arbitration and present our prototypical implementation for a set of decision objectives as a proof of our concept. Section 5.5 deals with the second tier of our decision concept and presents *GAP*, a scheduling approach to the problem of allocating network resources to the individual applications. A particular feature of *GAP* is the option to allocate applications to network bundles, as it has been presented in chapter 4, or to explicitly defer application requests in situations with constrained network resources. The performance of our approach is evaluated and compared to other possible strategies for dynamic network selection. We present the results of this evaluation in section 5.6 and discuss them in section 5.7. Finally, in section 5.8 this chapter closes with a summary of the different aspects that were addressed in this chapter and an overall discussion of the results that have been achieved.

5.1   QoS Characteristics

The first challenge on the way to a decision concept is the analysis of metrics and characteristics that make the quality of a network ratable with respect to user and application requirements. For this, we have to account for a variety of inputs and context information that may either be measured at the mobile device, or can be provided by external data sources. Location-based information about both, the mobility of the device and expected networks and characteristics can further be used to improve the final decision. Actually, there is already some research work on the specification and classification of QoS metrics. Chalmers and Sloman summarize the results of related work about QoS concepts with the focus on mobile computing environments [241]. They propose two classes of QoS categories: technology-related and user-related ones. The former class comprises all characteristics that deal with technical aspects describing requirements for an application to work as expected, such as the throughput or the delay. The latter class includes characteristics that map certain user expectations on the operation of applications and the ABC service itself. In contrast to the technology-related characteristics, these metrics might not be measured precisely. They may require tradeoffs in weighting certain QoS metrics for either a specific application, or even across concurrent applications that compete for the available network resources. On the basis of [241], we identified a set of QoS categories stating relevant characteristics affecting the network selection process. Figure 5.1 illustrates these categories and states further QoS metrics belonging to them.

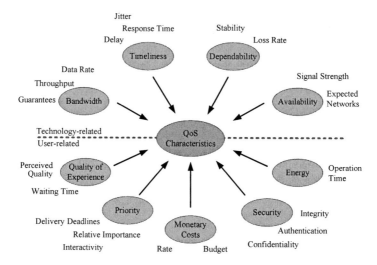

Figure 5.1: QoS characteristics in mobile environments

5.1.1   Technology-related QoS Categories

The technology-related QoS categories describe technical parameters stating certain conditions that are required for the application to meet its task. Most of them are obvious and stand for classical QoS requirements. They couple application requirements with network characteristics and allow for evaluating whether a certain network is able to serve an application or not. In general all of the metrics used inside a technology-related QoS category can be measured quantitatively and thus can be mapped directly to the appropriate network characteristic. In the following we discuss the different QoS categories separately and derive suitable metrics to implement them.

Bandwidth

The category *Bandwidth* stands for all metrics dealing with the amount of data that can be delivered in a given time. Thus, for measuring metrics that allow for comparing heterogeneous networks, one has to define a common notion of both parameters. The bandwidth can be determined at various layers of the ISO/OSI protocol stack. At the lower layers it states the maximum amount of data that can be transferred in a given time interval. However, this value is generally higher than the application layer throughput that is perceived by the applications. It includes the protocol overhead as well as further constraints as, for instance, the size of application data units. Additionally, there are certain differences in the methods for medium access between the network technologies. They differ in whether the available bandwidth is allocated to a dedicated user, or whether a user has to compete with other users for it. Moreover, several technologies for mobile communications are characterized by asymmetric link characteristics. Thus, the achievable throughput differs depending on the direction of the data flow.

Timeliness

Timeliness covers all aspects regarding to timely delivery of data. Especially applications with real-time requirements might attach special importance to this QoS category. On the one hand, timeliness is affected by the end-to-end delay between sender and receiver. However, especially streaming applications will also account for jitter that is the variation of the delay. A further parameter regarding the timeliness can be the response time of the network (for instance the round-trip time) as a measure of how long it may take until the response to a request is received.

Dependability

Dependability states how reliable a certain network is or has to be. One aspect to this issue is the rate of data that is lost or corrupted during the transmission. Further aspects are statistics about the network stability in terms of availability. This can be the average time a network was available in the past and how frequent connection and disconnection events occurred. This measure is specifically of interest, for instance, when rating mobile ad-hoc networks or delay tolerant networks with respect to certain application requirements.

Availability

Finally, the last category concerns about availability aspects. In contrast to dependability this category focuses on timely aspects regarding to the current or future availability of a network. Actually, there are two metrics of interest in this category. First, information about the expected time to disconnection might be used to minimize handovers between networks if an application establishes respective requirements. Otherwise, the time to connection may be used as an indicator for finding an alternative network. However, in some scenarios it might not always be necessary to transfer data immediately, which may allow for increasing the overall efficiency of network usage. More interesting in these terms is the expected time when a connection to a network is available. Thus, if an application is able to state a deadline until data has to be delivered, this QoS metric makes it possible to search for alternative transmission opportunities besides those networks that are currently available.

5.1.2   User-related QoS Categories

In contrast to the aforementioned technology-related QoS categories, the modeling and measurement of user-related QoS categories is much more imprecise. These categories include QoS metrics that are much fuzzier than the quantifiable technical characteristics and allow for certain margins in their rating. In addition, the parameters, particular features and capabilities vary clearly between different networking technologies. This makes the handling of these characteristics within the decision process much more difficult.

Quality of Experience

Actually, there are multiple definitions of what is understood by Quality of Experience (QoE). The ITU-T defines QoE as "The overall acceptability of an application or service, as perceived subjectively by the end-user" [242]. Muhammad et al. state the difference between QoS and QoE as "the aim of the network and services should be to achieve the maximum user rating (QoE), while network quality (QoS) is the main building block for reaching this goal" [243]. Finally, Kilkki gives a more general definition in [244]: "the basic character or nature of direct personal participation or observation". He proposes to distinguish between Quality of Experience, Quality of User Experience and Quality of Customer Experience depending on the role of a person.

All these definitions agree in the fact that QoE is a subjective measure stating somehow the experiences of a person with a certain service or applications. Actually, it is more a general term combining different facets of a person's perception of service quality. With respect to our field of application, QoE includes the user's satisfaction with the services provided by a certain applications. This could be, for instance, the perceived quality of the delivered content or the waiting time for a certain amount of data to be delivered.

In our notion of QoE, it is an indirect factor that affects the QoS required by applications. To illustrate this aspect, figure 5.2 shows exemplarily the possible correlation of throughput and QoE for three types of applications. The left graph shows a typical situation for a file transfer or web browser. Both applications are generally able to work at a wide range of data rates. Nevertheless, an increasing bandwidth reduces the time a user has to wait for the requested information. Thus, at higher data rates he will perceive a higher subjective quality. Other applications may require a minimum bandwidth in order to be able to work and provide a constant QoE as shown in the middle of the figure. Finally, there may be, for instance, multimedia streaming applications that offer different levels of video quality. In such cases, the correlation between bandwidth and QoE will form a step function depending on the number of supported quality levels (as shown on the right).

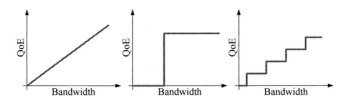

Figure 5.2: Schematic correlation between QoE and throughput

This small example also shows the crux of meeting a certain level of QoE. On the one hand, the acceptable QoE highly depends on the user itself and his individual "level of frustration". On the other hand, QoE highly depends on the application being used and probably even the respective situation. Within our work, we do not address questions on the adaptability of application content, as for instance the quality of a video stream. The advantages of such techniques need to be managed separately. Thus, we do not aim at making QoE quantifiable and finding a tradeoff in terms of the QoE between different applications inside the network selection process. However, this assumption will not limit the applicability of our approach as an application may change its requirements between consecutive iterations of the decision process and thus react to earlier decisions. Besides, it may also provide a set of alternative configurations that may be rated independently.

Priority

A user will not ascribe equal importance to all applications running on its mobile device. For instance, if he participates in a business meeting via a video conference, it will be more important to him to have a reliable video and especially audio transmission during this conference than downloading files in the background. Thus, a user may assign different priorities to applications in order to account for such differences in the user's perception. Actually, this level of importance may change depending on the current context and the current interests of the user.

Priorities also play a role for weighting the different QoS characteristics with respect to the application demands. Delay-critical applications like online gaming and VoIP may put a higher weight on delay and jitter than e-mail or web browsing. Thus, the weighting of different criteria has to be application-specific to achieve a high correlation between application needs and network capabilities.

Monetary Costs

Network providers offer different models to bill for network usage. With the advent of powerful mobile devices for Internet usage, flat rates gain increasing popularity. Some providers restrict the usage of their flat rate by reducing the provided QoS level, for instance the data rates, if a certain amount of data traffic is exceeded. Other models are volume tariffs that may either allow for using a certain amount of data traffic or for accessing the network service for a specific period of time. Finally, users may be charged by their actual network usage. Again, the user has to pay for the data traffic he caused or the time he was connected to the network.

A user has typically precise ideas on how much he is willing to pay. Thus, he may want to differentiate between applications or state a maximum budget for network usage. The most challenging task with this category is the quest for suitable metrics mapping the different accounting models onto parameters that cover all possible accounting models and can be easily understood and adapted by the user.

Security

Network security is an important aspect in wireless and mobile communications, as eavesdropping of data sent on a wireless communication channel is not a challenging task. Thus, in several situations, a user may want applications to use only those networks that provide at least a certain level of security. In our scenario, one can generally distinguish between three different aspects of security. The probably most important one is confidentially. It is typically implemented by using encryption techniques for the data transfer on the wireless channel or even the whole association between the sender and the receiver. A further aspect is authentication in order to proof either the identity of a user intending to use a specific network and/or the identity of a certain service provider or network access point. Finally, a third aspect can be the integrity of the wireless network, assuring that modifications of data transmitted through the network (or only the first wireless hop) are precluded or at least detected.

In wireless infrastructure networks, the security aspects generally focus on the first hop from the mobile device to the wireless access point. Using other networking paradigms as for instance Mobile ad-hoc networks or store-carry-forward networks, one might differentiate between features that provide security hop-by-hop or in the whole wireless network.

Energy

Mobile wireless devices are generally powered by rechargeable batteries. Only in special situations as, for instance, when driving by train or car users will connect their devices to a power outlet. As the capacity of the batteries is limited, users may be interested in maximizing the battery life. We classified energy into the user-related QoS categories, as it is depends on the user's objectives whether to maximize the battery lifetime or to make full use of the heterogeneous communication environment.

One contribution to the former target is to reduce the number of network interfaces being used. With respect to our network selection process, this might mean that it is beneficial to assign as many applications as possible to one certain network, before activating a further network interface. Further, there are clear difference in the energy consumption of using certain access networks for communication [245–247]. Thus, the selection process may take these differences into account for deciding on which network to use.

5.1.3 Classification of QoS Categories – Device vs. Application Domain

All of the aforementioned QoS categories (and probably even further ones) have effects on how good the application and user requirements are met. Thus, they affect the quality of the network selection process. However, it might not be enough to evaluate all of these parameters with respect to the domain of an individual application. Some parameters have to be evaluated across multiple applications running on the device.

Figure 5.3 illustrates the classification of the different QoS categories to the application and device domain. The application domain includes all QoS categories that need to be evaluated with respect to individual applications. In general, all technology-related QoS

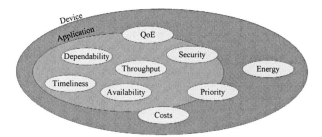

Figure 5.3: QoS domains

categories belong to this domain as they describe individual characteristics that are specific to the application under consideration. To give an example, each application has its own bandwidth requirements in order to provide a certain service to the user. For the user-related parameters, things are different. One the one hand Quality of Experience states a certain level of service quality for a specific application. On the other hand, if a user runs multiple applications concurrently, he will aim at maximizing the overall QoE for the whole set. This may imply that some applications have to cut back for the benefit of others. Security aspects are mainly related to this domain as well. A user or a company may implement security policies with respect to individual applications or all applications on the device. However, global policies typically do not depend on the number and characteristics of any concurrent applications. Thus, these global policies can be implemented in the application domain of the decision process. Priorities play a role in both domains. As mentioned before, they may state the importance of certain characteristics for the individual applications, but also state the significance of applications to the user. The same also holds for costs. A user may define individual cost budgets for applications. In addition, he may state the maximum amount of money he is willing to spend. Finally, energy defines a QoS category that primarily relates to the device domain as the minimization of energy consumption and the number of active networks is a cross-application objective.

5.2 Decision Tradeoffs

In the introduction to this chapter, we already pointed out that there is almost no reasonable chance to find exactly one optimal configuration for the decision process that provides always the best result in any possible scenario. The definition of what is "best" relates always to the subjective interpretations and weighting of the different decision objectives. This can be highly specific to the particular needs a user has at the moment. Additionally, there is a huge variety of applications, each having their specific notion on how important a specific objective might be. Several objectives and aims for the decision process are not in the same line and thus require reasonable tradeoffs to account for all relevant decision dimensions. In this context, we want to emphasize two major aspects:

▶ decision objectives that are diametrically opposed and

▶ the question whether a more precise modeling of parameters directly results in more accurate decision results.

In the following, we discuss both aspects with respect to their relevance on the quest for the best decision.

5.2.1 Weighting of Decision Objectives

In the previous sections we introduced a large set of QoS categories and their relation to application-specific and cross-application objectives. However, these QoS categories are not necessarily targeted at the same common objectives. Some of them may even act directly opposed to each other. As illustrated in figure 5.4, this fact holds especially for three different dimensions of optimizations, the perceived QoE per application, the number of applications being served and the general costs, for instance in terms of money and energy, for network communications. When basing the decision only on application-oriented objectives that are evaluated separately from the demands of concurrent applications, one might find at most a set of local optima for each individual application. However, in situations where the actual application demands are higher than the available resources, or where one access network has a significant higher attractiveness than others, this approach will lead to misestimations

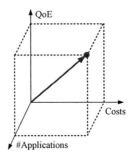

Figure 5.4: Tradeoffs for network selection

and thus, in the end, to wrong decisions. On the other hand, maximizing solely the number of applications to be served at the same time does not necessarily correspond with the user's QoE expectations. Finally, the aim of minimizing costs is generally conflictive with the objective to make full use of communication resources. Although our example in figure 5.4 focuses only on the user's view, there might be similar interests for other players in the communication ecosystem. A network provider that operates multiple access networks and offers different service levels might also have its own interests in regard of which network is used by its customers. Thus, the model of conflictive objectives may finally end up with even more dimensions.

To sum up, a network selection process requires reasonable tradeoffs between all of these objectives and thus has to find compromises that live up to expectations. Thus, a decision strategy should not solely rely on a fixed rule set or a simple weighted summation of normalized QoS metrics. It must provide a high degree of flexibility to balance different possible options depending on the current situation.

5.2.2 Precision vs. Complexity

A practical issue when implementing the aforementioned QoS categories as metrics in a decision process is the tradeoff between precision and complexity. Naturally, one might aim at a most precise modeling of requirements and network characteristics to get highly accurate inputs as basis for the actual decision. However, this desire is limited by two major reasons. First, it will hardly be possible to measure all required parameters at a high level of accuracy in the field. Information provided from different networking technologies and providers will typically vary in terms of granularity and accuracy. Moreover, mobility of the mobile device and changes in the environment will lead to frequent changes in the measured characteristics. Second, a huge amount of individual decision parameters requires respective definitions from the applications and users stating the demands on the parameters. This clearly increases the complexity of both interfaces, for the application and for the user. It can be expected that neither users are willing to configure a large and fine-granular set of QoS characteristics, nor will application programmers implement these parameter sets, although the applications can cope with large ranges of QoS characteristics. Thus, the question to be answered is whether a higher number of QoS parameters to be considered in the decision process, really justifies the additional increase in complexity.

A general rule for designing the decision process is to keep the number of parameters as low as possible and as high as necessary. This reduces the overhead (for instance in terms of processing time and memory usage) caused by the network selection process. Second, the fluctuating characteristics in wireless networks are opposed to a fine-granular modeling of characteristics and requirements.

5.3   The muXer Decision Concept

In section 3.4 we already derived a set of design issues for our *Decision Engine*. In brief, we identified the following key requirements:

► a modular and flexible concept to be able to easily adapt to different communication scenarios and to allow for simple integration of additional decision objectives,

► the support of highly heterogeneous input parameters and objectives at different levels of complexity, and

► an approach that accounts for both the requirements of individual applications and the cross-application optimization objectives.

In section 3.4.2 we already introduced the arbitration concept that is intentionally designed to provide a high level of dynamics, flexibility and responsiveness. Moreover, in section 3.4.3 we presented the basic idea of our two-tier approach. Now, we get back to this concept and go into the details of the muXer decision process. Figure 5.5 shows the generalized decision concept in more detail. As mentioned before, it is based on two tiers.

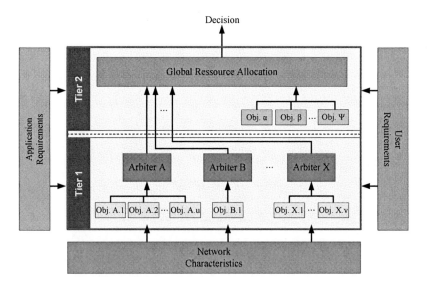

Obj. = Objective

Figure 5.5: The muXer decision concept

The arbitration tier (tier 1) is shown in the lower part of the figure. It consists of a set of arbiters that decide on different application-oriented decision factors as, for instance, whether certain networks meet the QoS requirements of an application. Every arbiter N makes use of a set of decision modules (*Obj. N.1, ..., Obj. N.u*), each implementing an objective with respect to the task or the control factor of that specific arbiter. In general, the decision modules act independently from each other. They can run asynchronously and may implement arbitrarily complex algorithms. The inputs to the decision process are application and user requirements as well as network characteristics. According to the basic concept of arbitration, all decision modules vote for the value of a certain factor that the arbiter focuses on. Afterwards, the arbiter merges and probably weights the different outputs to come to a final result. The results of the first tier are application-centered and thus focus on the requirements of the individual applications. These results go into the second tier, the global resource allocation process. Here, we combine the results for different applications and networks, to find an overall solution to the decision problem. This solution may be affected by additional cross-application optimization objectives (*Obj. α, ..., Obj. Ψ*) defined by the user. Examples for this might be the overall monetary costs or the available energy budget. The final output of the *Decision Engine* is a mapping of applications to a set of i networks, with $i \in \mathbb{N}_0$ as it is illustrated in figure 5.6.

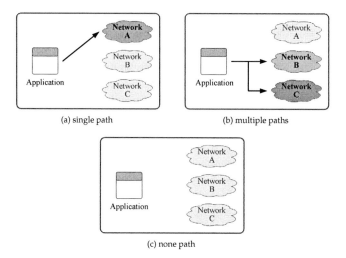

(a) single path   (b) multiple paths

(c) none path

Figure 5.6: Possible results of the muXer decision process

In general, the concrete implementation of different arbiters and decision modules at both tiers of our concept may depend on specifications of the network or service providers as well as the capabilities of a mobile device. To give an example: if the mobile device is equipped with the facility to determine its current position, it may make use of context information, such as connectivity maps, that can be either gathered by its own experiences in the past or may come from external sources like coverage maps that are provided by the network operator. Moreover, users may state a set of parameters that are important to them. In the following we will present our proposed implementation of a set of basic arbiters and decision modules for the application-oriented decision phase. Afterwards, we describe GAP, a scheduling approach to the global resource allocation problem.

5.4   Application-oriented Arbitration

The first tier of our decision process has to manage the various objectives for the individual applications. As stated before, one elementary component in making the application requirements ratable and comparable for the decision process is the concept of arbitration. In section 3.4.2 we already introduced the general idea behind this concept. In section 5.4.1 we come back to this issue to elaborate on the details on arbitration and how it is used to come to decisions. Afterwards, we present our implementation of the application-oriented arbitration process in sections 5.4.2 to 5.4.4. Finally, we show some evaluation results regarding the output of the first tier in the muXer decision process.

5.4.1   General Procedure of Arbitration

As already mentioned in section 3.4.2, the arbitration concept, as it is described by Rosenblatt [202], includes two basic components:

▶ an arbiter and

▶ a set of m decision modules.

Figure 5.7 shows a schematic representation of the decision process. An arbiter is always responsible for one certain control parameter κ. The basis for the arbitration process is a field $P = \{p_1, \ldots, p_n\}$ of discrete candidate values for this parameter. In the end, the arbiter has to decide on one of these values from the interval ($\kappa = p_i \in P$). For this purpose, it gets input from the set of decision modules. Each of these modules assigns a vote to every $p_i \in P$ with respect to the particular objective the decision module focuses on. The votes come from a given interval $[v_{min}, v_{max}]$ and their semantics are well-defined. The way how a particular vote is derived is fully encapsulated in the individual decision module and can be arbitrarily complex.

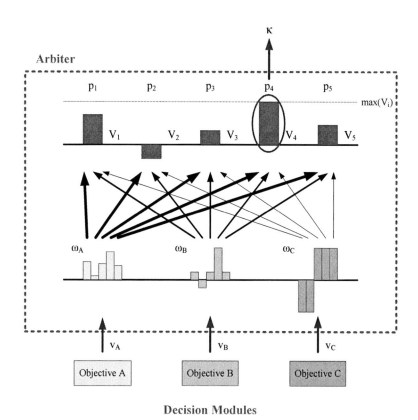

Figure 5.7: The general concept of arbitration

For all m decision modules, the arbiter determines a weighted sum V_i of all votes v_{ij} to value p_i according to the following equation:

$$V_i = \frac{\sum_{j=1}^{m} \omega_j \cdot v_{ij}}{\sum_{j=1}^{m} \omega_j} \quad \forall i \in \{1, \ldots, n\} \tag{5.1}$$

The arbiter has the optional opportunity to adapt the weights dynamically according to any external effects, further input parameters or the results of other arbiter or decision modules. Further, it may, for instance, smooth the gathered results across different parameter values V_i to interpolate between them, if this is advantageous to the arbiter's control parameter.

In the next step, the arbiter chooses that value for the control parameter that received the highest overall vote:

$$\kappa = p_{\phi} \mid V_{\phi} \geq V_i \quad \forall i \in \{1, \ldots, n\} \tag{5.2}$$

If there are multiple values of the parameter that have the same amount of votes, the arbiter may resolve this conflict by either explicitly choosing one option, for instance the highest value, or it may interpolate between the respective candidate values and choose a mean value. Alternatively, the arbiter may choose other methods to come to the final output depending on the characteristics of the specific control factor, or it does not make any final decision at all. In the latter case, it may simply forward the result being achieved to the next higher level in the hierarchy of the decision architecture and delegate the final decision to this entity.

5.4.2 Implementation Concept

In section 5.1, we already discussed potential objectives for the decision process and their specific relevance. We argued that there are two classes of QoS characteristics: Those that describe individual application requirements and those that have an effect across all applications running on the device. In addition, there are certain metrics that effect aspects in both domains. Based on these findings, we concluded that there are two basic types of arbiters needed for the network selection process:

- ► a *QoS Arbiter* and

- ► a *Priority Arbiter*.

The *QoS Arbiter* addresses all aspects related to the individual requirements of applications and votes for certain networks to be used, while the *Priority Arbiter* votes for the importance of applications to the optimization objective. Both arbiters provide the basic inputs that are needed for a global resource allocation process.

Implementations of the muXer decision process might include further arbiters besides these basic ones. For instance, service or network providers that offer ABC services or allow for using multiple access networks may implement their own policies and service level agreements into a separate arbiter. This way, those providers may have the opportunity to affect the decision process on the mobile device. To give an example, network operators may shift standard users to a different access network or limit their capabilities if additional resources are required to serve a premium user. As second option, it would be possible to implement a further arbiter that relates to content adaption aspects in order to add a further dimension to the solution space of the decision problem. As an application's QoE may vary with the network resources being provided, it is possible to use this parameter as an additional constraint in the overall optimization objective. In the scope of this thesis, we excluded the aspect of content adaptation as it depends highly on the user, the respective applications and probably even the actual context.

However, these additional options require extensive research that goes beyond the scope of this thesis. Thus, their further investigation and evaluation is left for future work. In the following sections 5.4.3 and 5.4.4, we present our prototypical implementations of the basic arbiters.

5.4.3 QoS Arbiter

The intention of the *QoS Arbiter* is to rate the candidate networks with respect to the specific needs of an application. As these needs are highly individual, there is always one dedicated *QoS Arbiter* for each application. This makes it possible to reduce the complexity of the arbiter module itself and to adjust parameters like the refresh rate and the relative importance of the individual objectives directly to the respective application.

Our prototype implementation to proof the general procedure of arbitration is based on the classification of QoS categories as presented in section 5.1. In general, the *QoS Arbiter* may use an arbitrary number of decision modules that might be implemented arbitrarily complex. However, the accurate design of these modules requires an in-depth analysis of the parameters for each objective and the effects of different network characteristics on the performance of an application. The design of such product-related modules exceeds the scope of this work. Thus, we decided to implement basic modules for eight decision objectives. They are examples on how such objectives might be implemented and demonstrate the general principle of the arbitration process. A comprehensive analysis on whether a more detailed and product-related design of decision objectives can raise additional optimization potentials is subject to future work.

Figure 5.8 shows the general design of our prototype *QoS Arbiter*. As mentioned before, it is initialized with a set of weights that may either be predefined standard values or can be given by the application itself. The objectives being used by the arbiter go back to the

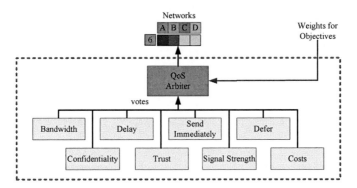

Figure 5.8: The muXer basic QoS Arbiter

QoS categories that we identified in section 5.1. Each decision module releases a vote $v_j \in [-128, 127]$ for every candidate network $n_j \mid j \in \{1, \ldots, p\}$. The vote indicates the adherence of the network's characteristics with the respective objectives. Thus, the output of each decision module k is a column vector v_{qos_k} with p elements. In the end, the *QoS Arbiter* combines all of these vectors. In our prototype implementation it determines the weighted sum of all results coming from the n decision modules.

$$V_{qos} = \begin{pmatrix} V_{qos_1} \\ \vdots \\ V_{qos_p} \end{pmatrix} = \frac{1}{\sum_{k=1}^{n} \omega_{qos_k}} \sum_{k=1}^{n} \omega_{qos_k} v_{qos_k} \qquad (5.3)$$

If optional policies enforce any exclusion criterions or specify any exceptions with respect to certain scenarios, one might diverge from this procedure and implement exclusion criterions or adapt the weights of particular decision modules dynamically. The vector V_{qos} is the final output of the QoS Arbiter that includes the overall suitability of the p candidate networks for the applications the arbiter focuses on. In contrast to the aforementioned procedure in section 5.4.1, the *QoS Arbiter* does not finally decide on which network is allocated to the application. This task is delegated to the second tier of the decision process.

In the following, we introduce the set of decision modules that are implemented in our prototype. All of the following functions for mapping network characteristic on votes are based on plausibility assumptions. Here, we will only present the shapes of these functions. Further details on how they are defined can be found in appendix D.

Bandwidth

For rating the bandwidth requirements of an application, we assume that the *Link Monitor* provides an estimate on the average throughput that can be achieved. This estimate might be measured at the mobile device either by passive monitoring or by active probes and with the general assumption that the wireless access network is the bottleneck of a network path to the correspondent node. As mentioned in section 5.1.2, there are different types of applications that tolerate a certain range of bandwidths. Thus, we expect an application to define an upper and a lower bound of the interval:

▶ the requested bandwidth bw_{req} and

▶ the tolerated bandwidth bw_{tol}.

Figure 5.9 illustrates the characteristic of our *Bandwidth* decision module prototype for a tolerated bandwidth of 300 kbit/s and a favored bandwidth of 500 kbit/s.

The decision module votes on the bandwidth bw_{net} that is actually provided by the network. If the available bandwidth is higher than the one tolerated by the application, the decision module releases a positive vote. The function was chosen to increase logarithmically with an upper limit of the maximum vote. The maximum positive vote is given for networks that provide a bandwidth that is greater than the one favored by the application with a small guard interval. On the other hand, if the bandwidth of a network is below the application's tolerated limit, the vote drops to lowest possible level within a guard interval of 10 % of the tolerated bandwidth. Thus, we chose a different function to model an exponential decrease, which results in the discontinuity that can be seen in the figure. In the case that an application does not state any bandwidth requirements, the decision module releases a neutral vote of 0.

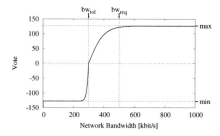

Figure 5.9: Voting on bandwidth requirements

The *Bandwidth* decision module evaluates the required bandwidth for up- and downlink separately. Afterwards, the module decides on the minimum of the votes that were determined for each communication direction.

Delay

Our delay decision module makes use of the average end-to-end delay that is provided by the *Link Monitor*. Comparing to the previous decision module, an application may define its requirements for two different parameters:

▶ the requested delay d_{req},

▶ and the tolerated delay d_{tol}.

The latter parameter states the minimal requirement that has to be met for a successful operation of the application. In contrast, the favored delay models the value that is actually desired to achieve the best quality of user experience. Whenever the experienced delay d_{net} of a network is lower than delay value that is favored by the application and a guard interval, the decision module will return the maximum possible vote. In the case the delay is between the favored and the tolerated value, the voting decreases until 0. As the application may still cope with delays that are slightly lower than the tolerated delay and to increase the robustness of the decision modules to delay fluctuations around the limits, we introduced a further interval $[d_{tol}, d_{tol} * 1.1]$. Thus, for network delays within this interval, the vote decreases exponentially to the lowest negative value. As in the decision module for the bandwidth objectives, we chose two different functions to model the required behavior. Afterwards, for delays that are even higher, the decision module will return the minimum possible vote. Figure 5.10 illustrates this behavior for our proof-of-concept. If an application does not state any delay requirements, the decision module will behave neutral and thus vote with 0. Again, the decision module handles up- and downlink separately and chooses the minimum vote.

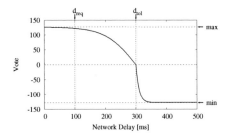

Figure 5.10: Voting on delay requirements

Signal Strength

The *Signal Strength* module targets at the expected availability of a network. It votes for the current signal strength of a wireless network and, thus, favors networks with higher signal strength over ones with weak signals. The absolute signal strength is a measure that is highly related to the technology and the actual network interface card that is being used [248, 249]. Thus, we use an abstract signal strength indicator SSI in $[0, 1]$ that has to be provided by the *Link Monitor*. It can be averaged over a certain time interval to get more stable values. As a second metric, we use the trend T of the signal strength within the past time intervals. We assume a minimum threshold for the signal strength to allow for communication. This threshold is defined to 0.1. From this threshold, the votes that are released by the decision module increase up to a maximum at a signal strength of 1. Furthermore, an application may define whether it prefers a conservative selection of networks or may tolerate risky decisions that have a higher chance of missing the actual objective. This is done by stating a risk level L_r in $[0, 1]$. An increasing risk level has the effect that the characteristic of the signal strength is moved towards lower values. Thus, networks with a weak signal will get better votes. Figure 5.11 illustrates the behavior of our prototype decision module for different risk levels and the signal strengths.

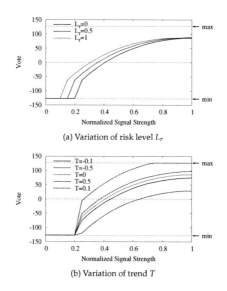

Figure 5.11: Voting on the network's signal strength

Defer or Send

To address the option to delay data transmissions until a later time, we designed two additional decision modules. First, the *Defer* module votes on candidate networks that are expected to appear in the future. The information about when a network may become available can be predicted based on mobility information of the mobile device and context information about the network coverage that may be, for instance, provided by the network provider or obtained by the mobile device in earlier traversals of the network's coverage area. The *Defer* decision module takes the level of an application's disruption tolerance L_{dt} and a deadline t_{dead} for the beginning of the data transmission as inputs. Based on this information that is provided by the *Link Monitor*, the module determines the difference between the application's deadline and the estimated time to connection t_{con} for all predicted candidate networks. If the network becomes available before the deadline exceeds, the module releases a positive vote. Otherwise, the network is voted negatively. As it is shown in figure 5.12, the voting of our prototype module is affected by the application's tolerance to disruptions.

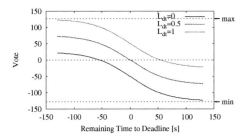

Figure 5.12: Voting on candidate networks for deferring an application request

In contrast to the *Defer* module, we implemented a second module that votes against deferring application requests. Thus, it votes on all networks that are available at the moment and determines the remaining time to an application's deadline t_{dead}. The vote for sending data immediately increases the closer the deadline approaches as is shown in figure 5.13.

Confidentiality and Trust

In section 5.1.2 we already pointed out that there are multiple aspects relating to security issues. For our prototypical implementation, we decided to vote in two of them: The level of *confidentiality* L_c that a network provides and the level of *trust* L_t. The former one is a

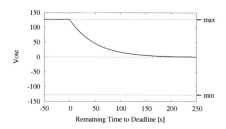

Figure 5.13: Voting on available networks to send data now

measure for the security of the wireless data transmission with respect to the preventing the interception of any information that is sent on the wireless channel. The latter measure indicates how much confidence the user shows in a specific network and its provider. Both aspects are implemented in separate decision modules that work in the same way. The network characteristics, as for instance the encryption techniques being used or the user's trust in a certain network provider, are mapped onto a set of five different levels: VERY LOW (VL), LOW (L), HIGH (H) and VERY HIGH (VH). Accordingly, the user has to state his own security requirements relating to a specific application in a similar way. To give an example, if we assume an unencrypted IEEE 802.11 WLAN network, it will probably be mapped onto the level VERY LOW in terms of confidentiality. In contrast, the level HIGH might be assigned to a different network that supports WPA2 – Personal [250] encryption technologies [25]. On the other hand, a public WLAN hotspot at the airport might be classified with the trust level LOW, while the user's personal WLAN access point at home will be rated with VERY HIGH.

The respective decision modules compare both levels and decide on one of three options:

▶ If the application does not state any specific requirements, the decision module behaves neutral and votes with 0 for all networks.

▶ If the network provides a security level that is higher or equal than the one requested, the module releases a highly positive vote.

▶ Finally, if the network provides a lower security level, the module votes highly negative.

Costs

The final decision module that we implemented for our proof-of-concept focuses on the monetary costs of network usage. Actually, there is a wide range of different rates for network access that result in different costs. For our prototype, we distinguish between four different classes:

► FREE,

► FLAT,

► BUDGET, and

► ONDEMAND (OD).

All networks that might be used at no charge receive the highest possible vote. The same policy holds for flat rates as they do not cause any additional costs besides the monthly fees that have to be paid anyway. Other rates that may cause additional costs to the user receive lower votes. On the one hand, the modules vote for rates that include a time or volume budget dependent on the level to which the budget has already been used. According to figure 5.14 (a), the vote for a network decreases the less amount of the budget remains available. On the other hand, networks that are charged by use are voted depending on their costs per volume (see (b)). Actually, the mapping of a network to one of these classes may vary over time. Thus, if the budget of a network is used up, the user may be charged on-demand.

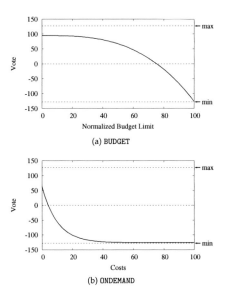

Figure 5.14: Voting on candidate networks for deferring an application request

Summary

To sum up, our implementation of the *QoS Arbiter* makes use of eight exemplary decision modules, each focusing on certain QoS requirements of the application. The parameters being used by these modules are summarized in table 5.1

Module	Parameter	Description
Bandwidth	bw_{req}	Requested bandwidth of an application
	bw_{tol}	Tolerated bandwidth of an application
	bw_{net}	Bandwidth provided by the network
Delay	d_{req}	Requested delay of an application
	d_{tol}	Tolerated delay of an application
	d_{net}	Delay provided by the network
Signal Strength	SSI	Normalized signal strength of a network
	T	Signal strength trend in the past
	L_r	Tolerance of an application to risky decisions
Defer / Send Now	t_{dead}	Deadline for beginning a data transmission
	t_{con}	Estimated time to connecting to a network
	L_{dt}	Level of an application's tolerance to disruptions
Confidentiality	L_{creq}	Required level of confidentiality
	L_{cnet}	Level of confidentiality provided by the network
Trust	L_{treq}	Required level of trust
	L_{tnet}	Level of trust provided by the network
Costs	R	Rate for network access
	L_{bud}	Level to which a volume budget is already used
	L_{cost}	Costs of network usage

Table 5.1: Parameters of the *QoS Arbiter*

5.4.4 Priority Arbiter

The priority arbiter decides on the benefit that an application has to the user with respect to the decision objectives. The concept goes back to the user-related QoS category stated in section 5.1.2. The applications running on the mobile device will typically not have an equal importance to the user. The knowledge about this aspect has two major consequences on the decision process. First, priorities can be used in situations, where application QoS requests exceed the network capabilities. Thus, the decision process may use the level of importance to decide which applications are actually allocated to the networks. Second, the priorities can further be used to decide which applications are deferred and have to wait until either the amount of network capabilities increases or other applications finish their transmissions.

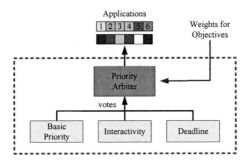

Figure 5.15: The muXer Priority Arbiter

Figure 5.15 illustrates our approach to this concept. The *Priority Arbiter* proceeds differently from the description in section 5.4.1. As the priorities are an abstract metric by themselves, the decision modules directly vote for a certain priority by choosing an appropriate level of their votes. In our prototypical implementation, each particular decision module of the *Priority Arbiter* votes for a level of an application's priority $p_u \in [-40, 39]$. The semantics of the votes is different from the one use for the *QoS Arbiter*, as we decided to base the *Priority Arbiter* on the priority concept used in UNIX-like operating systems. Thus, lower priority values indicate a higher importance for the respective application. We take a basic process priority as the basis and allow for priority up- and downgrades depending on other objectives. The votes of the different decision modules are weighted and merged. In the end, the final vote is chosen to be the priority of the respective application. Our prototype implementation of the *Priority Arbiter* includes three decision modules. We assume that their results have equal importance and add them up to the final output. Details on these decision modules are presented in the following sections.

Basic Priority

In related work on Quality of Service, applications or network services are often differentiated in a set of classes. Such concepts are, for instance, used in UMTS [111] and IEEE 802.11e [26]. Both allow for a differentiation of four QoS classes: background, best effort, video streaming, and audio. In our prototype module, we lean on the UNIX priority concept. Thus, the module votes for an priority within the interval [-20,19]. If the application does not state any information about its application class, the decision module behaves neutral and votes with 0. Further, the module implements a UNIX-like nice level to indicate a user-related level of an application's importance. The given nice level results in a priority up- or downgrade between $[-10, 10]$.

Interactivity

If the user interacts with an application, for instance a web browser, it may expect an immediate response. Thus, we introduced an additional flag in the application requirements, which indicates that an application interacts with the user at the moment. If this flag is set, the application receives a priority upgrade of -10 that is added to the basic priority. Thus, such applications are preferred over other ones and may have a higher probability to be served with the requested resources.

Deadline

Finally, we implemented a further decision module that votes for the remaining time to a deadline given by the application. It votes for a priority upgrade or downgrade in $[-10, 5]$. The interval was chosen in this asymmetric way to underline the different importance of this objective for the cases where the deadline is approaching and the deadline is far away respectively. We assume that in the former case, the objective has a higher relative importance to the overall result and applications get priority upgrades of up to -10. In the latter case the deadline is of less importance with respect to the other objectives. Thus, the priority downgrades are expected to be smaller. Figure 5.16 illustrates the characteristic of this decision module for one exemplary configuration.

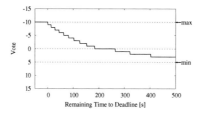

Figure 5.16: Deadline-dependent priority upgrade

Summary

The parameters being used by the three exemplary decision modules of the *Priority Arbiter* are summarized in table 5.2

Module	Parameter	Description
Basic Priority	p_{basic}	General level of an application's importance
Interactivity	I	Flag for indicating whether an application interacts with the user
Deadline	t_{dead}	Deadline for beginning a data transmission

Table 5.2: Parameters of the *Priority Arbiter*

5.4.5 Situation-based Evaluation

Analyzing the actual requirements of different applications and their behavior in networking scenarios with varying conditions in detail would need a huge measurement campaign which is, due to the required effort, beyond the possibilities of this thesis. Nevertheless, to demonstrate the concept of the arbitration process and the rating of different networks, we examined two exemplary scenarios. The first scenario models a communication situation as it may appear at home. It is intended to demonstrate the general voting on available networks with different QoS characteristics. The second scenario deals with the aspect of networks that are expected in the future. It models a city bus ride and demonstrates exemplary results of the QoS Arbiter at three different points in time.

In each of these scenarios, we assume three different applications that want to access the Internet. First, there is the user's E-mail client that requires a high level of trust and confidentiality from the access network to be used. In weighting the different decision objectives, the minimization of costs is a major goal. Second, the user runs a file download in the background. This application has very relaxed bandwidth requirements and does only require a low security level. Again, costs are an important factor for this application. Finally, the third application is a video conference that has higher bandwidth and delay requirements compared to the previous applications.

The detailed characteristics of the modeled applications are shown in table 5.3. In our evaluation, the set of application requirements includes the application's risk level and the level of disruption tolerance. We also model different bandwidth requirements for up- and downlink. For simplicity reasons, we do not differentiate between up- and downlink for the delay requirements. Finally, we defined a deadline and security requirements for the applications.

Application	L_r	L_{ul}	bw_{req} [Mbit/s] DL/UL	bw_{tot} [Mbit/s] DL/UL	d_{req} [ms] DL/UL	d_{tot} [ms] DL/UL	t_{dead}	L_{creq}	L_{treq}
E-mail	0.8	1	0.04 / 0.04	0.03 / 0.03	-	-	+10 min	H	H
File Download	1	1	0.30 / 0.005	0.06 / 0.005	-	-	+5 min	L	L
Video Conference	0	0	0.4 / 0.4	0.36 / 0.36	100 / 100	150 / 150	NOW	H	H

Table 5.3: Application characteristics in the evaluation scenarios

Table 5.4 summarizes the individual weighting of the decision objectives for each scenario. These are results from applying a plausibility analysis with a pair-wise comparison of the importance of each objective to the application. The relative weights are presented as percentage values.

Application	Bandwidth	Delay	Signal Strength	Defer	Send Now	Costs	Confidentiality	Trust
E-mail	3.23	3.23	3.23	22.58	3.23	32.26	16.13	16.13
File Download	2.44	4.88	4.88	24.39	4.88	48.78	4.88	4.88
Video Conference	14.63	14.63	21.95	14.63	14.63	0	9.76	9.76

Table 5.4: Weighting of decision objectives [%]

Home

The first scenario represents a communication scenario at the user's home. Our user can choose from four different networks. First, he may connect to his own private WLAN hotspot that is connected to its local ADSL Internet access. A second option is to use an open WLAN that is operated by one of its neighbors. Third, the user may decide on using his UMTS modem to get Internet access. Finally the last option is to connect to a WiMAX Metropolitan Area Network. During the arbitration process all networks are voted individually, regardless whether they belong to one interface that may not be able to serve multiple networks at the same time. This is an issue which is resolved in the second tier of the decision process. The exemplary characteristics of these networks are summarized in table 5.5.

Network	bw_{net} [Mbit/s] DL/UL	d_{net} [ms] DL/UL	SSI/T	t_{con} [min]	L_{cnet}	L_{tnet}	R	L_{bud}	L_{cost}
$WLAN_{home}$	4 / 0.38	20 / 20	0.8 / 0	-	H	VH	FREE	-	-
$WLAN_{neighbor}$	1 / 0.32	25 / 25	0.2 / 0	-	VL	L	FREE	-	-
$UMTS$	0.26 / 0.047	125 / 125	0.5 / 0	-	H	VH	BUD	0.6	-
$WiMAX$	2.5 / 0.5	141 / 141	0.7 / 0	-	H	H	OD	-	45

Table 5.5: Networks in the *Home* scenario

The resulting votes for the configuration of applications and networks in the home scenario are illustrated in figure 5.17 (a). One can see that the user's private WLAN access point receives the highest preference for all applications. This results from the fact that it provides a large amount of network resources at no additional costs and a very high level of trust and confidentiality. For the E-mail application, the arbiter gave low ratings to the neighbor's WLAN and the WiMAX network. The reasons for this are twofold. The public WLAN of the neighbor is not secured and as the user does not know his neighbor well, he does not trust the access point. On the other hand, the use of the WiMAX network would result in higher costs as it is charged on demand. This latter aspect is also the reason for the negative rating of the WiMAX network for the file download. The video conferencing application puts higher demands on the bandwidth and delay characteristics that are provided by the network. In addition, availability is of higher importance and handled more conservatively than in the case of the previous applications. For these reasons, the WiMAX network receives a higher voting despite of the high costs. In contrast, the UMTS network gets the lowest positive rating, as it is not able to fully meet the bandwidth and delay requirements of the application. Nevertheless, it may be used together in a bundle with other networks. Thus, a positive voting is still reasonable.

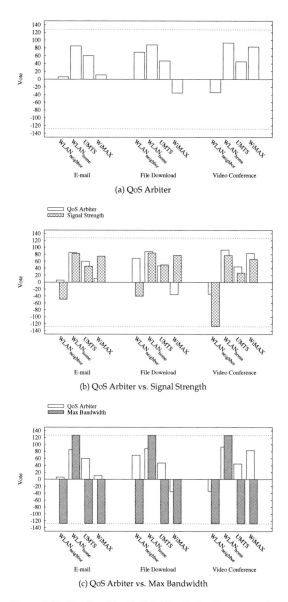

(a) QoS Arbiter

(b) QoS Arbiter vs. Signal Strength

(c) QoS Arbiter vs. Max Bandwidth

Figure 5.17: Results of the QoS Arbiter in the *Home* scenario

In figures 5.17 (b) and 5.17 (c) we compare the rating of our prototype *QoS Arbiter* with those of two other approaches that are commonly used. The first one (b) is based solely on the signal strength and thus relies on the output of the *Signal Strength* module. The second one (c) chooses the network with the maximum bandwidth. Thus, it releases the highest possible vote to this network and the lowest possible vote to other networks. One can see from the results that both alternative strategies would also prefer the user's private WLAN, as it provides the highest signal strength and bandwidth. If we would select the network with the highest performance per application and this network would be able to serve the three applications concurrently, all strategies would have the same results. Nevertheless, we can see differences in the applications' preferences with respect to the other networks, if we compare the results with those that are shown in figure 5.17 (a). Taking the E-mail application as an example, the signal strength strategy rates the WiMAX network quite high, while the *QoS Arbiter* releases a low positive vote. This results from the fact that the use of the WiMAX network causes high costs and the user defined that cost minimization is an important issue to the E-mail application. Another example is the rating of the $WLAN_{neighbor}$ network for the file download. Here, the network is rated negatively by the signal strength strategy as it provides a weak signal level. However, as the file download is disruption tolerant and the network provides high bandwidth at low costs, it is rated clearly positive by the *QoS Arbiter*.

Bus Ride

Our second scenario models a bus drive through the city. We chose this scenario to demonstrate the rating of networks that may become available in the future. Thus, in this scenario, we evaluate the communication at three different points in time. At time t_0, the mobile device may get Internet access via *GPRS* or the $WLAN_B$, which is an open access point by an unknown provider. Next, at time t_1, a second $WLAN_A$ hotspot becomes available. Here, the user knows the provider well. Finally, at time t_2 the user enters an area with HSDPA coverage. Thus, the GPRS link disappears and the radio switches to HSDPA. The detailed characteristics of this scenario are summarized in table 5.6. Empty cells in the table indicate that the respective value has not changed compared to the previous time step.

The resulting votes for the three situations are shown in figure 5.18. At time t_0 only two candidate networks are available: *GPRS* and $WLAN_B$. For the E-mail application, the Arbiter releases high ratings on the networks that are predicted to appear in the future, as they are expected to meet the application requirements better than the available ones. The download application prefers to wait for the $WLAN_A$ network as well. It provides a higher level of trust and confidentiality and thus received a higher rating than the available $WLAN_B$ network that provides equal communication characteristics. For the video conference, none of the networks is really well suited. As it is not disruption tolerant, the expected networks are

Network	time	bw_{net} [Mbit/s] DL/UL	d_{net} [ms]	SSI/T	t_{con} [min]	L_{cnet}	L_{fnet}	R	L_{bud}	L_{cost}
GPRS	t_0	0.04 / 0.02	400	0.4 / -0.1	-	VH	V	OD	-	0.25
	t_1			0.8 / 0						
	t_2	-	-	-	-	-	-	-	-	-
HSDPA	t_0	0.825 / 0.36	50	0 / 0	+5	H	VH	OD	-	15
	t_1				+3					
	t_2			0.8 / 0	-					
$WLAN_A$	t_0	0.85 / 0.5	50	0 / 0	+2	L	H	FLAT	-	-
	t_1			0.3 / 0.1	-					
	t_2			0.7 / -0.2						
$WLAN_B$	t_0	0.85 / 0.5	50	0.2 / 0.15	-	VL	VL	FREE	-	-
	t_1			0.5 / -0.1						
	t_2			0.1 / -0.1						

Table 5.6: Networks in the *Bus Ride* scenario

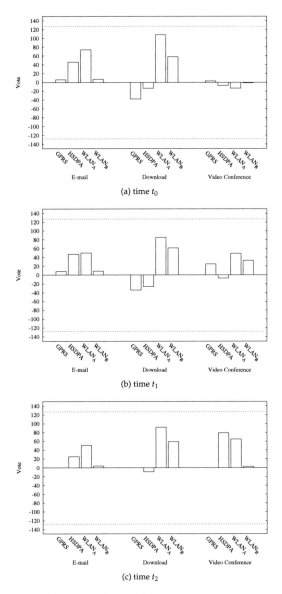

Figure 5.18: Results of the QoS Arbiter in the *Bus Ride* scenario

rated with negative votes. The $WLAN_B$ network does not meet the requirements for trust and confidentiality. Besides, the signal strength is quite low although the trend is increasing. Only the GPRS network receives a slightly positive voting. It is available and has average signal level, but does not provide enough bandwidth to serve the applications.

At time t_1, the $WLAN_A$ network becomes available. Again, the E-mail application and the download prefer this network at most, as it meets most of the application's requirements. Another aspect is the approaching deadline of the download that results in small vote upgrades for networks that are available. In the case of the video conference, one can see a clear change of the ratings. This has two reasons, first the signal strength of the GPRS and $WLAN_B$ networks have stabilized at a clearly higher level. Second, as the $WLAN_A$ network is now available and meets most of the requirements it receives the highest voting of all four networks.

Finally, at time t_2, the GPRS link switches to $HSDPA$. This does not have significant effects on the results for the E-mail application and the download. However, for the video conference the network with the highest level of preference is now $HSDPA$, as it fully complies with the application's level of confidentially and the higher costs are not relevant for this application.

Figure 5.19 shows again the comparison of the results for the *QoS Arbiter* to the strategies based solely on either the signal strength or the maximum bandwidth at time t_0. Here, we can see even stronger differences between the results compared to the previous scenario. As the $HSDPA$ and $WLAN_A$ networks are not available at the moment, both are rated highly negative by the alternative strategies. For the E-mail application and the download, the signal strength-based strategy prefers to use the GPRS network. However, this network provides only a low performance at quite high costs. As the applications do not have to communicate immediately, it is advantageous to wait for the upcoming alternatives. The maximum bandwidth strategy prefers at time t_0 the public $WLAN_B$ network. However, this network provides only a very low level of confidentiality and trust, why it is devaluated by the *QoS Arbiter*.

In the next step, we also demonstrate the behavior of the *Priority Arbiter*. Table 5.7 summarizes the priorities that were obtained for the individual applications at the modeled points in time. According to our priority schema, negative values indicate a high priority and increasing values correspond to lower application priorities. We assume that all three objectives of the arbiter are weighted equally. One can see that the priorities of the E-mail application and the download increases the closer the deadline approaches. In contrast, the video conference receives a constant priority, as it requires immediate and continuous Internet access.

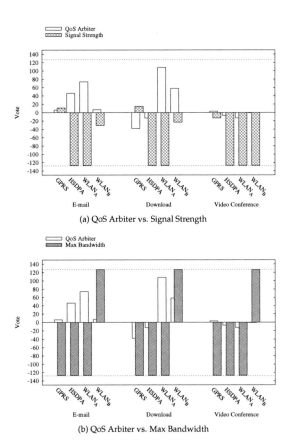

(a) QoS Arbiter vs. Signal Strength

(b) QoS Arbiter vs. Max Bandwidth

Figure 5.19: Comparison to other approaches at time t_0

Application	t_0	t_1	t_2
E-mail	14	13	11
File Download	10	6	-1
Video Conference	-30	-30	-30

Table 5.7: Application priorities in the *Bus Ride* scenario

Discussion

Our situation-based evaluation of the *QoS Arbiter* demonstrated the muXer ar"-bi"-tra"-tion-based voting concept in two different scenarios. The first one was static, while the second scenario focused on changes in the network characteristics and the rating of expected networks over simulated time. Obviously, this evaluation is just a proof-of-concept with the only intention to show how the general procedure works. We only chose one exemplary set of decision modules and configuration parameters. Thus, the results do not allow any conclusions on the quality of the votes that are released by the decision modules. However, the detailed parameterization of the decision modules and their weighting require further research work that is out of the scope of this thesis. Especially, the evaluation of the effects and benefits of particular decision modules on the overall decision result and the performance of individual applications in different networking scenarios are promising research topics that require intensive work to find reasonable sets of parameters that meet the application requirements best. For this, extensive real-world measurement campaigns are required.

5.5 Global Resource Allocation

The application-oriented rating discussed in the previous section 5.4 focuses on the needs of isolated applications only. Thus, the global arbitration has to map the set of locally optimal ratings onto a global optimum for all applications running on the mobile device. To reach these goals, the global arbitration process has to account for the application preferences determined during the application-oriented rating as well as further cross-application optimization goals as, for instance, the overall costs and energy constraints of the mobile device.

The remaining part of this section discusses the requirements and design issues for the global arbitration process. Afterwards, related work and candidate algorithms are presented and evaluated with respect to the requirements. Section 5.5.4 introduces the *GAP* algorithm that bases on application priorities, votes, and optimization constraints. Finally, the section closes with an evaluation of the approach's characteristics.

5.5.1 Requirements and Design Issues

The global arbitration process combines the application-specific ratings and generates and decides on the final mapping of applications and communication networks. This process has two major goals: First, to ensure an efficient utilization of the communication capabilities and second to avoid overloads of networks that may lead to decreased application performances. To perform these tasks, the process has to meet the following requirements:

Optimality: One of the main goals of the algorithm is to make use of the full capacity that is available for communication. Thus, the global arbitration process should use this capacity to the best and make as many applications active as possible. At the same time, the algorithm always has to consider the application-oriented ratings and should not schedule an application to a network that was deprecated as the result of the previous decision phase.

Complexity: The algorithm should be as complex as needed, but as simple as possible at the same time. One the one hand, a certain level of complexity is needed to handle the different optimization goals and to find good solutions to the decision problem. It should use memory and processing resources economically, as mobile devices are often less powerful devices.

Scalability: One important aspect for the algorithm is its scalability. It should scale well with an increasing number of applications and networks, both resulting in a higher number of possible configurations.

Responsiveness: Our decision concept was intentionally designed to provide a high responsiveness, by employing the concept of asynchronous decision modules. Thus, the resource allocation process should target at the same aim and should find a solution to the problem within a short period of time.

In the following, we analyze possible candidate algorithms for the overall optimization of the application-oriented ratings referring to their ability to meet these requirements.

5.5.2 Formal Problem Statement

Assume that we have a given set of m applications $A = \{a_1, \ldots, a_m\}$ running on the mobile device. Each of these applications requests a specific bandwidth Bw_i with $i \in \{1, \ldots, m\}$. Furthermore, we assume to have a set of p networks $N = \{n_1, \ldots, n_p\}$, each having a particular bandwidth capacity cap_j with $j \in \{1, \ldots p\}$. Furthermore, the mobile device is equipped with a given set of q interfaces $E = \{e_1, \ldots, e_q\}$. Via each of these Interfaces it is possible to access a subset of the available networks. This means that the set of networks that are accessible via interfaces e_k can be states as $F_k \subseteq N$. The actual use of one of these interfaces e_k to connect to network n_j incurs a certain amount of costs $costs_{jk}$. As our approach accounts for using network bundles, the bandwidth that is requested by application i may be split-up in portions x_{ij} that are assigned to a specific network j. Finally, the *QoS Arbiter* in the first tier of the decision process provides us with a set of votes $qosVote_{ij}$ for all possible combinations of applications $a_i \in A$ and networks $n_j \in N$. In addition, the *Priority Arbiter* states a set of priorities $prio_i$ with $i \in \{1, \ldots, m\}$ indicating the importance of an application a_i.

For mapping of applications to networks, we aim at meeting the following optimization goals:

1. Maximize the number of applications that are served at a time.

2. Meet the application requirements and priorities as good as possible.

3. Minimize the number of networks being used.

Mathematically this problem ends up in a scheduling problem with splitting jobs. For any given scenario, it can be formulated as the following linear programming problem:

$$\text{Maximize} \quad \frac{1}{|A|} \sum_{i=1}^{m} \sum_{j=1}^{p} \left(qosVote_{ij} \cdot \frac{x_{ij}}{bw_i} \cdot prio_i \right) - \frac{1}{|N|} \left(\sum_{j=1}^{p} y_j \cdot costs_{jk} \right) \quad (5.4)$$

Subject to

$$\sum_{i=1}^{m} x_{ij} \leq cap_j \quad \forall j \in \{1, \ldots, p\} \quad (5.5)$$

$$\sum_{j=1}^{p} x_{ij} = z_i \cdot bw_i \quad \forall i \in \{1, \ldots, m\} \quad (5.6)$$

$$\sum_{n_j \in F_k} y_j \leq 1 \quad \forall k \in \{1, \ldots, q\} \quad (5.7)$$

$$\frac{\sum_{i=1}^{m} x_{ij}}{cap_j} \leq y_j \quad \forall j \in \{1, \ldots, p\} \quad (5.8)$$

$$y_j \leq \sum_{i=1}^{m} x_{ij} \quad \forall j \in \{1, \ldots, p\} \quad (5.9)$$

$$\frac{\sum_{j=1}^{p} x_{ij}}{bw_i} \leq z_i \quad \forall i \in \{1, \ldots, m\} \quad (5.10)$$

$$z_i \leq \sum_{j=1}^{p} x_{ij} \quad \forall i \in \{1, \ldots, m\} \quad (5.11)$$

where

$$x_{ij} \in \mathbb{N}_0 \mid x_{ij} \leq cap_j \quad \forall j \in \mathcal{N} \quad (5.12)$$

$$y_j = \begin{cases} 1 & \text{if network } j \text{ is used} \\ 0 & \text{else} \end{cases} \quad (5.13)$$

$$z_i = \begin{cases} 1 & \text{if application } i \text{ is successfully assigned to any network} \\ 0 & \text{else} \end{cases} \quad (5.14)$$

186   5. An Arbitration Concept for Dynamic Network Selection

Parameter	Description
A	Set of applications
$|A|$	Number of applications
N	Set of networks
$|N|$	Number of networks
E	Set of network interfaces
F_k	Set of networks that can be accessed via interface k
$qosVote_{ij}$	Vote of the *QoS Arbiter* for application i and network j
bw_i	Bandwidth requested by application i
x_{ij}	Bandwidth being allocated at network j for application i
$prio_i$	Vote of the *Prio Arbiter* for application i
y_j	Flag indicating whether network j is used ($y_j = 1$) or not ($y_j = 0$)
$costs_{jk}$	Costs of using network j via interface k
cap_j	Bandwidth capacity of network j
z_i	Flag whether network resources are allocated to an application i during the scheduling process ($z_i = 1$) or not ($z_i = 0$)

Table 5.8: Parameters of the formal problem statement

Table 5.8 summarizes the parameters different parameters being used in our problem statement. Equation 5.4 states the actual objective function. It depends on a set of constraints. First, the amount of bandwidth that is scheduled to any network j must not exceed the available capacity of this network (5.5). Thus, for each network j we add up all amounts of bandwidth x_{ij} that have been allocated to any application i. The result must be lower than the bandwidth capacity cap_j of network j.

Second, an application can only get all of its requested bandwidth or none. It is not possible to assign only parts of the requested bandwidths to any application. As it is shown in equation 5.6, we iterate through all networks and add up the amount of bandwidth that has been allocated to application i. The result must be either zero, if the application request is deferred ($z_i = 0$), or it must be equal to the requested bandwidth bw_i ($z_i = 1$).

In our problem statement, we assume that it is only possible to use one network per interface. Equation 5.7 ensures that this restriction is met. We iterated through the set F_k

of all networks and that are accessible via an interface e_k and add up the flags whether a network j is active ($y_j = 1$) or not ($y_j = 0$). The results must equal to or less than one.

Equations 5.8 to 5.11 are needed to control the auxiliary variables y_j and z_i that indicate whether a network and application is used respectively. First, equation 5.8 ensures that no networks are overloaded. Thus for each network j, the ratio between the sum $\sum x_{ij}$ of the amount of bandwidth that is allocated to any applications and the network capacity cap_j must either be equal to zero in the case that the network is not used ($y_j = 0$). Otherwise, if the network is used ($y_j = 1$), the ratio must be equal to or lower than one to avoid overload situations. Second, equation 5.9 is responsible for switching the flag y_j off. If no bandwidth of any network j is allocated to any application i the network is not used ($y_j = 0$). Equations 5.10 and 5.11 describe a similar approach for the flag $z_i \in [0,1]$. The ratio between the amount of the application's bandwidth that is reserved at any networks and its requested bandwidth must either be equal to zero if the application request is deferred ($z_i = 0$), or it must be equal to or lower than one in the opposite case ($z_i = 1$). In addition, z_i must be set to zero if no bandwidth of an application is scheduled to any networks (equation 5.11). Finally, equations 5.12 to 5.14 state additional conditions to the values of parameters.

The previous formulation is an idealized representation of the actual problem statement for two reasons: First, it does not consider the fact that the splitting of an application's requested bandwidth onto multiple networks is bounded by the characteristics of the networks being bundled, which were analyzed in section 4.4.4. Thus, increasing differences in these characteristics result in a lower efficiency of network bundling. Second, it does not account for any aspects relating to the time that resources of a network are occupied by an application.

In the end, our optimization problem compares to scheduling approaches to unrelated parallel machines with job splitting. Several variants of this optimization problem have been discussed in previous research work, for instance in the area of operations research [251–260]. All of them were shown to be NP-hard. Thus, one can assume that our problem is NP-hard as well and that it is practically impossible to find an optimal solution within polynomial time. Instead, we need to find a reasonable heuristic that results in a good schedule, but still ensures a reactive behavior of the whole decision concept.

5.5.3 Candidate Algorithms

So far, there are no comparable approaches to the muXer global resource allocation concept in related work on dynamic network selection. Nevertheless, the decision problem is similar to other QoS scheduling problems in the processor or network domain as well as to the aforementioned machine scheduling problems. Candidate algorithms to solve the decision problem must manage with the following set of constraints that result from the muXer decision concept:

- ► All resources are rated with scores. Those scores are an abstract metric for the individual profit, which a specific resource has with respect to the application requirements. Applications should only be scheduled to resources that are scored above a minimum threshold.

- ► For each application to be scheduled, there might be multiple candidate resources it can be assigned to. These resources differ in their characteristics and may even show asymmetric characteristics in up- and downlink direction.

- ► Applications may not only be scheduled to a single resource, but may be spread over multiple ones.

- ► Applications may have particular benefits to the user and thus should be handled accordingly.

These constraints clearly increase the number of dimensions as well as the complexity of the decision problem. From related work, we identified multiple candidate algorithms that might be used to solve the decision problem. The following list makes no claim to be complete, but it gives an overview on the variety of possible options:

Graph Algorithms

One possible option with some relaxations could be the mapping of the decision problem with all possible solutions onto a graph representation. Afterwards, one has to find the shortest path in the graph to find the optimal solutions. Actually, there are multiple options to solve this problem. Two examples are given in the following:

Backtracking: The backtracking algorithm is based on a depth-first search [261] and tries to find an overall solution to the given decision problem gradually. For this, backtracking creates partial problem solutions and checks whether there is a chance to reach the overall goal with them. If not, the algorithm searches for alternative solutions and may even revert to an earlier state of the solution. Otherwise the algorithm continuous its search in this direction and extents the intermediate solution until it found the final result. If it is not required to find the optimal solution, backtracking allows for defining a weighting function that determines the utility of a solution with respect to the decision problem. Thus, the algorithm may not result in an optimal solution, but one that is sufficient to solve the problem.

Ant Colony Optimization: The ant colony optimization algorithm is inspired by the behavior of ants seeking for food [262]. It implements a metaheuristic, which aims at finding solutions that are near to the optimum. An advantage of the ant colony optimization is that it allows for dynamic adaptations if the graph changes.

The disadvantage of the use of graph algorithms is the fact that even with a moderate number of applications and networks, the number of candidate solutions increases exponentially in the context of our concept for network selection. This results in high requirements of memory resources and clearly increased complexity in finding the optimal solution. Finally, as the mobile communication scenarios might be subject to frequent changes in the communication environment, such a solution would cause significant overhead for the continuous adaptation of the graph.

Linear Programming

Another option would be the use of linear programming techniques to solve the optimization problem. As our optimization problem is formulated as a set of linear equations, we can use, for instance, the simplex algorithm [263] to solve this problem in a numerical way. As some of the variables are required to be integral, one might use the branch and bound [264] or branch and cut method [265] which combines branch and bound with cutting plane methods. Both relax the integral constraint in the first place and divide the original problem into linear programming problems that can be solved using the simplex algorithm until either an integral solution is found, or the complete solution space has been searched. Alternatively, one may define a quality estimator that indicates whether a found solution is good enough to meet the optimization problem.

The linear programming approach is supposed to find an optimal solution to the decision problem, but there is no guarantee that this solution is found in polynomial time. Thus, it may take a long time to find an optimal solution for the decision problem. Moreover, if the initial problem is split up into a large number of sub problems, this may generate a large overhead for managing all of these sub problems that have to be solved one-by-one using the simplex algorithm. The computation time might be reduced by stating a quality estimator that relaxes the constraint of finding an optimal solution to the objective of finding one that is close to the optimum.

Classical Scheduling

Furthermore, there are numerous scheduling approaches to the decision problem that process the application request in a certain order. The following list illustrates the range of possible candidate schedulers that work on different metrics:

Priority-based Scheduling: The concept of priority-based scheduling assumes that each item to be scheduled has a predefined priority. Based on this, the items are handled in the order of their priority and allocated to the available resources.

Latency-based Scheduling: Latency-based scheduling tries to minimize the average cycle time of an application. Thus, it prefers applications that use resources for a shorter time over applications that block resources for longer periods of time. A classical candidate of this class of scheduling algorithms is Shortest Job First (SJF).

Priority- and Latency-based Scheduling: This algorithm combines the previous scheduling strategies. It handles applications in the order of their priority and their expected time for using the resource.

Deadline-based Scheduling: Deadline-based schedulers operate on the basis of deadlines that are assigned to the applications. Applications with shorter deadlines will be scheduled prior to applications with deadlines lying further ahead. This strategy aims at ensuring the strict adherence to the predefined deadlines. A prominent example of a deadline-based scheduling algorithm is Earliest-Deadline First (EDF) [266] that is being used for tasks with real-time requirements.

These scheduling approaches will not necessarily find an optimal solution to the decision problem. However, they have the great advantage of having a very low complexity and can be expected to scale well with increasing numbers of networks and application.

Discussion

This list of candidate strategies is not exhaustive and it might surely be extended by further approaches. All of these possible candidate concepts have their own advantages and disadvantages. Table 5.9 summarizes their characteristics with respect to the requirements stated above. The fulfillment of each requirement is evaluated according to a scale of three levels:

+ the requirement is fully met,

o the requirement is partly met, and

- the requirement is not met.

It becomes clear that none of the approaches meets all of the requirements. Graph algorithms may find an optimal solution, but at the costs of a high complexity and exponential worst-case running times. Depending on what kind of heuristic is used, the runtime may be reduced at the costs of a lower optimality. In addition, the concept of periodically generating graphs with all possible configurations does not scale well for increasing numbers of applications and networks. For muXer, such a behavior is inacceptable as it is contradictory to the arbitration concept with asynchronous decision modules that are intended to provide a high level of responsiveness.

The linear programming approach is also able to find optimal results by solving a linear programming problem. As input it requires a set of linear equations that state the optimization objective. The effort for determining this set is expected to be much lower than in the

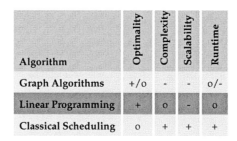

Algorithm	Optimality	Complexity	Scalability	Runtime
Graph Algorithms	+/o	-	-	o/-
Linear Programming	+	o	-	o
Classical Scheduling	o	+	+	+

Table 5.9: Comparison of candidate algorithms

previous case. The simplex algorithm can be expected to solve practical decision problems in a reasonable amount of time, although there is no guarantee that it is able to solve them in polynomial time.

Finally, we presented a set of classical schedulers working on different metrics that will not necessarily find the optimal solution to the decision problem. However, they have the great advantage that they are simple, lightweight and scale well even in larger scenarios.

The decision of which approach to chose for muXer is again a tradeoff between precision and complexity as stated in section 5.2.2. On the one hand, it is desired to achieve the best possible configuration of applications and networks. On the other hand, mobile devices provide often a limited amount of resources and processing power. This aspect tip the scale for basing the global resource allocation in muXer on a classical scheduling approach that proposes good runtime behavior and comparable low levels of complexities paired with the abilities to make reasonable decisions. Thus, we use a classical scheduling approach as a basis for the muXer global resource allocation. In our later evaluation, we will compare our approach to a linear programming technique in order to state the distance to the optimal result and thus to evaluate whether our tradeoff was chosen wisely.

5.5.4 The muXer Global Arbitration Process

The *muXer Global Arbitration Process* (GAP) is designed, on the one hand, to utilize the communication capabilities efficiently and to maximize the number of applications being served, but on the other hand to respect the individual application requirements as well.

Inputs

Besides the list of applications and networks, the process is based on a set of further input parameters:

Application-oriented rating: The application-oriented rating is the output of the *QoS Arbiters* (section 5.4.3) in the first tier of the decision process. It is represented by a matrix containing the applications' votes for each network.

Application priorities: The application priorities come from the *Priority Arbiter* presented in section 5.4.4. They allow for defining the relative importance of an application with respect to other applications. As certain applications have a higher or lower importance, they might be handled differently by the scheduler.

Bandwidth requirements: The bandwidth requirements of an application are needed to check whether a network that is preferred by the application is actually able to provide sufficient remaining capacities to serve this application.

Architecture

The *GAP* architecture is made up of five components (see figure 5.20). The *Scheduler* runs the actual network selection process. It may use additional decision modules that implement global objectives relating to cross-application issues as, for instance, overall costs or energy consumptions. Details on this concept are explained later in this section. The modules are managed by a *Vote Adaptation* arbiter. Whenever the *Scheduler* wants to assign an application to a specific network, it firstly asks the *Bandwidth Manager*.

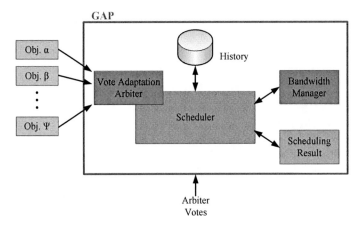

Figure 5.20: The GAP architecture

The *Bandwidth Manager* keeps track of free and used capacities of the candidate networks. For this, it receives requests from the *Scheduler* and checks whether they can be served. If this is the case, it reserves the requested bandwidth on this network. The final results are passed to the *Scheduling Result* component that collects all information about decisions being made by the scheduler. Moreover, it offers various functionalities for generating the final decision outcome and managing the resulting configurations. In addition, the *GAP* architecture includes a *History* module that stores a certain number of results that have been achieved in previous scheduler runs. This *History* is used to make dynamic adaptations in the current scheduling run, for instance to determine a handover hysteresis for applications that already use one or more networks.

In the prototypical realization of *GAP* all bandwidth reservations that are done by *Bandwidth Manager*, as described above, are virtual ones. This means that the *Bandwidth Manager* subtracts the requested bandwidth from the network's available capacity. The implementation of "real" network reservations and QoS guarantees [267] are out of scope at this point. They could be an option for future research work, but will typically require the support of the network infrastructure. While reservation of bandwidth for single network paths within the *Bandwidth Manager* is almost straight forward, it is more complex in the case of multipath transfer. Here, the requested bandwidth has to be split-up onto the single paths included in the bundle. As the results in section 4.3 indicate, this ratio depends on the specific characteristics of the bundled networks. Nevertheless, the current implementation only spreads the requested bandwidth proportional to the free capacity of a network. A more complex and accurate function describing the distribution of application data on network bundles is subject to the parameterization of the system in a deployment scenario.

Scheduling Process

In the following, we describe the actual scheduling process that is implemented in *GAP*. It handles applications in prioritized order and assigns one of three possible decision options to them: assign

1. allocate a single network for communication to the application,

2. allocate a bundle of multiple networks for communication to the application, or

3. defer an application request to wait for any further opportunities later in the future.

The choice of the third option may result from two different reasons. An application might either be put aside because none of the possible candidate network actually meets the application requirements or because the preferred networks do not offer enough remaining capacities to satisfy the bandwidth requirements of the application.

Figure 5.21 gives a generalized overview about the working of the scheduling approach implemented in *GAP*. The process itself is split-up into four stages. The first one is called

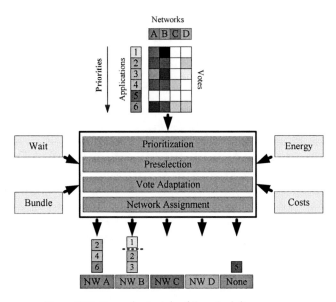

Figure 5.21: General principle of the scheduling process

Prioritization and is responsible for sorting applications with respect to their priorities that were determined by the *Priority Arbiter*. The *Scheduler* itself has the opportunity to make any further adaptation of these priorities, for instance, based on previous decision results, if there is any respective objective in the decision process. According to our arbitration concept, such an objective would be implemented as a decision module that votes for certain adaptations. In the remaining part of the process, the algorithm handles all applications according to the order that was determined in this stage. The *Priorization* stage is followed by a *Preselection* stage. Here, the algorithm filters out those networks that do not meet the application requirements at all. This decision is based on a minimum threshold for application rating that has to be exceeded by a network. Further on, only the remaining, i.e. preferred, candidate networks are evaluated for each application. In the next stage of our process, that is called *Vote Adaptation*, the network ratings of an application are adapted according to additional global objectives. In general, a variety of such objectives is conceivable and can be modularly integrated into the decision process. Finally, in the *Network Assignment* stage, the algorithm decides on the actual allocation of network resources to the application.

After introducing the general organization of our scheduling process, we now turn to the detailed description of the workflow, which is shown in figure 5.22. In the following, we introduce the individual steps that are traversed to schedule the application requests:

1. First, for each application, the algorithm obtains the respective priority from the result of the *Priority Arbiter*. Afterwards, it checks whether there are any global objectives that lead to an adjustment of this priority level. One possible option for such an objective is the time that an application request was deferred in previous scheduling runs. Such an approach may be used to improve the fairness of the scheduling process with respect to applications that have almost similar importance to the user, but already wait for some time to get network access.

2. Second, all applications, the algorithm has to decide on, are added to a global priority queue according to the priorities that are determined in the previous step. The order of applications within this queue defines the processing sequence of applications within the remaining part of the scheduling process.

3. Next, the scheduler iterates through the global priority queue of applications. As long as there are further applications to schedule, the algorithm fetches the next one from the queue and proceeds with its normal operation. Otherwise, the scheduling process is finished and the final result can be forwarded to the *Path Management* module in the muXer architecture.

4. For every application, the scheduler starts with extracting the corresponding results of the arbitration process in the first tier from the input matrix. In our prototypical implementation these are only the results that have been determined by the *QoS Arbiter*.

5. In the next step, the scheduler determines the list of networks that are preferred by the application based on the amount of votes that a network has received. As already mentioned above, this list is a subset of all networks and includes only those that are rated above a certain threshold. The threshold ensures that only networks with a minimum level of acceptance are considered as possible candidates for data transmission and thus are able to meet at least basic QoS requirements of the application.

6. The application-oriented rating of certain networks may be subject to further adaptations if any global objectives provide additional aspects that have to be considered in the decision-making process. This step implements the interface for global optimization objectives based on the arbitration concept. By increasing or reducing the votes, the level of preference for certain networks may be changed. Subsequently, this may results in a different processing sequence of candidate networks. Details on how this adaptation is implemented are given later on in a separate subsection.

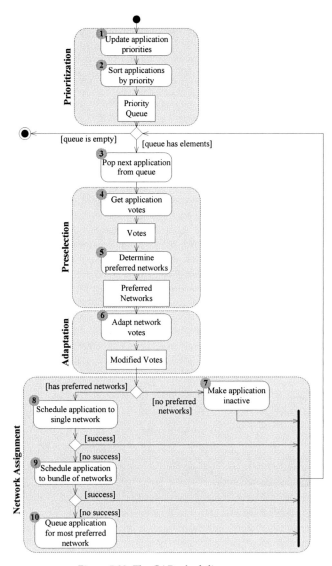

Figure 5.22: The GAP scheduling process

In the end, the remaining networks that are voted above the aforementioned threshold are added to a queue and sorted in descending order with respect to their level of preference that is expressed in the amount of votes a network drew in. This order states the sequence in which the algorithm evaluates all candidate networks.

7. Before the algorithm proceeds, it first checks if there is actually at least one network in the queue of preferred networks. If the queue is empty, all candidate networks were voted below the predefined threshold and do not meet the application requirements at all. In this case, *GAP* sets the application to the status INACTIVE and defers its request for network resources for now.

8. Otherwise, if an application has at least one preferred network, *GAP* continues and tries to schedule the application. First, it tries to find a single network that is able to serve the application. Figure 5.23 illustrates the steps that are performed in this case. For each iteration, *GAP* takes the most preferred network of the remaining ones and asks the *Bandwidth Manager* to reserve the requested bandwidth on this network. If this reservation is successful, the application is set to the status ACTIVE, the respective network is assigned to that application and the schedule starts a new iteration with the next application. Otherwise, the network currently under investigation is skipped and the algorithm probes the next best network.

On the one hand, this procedure ensures that networks are not used beyond their capacity limits. On the other hand, it is possible to schedule applications to less preferred networks that still meet the application requirements to some extent, thereby increasing the number of applications that can be made ACTIVE.

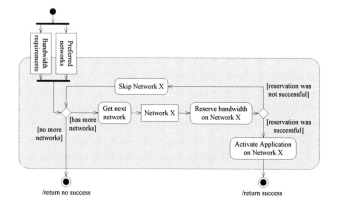

Figure 5.23: GAP: Schedule an application to a single network

9. If the previous step was not successful and an application has more than one preferred networks, *GAP* tries to find a bundle of networks as an alternative for communication. In doing so, it first adds the two networks with the highest preference to a virtual bundle and asks the *Bandwidth Manager* for a bandwidth reservation. In the case that this reservation is successful, *GAP* assigns the resource of these networks to the application and sets it to ACTIVE. Otherwise, it adds further preferred networks (if any) to the bundle and repeats the procedure until there are no further preferred networks or a suitable bundle of networks is found. The whole process is shown in figure 5.24. This procedure for choosing bundles may potentially lead to bundles with higher number of networks. However, it has the advantage that it ensures a better scalability and processing time with an increasing number of candidate networks.

In our prototypical implementation, we consider the option of using multipath transfer only as the second best alternative. The reason for this is the additional overhead that is caused by concurrent multipath transfer in terms of splitting and reordering data (see chapter 4.3).

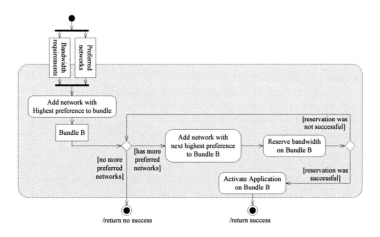

Figure 5.24: GAP: Schedule an application to a bundle of networks

10. Finally, if the network assignment process was neither able to find a single network nor a network bundle that provides enough capacity, the respective application gets the status DEFERRED. This status implicates the fact that no resources are allocated to the application in this scheduler run. Furthermore, the application is added to the waiting queue for the network it preferred at most. An application's position in this

waiting queue depends on its priority, the level of preference and, if known, the time it is expected to use the network. This aspect has two consequences on the further operation. First, the application may succeed to any application that releases its resources of the network. This can be done even without the necessity of a complete new run of the scheduler, if there are enough resources to serve the applications. Otherwise, the time an application is queued may also be used as a further metric in the *Vote Adaptation* stage during the subsequent scheduler runs. However, this issue is left for future optimizations of the scheduling process.

Vote Adaptation

In the previous subsection, we introduced the general workflow of *GAP*. However, so far we left out, how the cross-application objectives are implemented within the stage of *Vote Adaptation*. Now, we make up for this and explain our approach to integrating global decision objectives.

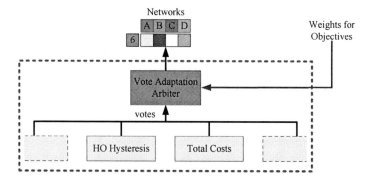

Figure 5.25: The concept of Vote Adaptation

To pursue our concept of a highly flexible and modular concept for combining different decision objectives and metrics, the vote adaptation process is also based on an arbitration concept. Thus, it allows for integrating and weighting different objectives in a simple way. Figure 5.25 shows the generalized concept. The *Vote Adaptation Arbiter* votes for additional up- or downgrades of the application-oriented votes. For out prototypical implementation of *GAP*, we designed two different decision modules. The *HO Hysteresis* module implements a hysteresis to avoid frequent handovers between different networks in successive runs of the scheduling algorithm. If an application i is already active, the decision modules votes for a bonus $v_{hyst_{ij}}$ to that network j or bundle of networks that is currently being used by the application. We set this bonus to a constant factor of 10 that is added to the respective networks. However, the actual parameterization will be subject to possible deployment scenarios and may even be chosen dynamically, for instance depending on the time an application is already using a specific network. Thus, this procedure is intended to minimize the probability of ping-pong effects [106].

Second, the *Total Costs* decision module focuses on reducing the overall costs of network usage. As a proof-of-concept, we implemented a decision module that aims at reducing the number of networks being used, but does not account for any overall limit of a cost or energy budget. Instead, we provide upgrades to networks that are already used by any applications. Thus, the idea is to fill those networks up that are already in use, before scheduling applications to any further networks that are idle at the moment. In our implementation, the bonus amounts to:

$$v_{cost_j} = \left(127 + 127 \cdot \frac{load_{UL_j} + load_{DL_j}}{2}\right), \tag{5.15}$$

where $load_{UL_j}$ and $load_{DL_j} \in [0,1]$ state the ratio of available and allocated resources on either the up- and the downlink of the respective network j. The effect of the *Total Costs* module on the final result is controlled by a weighting factor $\omega_c \in [0,1]$. This factor controls the importance of cost reduction to the user that may choose an arbitrary value between "no cost reduction at all" and "maximum cost reduction". Adding a constant factor of 127 to the application-oriented vote ensures that any network that got a positive voting in the first tier of the decision process and to which the scheduler already assigned an application within the current run will be preferred with respect to the other applications in the case ω_c is maximum. The second term represents a proportional share that increase with the load of the network. It aims at trying to fill networks up to their full capacity. This way, our approach of cost reduction will not actively limit the number of networks being used or the number of applications that gain network access. It just gives the objective of using a minimal number of networks to schedule the applications a higher importance with respect to the aim of choosing that network that meets all application-oriented requirements best.

In summary, the final output of the *Vote Adaptation Arbiter* for an application i and a network j is:

$$v_{adapt_{ij}} = v_{hyst_{ij}} + \omega_c \cdot v_{cost_j} . \tag{5.16}$$

The implementation of these modules is intended as a proof of concept. Future work may analyze the effects of cost and energy constraints on the communication performance and network decision strategies in more detail.

Output

In the end, *GAP* returns the *Scheduling Result* that is made up of three different parts:

1. a list of INACTIVE applications that do not prefer any network at all,

2. a list of ACTIVE applications that are scheduled to a specific network or a network bundle, and

3. a list of DEFERRED applications that are added to a waiting queued of a specific network.

Further on, this output is processed as follows: First, the result is passed to the *Path Management* module (see section 3.5), where it is analyzed and compared to the current configuration. If required, the *Path Management* module initiates handovers or bundles, and freezes the data transfer of applications that were not set to ACTIVE by the *GAP* scheduler. Second, the result is added to the *History* of the scheduler and is used again in subsequent iterations of the process.

5.5.5 Triggers for Scheduler Iterations

The previous description of the workflow of *GAP* describes one run of the process. In practice, this process is repeated continuously in order to adapt to changes in the communication environments, the number and characteristics of applications that want to use network resources or of any further input parameters to the decision process. To trigger new scheduler runs, we can distinguish basically between two possible options:

1. **time-based**
   In this case, new runs are triggered regularly within certain periods of time.

2. **event-based**
   Using an event-based approach, new scheduler runs are triggered by external events. Those events may result from new applications that want to use network resources, applications that finished their data transmissions or clear changes in the networking conditions.

The first option has the advantage to be easy to implement. However, it may result in higher scheduling overhead than the second option in scenarios with low dynamic or worse responsiveness. Especially on small mobile devices, an asynchronous behavior can help to increase the overall system performance. But, this gain highly depends on the design of trigger events and respective thresholds. They have to be realized in a way that the number of unnecessary scheduling runs is reduced and the scheduler still shows enough responsiveness to react to changes in the input parameters immediately. To analyze the core functionalities of *GAP* and the whole muXer decision process, we rely on a time-based approach. The design of reasonable triggers and event-based execution of the scheduler depends on many factors of the real implementation platform and the real communication systems being used. This issue remains for future studies.

5.5.6 Improvement Potentials

GAP is intentionally designed to allow for future optimizations and additional optimization goals. In this section, we present some further improvements that may optimize the efficiency and accuracy of the scheduler, but do not belong to the core functionalities of GAP as they rely on technical specifications of the concrete implementation platform or touch additional research areas that are out of the scope of this thesis and, thus, have to be analyzed in future work

Content Adaptation

In the current stage, each application that requires network resources provides one set of parameters as input for the decision process. Based on the votes for specific networks, *GAP* tries to schedule the application to a network that meets the application requirements. In some cases none of the preferred networks may provide enough capabilities to serve this application. In this case the application is queued and has to wait for upcoming opportunities. To reduce the number of queued applications and to make use of remaining capacities, the decision engine may provide feedback to the application and may ask whether it can manage with lower resource supply or wants to wait until enough resources are available. On the other hand, it would also be possible that an application defines a set of resource requirements from the very beginning that represents different operation modes. Actually, there are a large number of applications that are well suited for context adaptation mechanisms. One example are streaming applications that may transfer video data at different bitrates and quality levels [38]. Another one would be a file transfers that is not bound to a specific data rate. However, the actual ability to adapt to certain available resources clearly depends on the specific application. To stick to the previous examples, the video streaming application may only operate at certain levels of data rate depending on the video codecs and configurations being supported. In contrast, file transfers may require only a minimum data rate in order to work properly. Every stepwise increase of the available bandwidth will reduce the time until a file is transferred completely, but has no further effects on the quality of experience. Finally, the willingness of the user to accept certain levels of service quality plays an important role as well. The integration of content adaptive functionalities into *GAP* requires extensive research on a reasonable API to the application for providing feedback on limited networking resources and the acceptance and capabilities of content adaptation techniques in dynamic heterogeneous networking scenarios. It has to be evaluated whether the significant increase of complexity resulting from the additional decision options is really justified by a respective performance gain. Moreover, the impact of such an approach on the stability of the overall process needs to be analyzed as well.

Energy Awareness

In the core functionalities of *GAP*, energy aspects are only considered together with costs in a joint optimization parameter. The goal is simply to reduce the number of active networks by serving as many applications as possible. In certain scenarios, especially for mobile devices with strong energy constraints, a more differentiated consideration of energy restrictions is needed to find a tradeoff between the use of networking resources and lifetime of the mobile device. As already mentioned in section 5.1.2, the energy consumption for communication clearly depends on the network technology being used as well as the communication characteristics. Therefore, the energy consumption at low signal levels can be expected higher than that at high levels as other coding schemes or retransmission mechanisms come into play. Besides, the actual hardware that is used has an additional effect as well. Thus, it can make a difference which and how many networks are used for communications. This optimization highly depends on detailed investigations of the energy consumptions in different communication scenarios and for different hardware components. For that reason it is left for future work and does not belong to the core aspects of *GAP*.

Resource Reservations

The *Bandwidth Manager* used in *GAP* currently makes only virtual reservation on networks being used to control how much capacity has not already been scheduled to other applications. However, this does not result in any real QoS guarantees for the applications. For this, additional reservation functionalities have to be integrated into the bandwidth manager. Classical approaches for this are Integrated or Differentiated Services [267]. However, these functionalities require a comprehensive implementation of these techniques in the network technologies being used and rely on additional protocols or protocol extensions. For that reason, they are excluded from the core functionalities of *GAP*.

5.6   Evaluation

To evaluate our network selection approach, we need reasonable metrics to state the quality and effectiveness of our arbitration concept. However, as mentioned in section 5.2 there may be multiple conflictive optimization objectives and the decision process needs to find a suitable tradeoff between them. The quality of a decision result always depends on the importance of the variety of objectives in a specific situation. Thus, it is hardly possible to find an objective measure that really states the performance of a network selection process in any possible scenario.

To cover a large range of possible scenarios and configurations, we decided to evaluate *GAP* in a simulative way by generating a large amount of random scenarios. In order to have a benchmark for stating the performance of our approach, we implemented a set of other possible strategies for network selection and compare their results with those of *GAP*. Some of these benchmark schedulers are used in related work, while others are more theoretical models that are only intended to be a performance scale.

In the following, we first introduce the set of benchmark schedulers in section 5.6.1 and the simulation setup in section 5.6.2. Afterwards, we describe the metrics that are used in the evaluation process and present the gathered results.

5.6.1 Benchmark Schedulers

Following, we present five strategies that were implemented for benchmarking. All of them provide the functionality to delay applications if the networks are not able to provide sufficient resources, while only some also allow for network bundling.

Vote: The *Vote scheduler* implements a strategy that solely focuses on the QoS vote. It assigns each application to the network that received the highest rating, as long as the network is able to serve the requested bandwidth. Otherwise, the application is queued and no communication resources are assigned. The scheduler does not account for network bundles. Comparable strategies are commonly used in related work on application-oriented ABC approaches [134, 149, 162].

True Random: The *True Random scheduler* distributes the applications randomly to the networks that are available. Hereby, the scheduler does not only account for single network assignments, but also for network bundles. For this, it builds a random set of networks. First, this set consists of one network that is chosen randomly from the available ones. Next, we model the functionality of network bundling by expanding this set by further network. This is done randomly as well. We choose a further network randomly and add it to the set with a probability of 50 %. If the network is added, the previous step is repeated. Otherwise, the algorithm stops this iteration and proceeds with the next step. The scheduler checks whether the generated set of networks provides sufficient capabilities. If this is the case, it assigns the application to this set. Otherwise, the application is added to the waiting queue.

Vote-aware Random: This scheduler implementation is derived from the previous one. However, in contrast to the *True Random scheduler* it accounts for the QoS votes and does only consider so-called preferred networks, which are voted above a predefined threshold for building the set of networks to be used by an application.

Maximum Bandwidth: The *Maximum Bandwidth scheduler* resembles a simple strategy as they can be found, for instance, in the Apple iPhone. It uses only the network with the highest bandwidth and schedules as many applications as possible to this network. If an application requests more bandwidth than the network's remaining capacity, its request is deferred and it must wait for future opportunities.

One Bundle: Instead of selecting certain networks, it would also be possible to combine all available networks to one logical communication link. Thus, this scheduler assumes that the data transfer of an application is spread across all available networks. In doing so, it neglects overheads that result from different characteristics of the bundled networks. Thus, the *One Bundle* scheduler implements an idealized strategy that aims at achieving a maximum level of network efficiency.

5.6.2 Simulation Setup and Scenario Characteristics

To get reasonable results, we analyze the algorithms' performance in a wide range of possible scenarios. Figure 5.26 illustrates the basic setup for the benchmark simulations. To our knowledge, there is no comparable approach of evaluating ABC approaches in the literature.

In the first step, we randomly generate sets of different communications scenarios. For this, the simulation setup implements a *Network Factory* and an *Application Factory* that generate a given number of networks and applications respectively with varying characteristics. Those characteristics are randomly chosen according to predefined specifications. Afterwards, the resulting sets of networks and applications are passed to the *Vote Factory*. For each possible combination of applications and networks, the *Vote Factory* derives an individual random rating that indicates the application's satisfaction with the QoS offered by the respective network. To obtain more reasonable ratings, the factory checks the network with respect to the application requirements (especially the requested bandwidth). Thus, networks that meet the application requirements are more likely to get a positive voting. On the other hand, if the requested bandwidth clearly exceeds the current network capabilities, this network is voted negatively. In a transition zone, between both cases, a network is rated low positive or low negative with a probability of 50 %.

The approach of generating random votes makes it possible to generate a large number of different scenarios without the need for explicitly choosing certain application requirements. As the arbitration concept in muXer is intentionally designed to abstract specific application characteristics and requirements from the following resource allocation process, this is a reasonable way of creating meaningful scenarios for evaluating the resource allocation process.

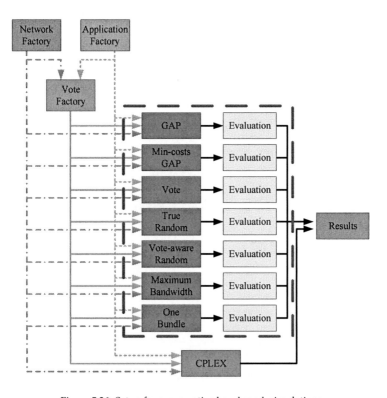

Figure 5.26: Setup for comparative benchmark simulations

The resulting scenario is passed as input to the different schedulers that decide on the allocation of network resources to the applications. In the next step, the results of each scheduling run are evaluated according to a set of performance measures. As a further benchmark, we implemented the optimization objective presented in section 5.5.2 as a mixed integer linear programming problem and passed it to the optimization software package ILOG CPLEX [268] to find an optimal solution with respect to the formal statement. Thus, these results are an indicator whether our decision of choosing an efficient and not necessarily optimal approach to the allocation problem, as being discussed in section 5.5.3, was a reasonable tradeoff.

For each evaluation run, we generated a set of 100 000 different scenarios and determined overall statistics. This way, the results cover a wide range of possible scenarios and the variations between multiple evaluations runs are minimal.

	Parameter	Value Range	
		min	max
Application Factory	Bandwidth	> 0 kbit/s	10 Mbit/s
	Priority	-20	19
	Interactivity Upgrade	-10	
Network Factory	Optimal Bandwidth	53.6 kbit/s	54 Mbit/s
	Available Bandwidth	10 kbit/s	22 Mbit/s
Vote Factory	Network Votes	-127	128

Table 5.10: Scenario settings for benchmark evaluations

The parameterization of the scenario factories is summarized in table 5.10. For the network characteristics we assumed GPRS as a lower bound and IEEE 802.11a/g as an upper bound of the range of possible networks. Thus, the optimal bandwidth bw_{opt} for a network is chosen within a range of 53.6 kbit/s and 54 Mbit/s. Furthermore, the *Network Factory* assigns each network an amount of bandwidth bw_{avail} that is actually available at the moment. This value is chosen in an interval between 10 kbit/s and $min(22 Mbit/s, bw_{opt})$. Again, these bounds refer to the maximum typical throughput that can be expected by using either GPRS [269] or IEEE 802.11a/g [270]. To get more realistic scenarios, we do not assume that available networks are uniformly distributed within this interval. During a measurement run in the city of Braunschweig, we collected performance data of IEEE 802.11g access points. We found out, that the median of the data rate was only 18 Mbit/s. According to [271] this results in a maximum throughput of about 12 Mbit/s. Moreover, we can expect that the average available bandwidth of networks in certain communication scenarios tends to be clearly lower. To give some examples, most WLAN hotspots will be connected to the Internet via ADSL links, which, on average, reduces the effective bandwidth that can be used. In addition, systems as, for instance, GPRS are characterized by a high coverage, but provide only a low bandwidth. Moreover, a user may have to share the access point with other users. For these reasons, we chose an appropriate distribution of the generated values that covers these aspects. The bw_{avail} parameter of the generated networks are chosen normally distributed with a mean of 0 and a standard derivation of 5 within the interval state in table 5.10 to get a more reasonable picture of reality.

The *Application Factory* generates a set of applications. For each application, the factory determines a fictive bandwidth demand between almost 0 kbit/s and 10 Mbit/s. The upper bound is chosen with reference to the streaming of an HD video. However, again the application requirements will typically not be equally distributed within this interval. Typical applications like Web Browsing or E-mail will work with clearly lower demands. Here, the required bandwidth is more a matter of the user's patience to wait for the data to be transferred. Thus, to account for these aspects, in our scenarios the requested bandwidth of applications is assumed to be log-normal distributed with a mean of two and a variation of 4. Thus, most of the simulated applications come with bandwidth requests lower than 1 Mbit/s.

Additionally, the *Application Factory* determines a priority for each application between -20 and 19, where -20 indicates the highest importance and 19 states highest unimportance. In addition, on average 20 % of the applications are considered to currently interact with the user and thus receive a priority upgrade of -10.

5.6.3 Evaluation Metrics

In the evaluation, we meet again the aforementioned problem that there is actually no general objective measure to state the performance of a dynamic network selection process, as the result depends on a variety of objectives and boundary conditions whose relative importance is highly subjective. Thus, we concentrate our evaluation on three different aspects:

1. a qualitative scoring,

2. the adherence to application requirements, and

3. the efficiency of using network resources.

The first metric is a qualitative measure on how well the scheduler meets the overall optimization objective that was introduced in section 5.5.2. The second aspect focuses on the

application requirements and the two questions of how many applications could be scheduled to all networks. The third aspect focuses on technical parameters and evaluates the results from the perspective of making full use of the available network resources. For this, we
analyze the overall number of networks being used and the network utilization. We further
evaluate the effects of bundling networks and deferring application requests on the decision
result by comparing scheduler variants with and without these features. Finally, we analyze
the impact of our basic approach to cost minimization that was introduced in 5.5.4 on the
number of networks being actively used by the scheduler and the adherence to application
requirements.

5.6.4 Quality of Decisions

As already mentioned before it is a very challenging task to state whether the result of the
decision process is optimal or not. For a really optimal result, the scheduler must possess the
global knowledge of all current characteristics and requirements as well as possible changes
in the future. Moreover, as we pointed out in section 5.2, there is always a need for a tradeoff
between the achieved Quality of Experience, the number of applications that can be served
at the moment and the costs that accrue for using network resources. The rating of decisions may clearly depend on the relative importance of all these aspects. Anyhow, to be able
to make the output of GAP ratable and comparable to other schedulers, we go back to our
formal problem statement in section 5.5.2. There, we set up an optimization objective for-
malizing the resource allocation problem in a simplified way. Now, we adopt this objective
to determine an abstract score that describes the adherence to this objective.

Our score is determined according to the following equation:

$$\frac{1}{|A|} \cdot \sum_{i \in A} \sum_{j \in \mathcal{N}} \left(vote_{ij} \cdot \frac{x_{ij}}{bw_i} \cdot prio_i \right) - \frac{1}{|N|} \cdot \left(\sum_{j \in \mathcal{N}} y_j \cdot K \right) \tag{5.17}$$

where

$$prio_i = \left((-1) * prio_{app_i} + 20 \right) + (-1) * prio_{interactive_i} \tag{5.18}$$

The first term of this equation represents the application-related score. It is determined as
a sum over all applications A and networks N that includes the vote that a certain network
j received for application i, the amount of bandwidth that is assigned to this network (x_{ij}),
the bandwidth bw_i requested by the application, and the priority $prio_i$ of the application.
The second term models the costs of using a specific number of networks, where $y_i \in [0,1]$
indicates whether network j is used or not. The importance of this term with respect to the
application-related score depends on the value of the cost factor K. In our evaluation, we
distinguish between two cases for this cost factor:

1. $K = 500$ (with costs)

2. $K = 0$ (without costs)

The first case is used to rate the performance of the schedulers with respect to the overall objective. We chose the value 500 for K by evaluation, to let the cost factor have a strong effect on the total score. The second case, in which K is zero, gives us only the score related to the application-specific requirements.

Figure 5.27 shows the comparison of the calculated scores between our set of benchmark schedulers for three different networking scenarios. We also determined an idealized optimum of the score by using the *CPLEX* solver to solve the optimization problem presented in section 5.5.2. The figure shows the median score that was achieved in all simulation runs. For *GAP* and the benchmark scheduler, we also provide error bars that show the 95

In the small scenario (a) the *One Bundle Scheduler* performs worst (-82) with respect to the total score with costs, which basically relies on the fact that it always use both networks that are available, while the single application in this scenario might also be served by using only one network. But, when only looking at the application-related score (without costs), the *One Bundle Scheduler* outperforms the *Max Bandwidth* and *True Random Schedulers*. In the small scenario, both strategies perform equally worse, while the *Max Bandwidth Scheduler* still achieves a higher application-related score. *GAP* and pure *Vote Scheduler* perform similar well in this scenario. Both achieve a score of 434. GAP's additional features do not have any effect in this scenario, as in most cases either of the networks will be able to serve the application. The *Vote-aware Random Scheduler* performs clearly worse with a score of 250. In this scenario it has a quite good chance to choose the network that is mostly preferred by the application.

In the second scenario with three networks and five applications, the differences between the schedulers increase. *GAP* achieves the highest median score of 887, followed by the *Vote Scheduler* with a score of 823. The order of the remaining schedulers stays almost the same as in the previous scenario. Just the *Max Bandwidth scheduler* does now also outperform the *True Random Scheduler*. The difference between *GAP* and the pure *Vote Scheduler* increases to 193 (1062 vs. 869). The other schedulers achieve clearly lower results. The score of the *Max Bandwidth Scheduler* is even lower than before (181).

In the third scenario with five networks and 15 applications, we get similar results compared to the previous one. Again, *GAP* receives the highest scores out of all schedulers, while the other ones perform worse with respect to the optimal scores.

In summary, the results show that *GAP* achieves the highest adherence to the optimization objective with respect to the other benchmark schedulers. In scenarios with a low number of networks and applications, the additional features of *GAP* do not take a clear effect. However, with increasing heterogeneity, *GAP* is able to distance itself from the other schedulers clearly. Another conclusion from the obtained results is that a common strategy like

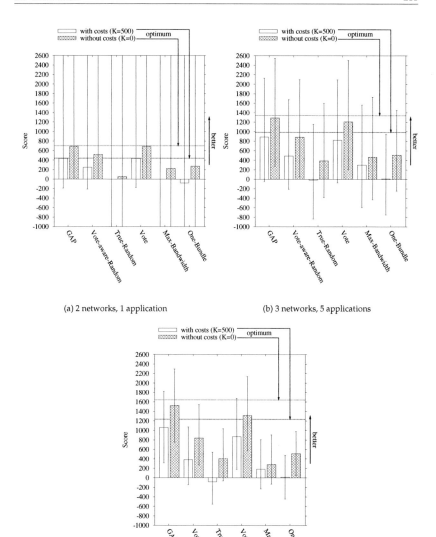

(a) 2 networks, 1 application   (b) 3 networks, 5 applications

(c) 5 networks, 15 applications

Figure 5.27: Qualitative scores for three different scenarios

Max Bandwidth, that can be found in some of today's mobile devices, reaches a clearly lower score throughout the different scenarios. If we only focus on the application-related scores, *Max Bandwidth* is only slightly better than the *True Random Scheduler* in scenario (b) and even worse in scenario (c). A *Vote-aware Random* strategy brings a clear advantage to a *True Random* approach, as it filters out those networks that are fully unsuited to the application requirements.

Compared to the optimal scores, which were determined by *CPLEX*, *GAP* performs very well. In scenario (a) it achieves only marginally lower scores (434 vs. 439). In this scenario, the vote scheduler was able to achieve similar results. With an increasing heterogeneity, *GAP* leaves the Vote Scheduler behind it. But, although the difference between the scores of *GAP* and the optimal scores increases as well, it amounts only to 173 points for the total score and to 116 points for the application-related score in scenario (c). In scenario (b), the differences are even lower (98 and 50 points respectively). There are two major reasons why the difference between *GAP* and the optimal score increases. First, in the way we formulated the optimization problem, *CPLEX* may split data flows up into arbitrary pieces. Depending on the characteristics of the bundled networks, this procedure might not be practical, as the bundling of networks goes along with an increased overhead for reordering data at the receiver. Therefore, an arbitrary segmentation of data flows comes with various disadvantages. In contrast, our implementation of *GAP* assumes a proportional allocation with respect to the remaining capacities of the networks in the bundle. Second, *GAP* does not implement any iterative improvements of the results. This was done to achieve a higher responsiveness of the scheduler and to improve its scalability with increasing number of networks and applications. In contrast, CPLEX searches through a large number of possible configurations and analyzes the cost-benefit ratio for each application to be scheduled. Thus, there are a considerably large number of decision results, where CPLEX allocates network resources to a lower number of applications, as the benefit of scheduling further applications does not compensate for the costs of using another network. Therefore, the total optimal score increase with respect to the *GAP* procedure.

5.6.5   Adherence to Application Requirements

Now, we analyze the output of the decision process in more detail with respect to the adherence to the application requirements. For this, we focus on two metrics:

► the number of applications that can be served, and

► the application-oriented rating of networks.

Scheduled Applications

Figure 5.28 illustrates the scheduling result with respect to the number of applications that are set to *active, deferred* or *inactive*. The first state indicates that the scheduler assigned a network to the applications that it might use for communication. An application is set to *deferred*, if there are not enough resources to serve the application. Finally, if none of the networks meets the application requirements at all, an application is set to *inactive*.

Figure 5.28 shows the average number of applications that are set to either of these states across all simulation runs. In scenario (a), the *One Bundle Scheduler* achieves the highest number of active applications. On average it was able to serve 0.946 applications. The *Max Bandwidth Scheduler* is slightly worse, with a value of 0.896 applications. In third place, the *True Random Scheduler* was able to serve 0.785 applications. The three vote-aware schedulers achieve almost similar results. GAP was able to set on average 0.738 applications to active, while the *Vote Scheduler* achieves a value of 0.727 and the *Vote-aware Random Scheduler* a value of 0.714. The major reason for their worse performance compared to the vote-unaware schedulers is the fact that all of them set on average 0.205 applications to inactive which is a share of 20.5 %. Thus, vote-unaware schedulers have the opportunity to choose from a large solution space to schedule applications to networks. However, the approach of inactive networks is intentionally desired, as those applications have not voted for any networks above a minimum threshold for the adherence to the application requirements. Thus, although one would schedule them to any network, these applications will not operate as expected or needed. With an increasing number of networks in scenarios (b) and (c) the average number of inactive applications reduces from 10.24 % to 3 %. This effect results from the fact that a higher number of different networks reduces the probability that an application assesses all networks to be fully unsuited. It goes along with an increased efficiency of the vote-aware schedulers. One can see that *GAP* is able to distance itself from the other schedulers and especially from the *Vote Scheduler* in scenarios (b) and (c). Especially in (c) *GAP* achieves the best results.

Table 5.11 lists the average share of applications being scheduled to any network in our three scenarios for different schedulers and compares them to the results that were achieved by our *CPLEX* simulations. In scenario (c) *GAP* was able to serve 81.06 % of the application requests, while the *Vote Scheduler* achieved only a ratio of 69.02 %. In the same scenario, *GAP* also outperforms the *One Bundle Scheduler* that was able to allocate network resources for 80.09 % of the applications. A general trend that becomes obvious is the fact that with an increased heterogeneity, the performance of random schedulers decreases as they tend to spread the applications across all available networks. This behavior results in a higher fragmentation of network resources. The performance of the *Max Bandwidth Scheduler* drops substantially from scenario (a) (89.63 %) to (c) (46.32 %). This fact ascribes to the increasing number of applications, whose total requirements exceed the capabilities of the network with the highest bandwidth. For the results obtained by *CPLEX*, we distinguish between

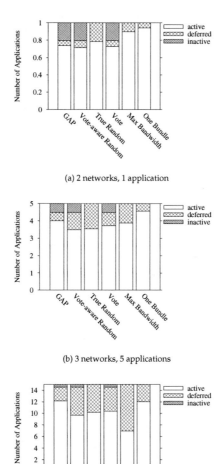

(a) 2 networks, 1 application

(b) 3 networks, 5 applications

(c) 5 networks, 15 applications

Figure 5.28: Number of scheduled applications for three different scenarios

Scenario	GAP	Vote-aw. Rand.	True Rand.	Vote	Max Bw	One Bundle	CPLEX (K=500)	CPLEX (K=0)
(a)	73.78 %	71.40 %	78.46 %	72.71 %	89.63 %	94.06 %	63.99 %	76.92 %
(b)	80.06 %	69.71	70.83 %	74.29 %	77.57 %	91.11 %	75.00 %	83.8 %
(c)	81.06 %	64.45 %	67.78 %	69.02 %	46.32 %	80.09 %	79.67 %	84.6 %

Table 5.11: Average share of scheduled applications

two cases: The total objective (K=500) and the application-related one (K=0). We can see that there is a clear difference between both cases. This emphasizes our previous findings related to the scoring result. The difference mainly comes from the fact that in the former case, *CPLEX* does not schedule applications to one or more networks, if the additional costs for using this network are higher or even equal to the benefit of the applications with respect to the optimization objective. However, we can see that *GAP* achieves a result between both variants that is a little bit closer to the applications-related result of *CPLEX*. This is not really surprising, as in our simulations we assumed no explicit cost reduction for *GAP*. In summary we can state that across all scenarios, *GAP* performs well with respect to the optimal result. Nevertheless, without additional cost reduction mechanisms, it tends to schedule more applications although their benefit to the optimization objective is lower than the respective costs. Actually this is a question of the aforementioned tradeoff between the costs, the QoE and the number of applications being served. Moreover, in our optimization objective, we assumed a constant cost factor. In practice, the real cost will be specific to the respective network and probably even the number of applications or the amounts of data that are allocated to this network. Thus, there will be a clearly higher dynamic that will have different effects on the decision results.

The aforementioned findings are emphasized by the results shown in figure 5.29 for varying numbers of available networks and applications that request network access. In scenario (a) we assume to have three networks available and varied the number of applications that try to gain network access from 1 to 20. The results show that the average number of active applications for the *Maximum Bandwidth Scheduler* already goes into saturation at a quite low number of applications and slowly approaches a maximum of 6.24 applications. The *One Bundle Scheduler* achieves the best results with respect to the number of active applications for a total number of 1 to 12 applications. In the scenario with 13 applications it achieves almost the same performance as *GAP*. Henceforth, it falls behind *GAP* and later on

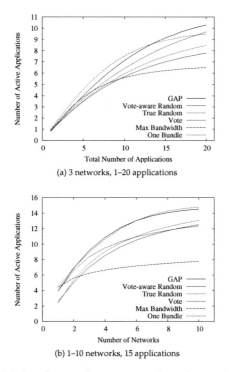

(a) 3 networks, 1–20 applications

(b) 1–10 networks, 15 applications

Figure 5.29: Scheduled applications for varying numbers of networks and applications

even behind the *Vote Scheduler*. The reason for this is that the available networks are not able to serve all application-requests at the same time. Thus, a smarter scheduling and selection of applications in combination with the application-oriented rating of networks results in a higher efficiency. In total, *GAP* performs well in all situations and achieves the highest efficiency in overload situations compared to the other benchmark schedulers.

Scenario (b) models the inverse case to (a). Here, the number of applications is fixed to 15, while the number of available networks varies from 1 to 10. We can see that *GAP* achieves a similar performance like the *One Bundle Scheduler*, which makes most efficient use of the network resources by avoiding any fragmentation. With an increasing number of networks, the *Vote Scheduler* clearly falls off with respect to *GAP*. In scenarios with more than 6 networks, it even performs worse than the *True Random Scheduler*. Later it also falls behind the *Vote-aware Random Scheduler*. The reason for this is that the *Vote Scheduler* only chooses that network which is voted best. However, in general certain networks will be more popular than others. Thus, the *Vote Scheduler* is not able to make full use of the available networking resources, although alternative networks might be only rated slightly lower. We can expect, that this effect increases the more applications prefer one specific network or even a dedicated set of networks. Further, the results in scenario (b) show again the aforementioned problem of the *Max Bandwidth Scheduler*. Due to its design, it is not able to make use of a higher number of available networks.

Preferred Networks

After focusing on quantitative aspects of the pure number of applications being served at one specific moment, we now turn to the analysis of qualitative aspects of the decision. Thus, we evaluate the accordance of the network an application is actually scheduled to with the results of the primary output QoS Arbiter. For this, we order all applications with respect to the application votes and determine the relative position of the respective network within this order, the so called level of preference. To give an example, if the level of preference is equal to 1, an application was scheduled to the network that received the highest vote. A level of preference equal to 3 indicates that the application was scheduled to the network with the third highest vote.

Figure 5.30 shows the obtained results for this measure. In all scenarios, the *Vote Scheduler* achieves the highest number of application that are scheduled to the network with the highest preference. This is not really a surprise, as that is exactly what the scheduler is designed for and should do best. Nevertheless, in all scenarios there is only a small difference between *GAP* and the *Vote Scheduler*. In scenario (c), the *Vote Scheduler* was able to allocate 69.01 % of all application requests to the network which is preferred most with respect to the QoS votes. *GAP* only reached a value of 62.03 %. But, as the *Vote Scheduler* defers all further requests, *GAP* is able to assign applications to other candidate networks. Thus, for

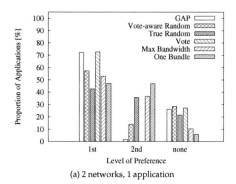

(a) 2 networks, 1 application

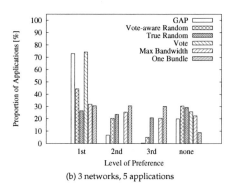

(b) 3 networks, 5 applications

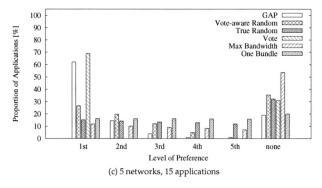

(c) 5 networks, 15 applications

Figure 5.30: Adherence to application-related requirements for three different scenarios

scenario (c), it schedules 14.34 % of all application requests to the second preferred network and 3.77 % of the application requests to the network with the third highest preference. In addition, GAP clearly outperforms the remaining schedulers that spread the applications more or less equally across the networks with respect to their level of preference.

Table 5.12 summarizes the average levels of preference for active applications. It emphasizes the fact that *GAP* performs very well in comparison to the other schedulers and reaches an average level of preference that is close to that of the *Vote Scheduler*, although being able to serve more applications at a particular moment.

Scenario	GAP	Vote-aw. Rand.	True Rand.	Vote	Max Bw	One Bundle
(a)	1.02	1.20	1.46	1	1.41	1.50
(b)	1.09	1.44	1.92	1	1.85	2.00
(c)	1.30	1.98	2.89	1	2.76	2.99

Table 5.12: Average level of preference for active applications

Figure 5.31 (a) illustrates the effects of a varying number of networks on the average achieved level of preference for the different schedulers. Taking the result of the *Vote Scheduler* as a basis, the level achieved by *GAP* increases very slightly with a higher number of networks and stabilizes at around 1.30. In contrast, the other schedulers show a linear increase of the average preference level. This increase is lower for the *Vote-aware Random Scheduler*, as this one filters out those networks that are fully unsuited. Figure 5.31 (b) shows the average level of preference that is achieved by *GAP* across all simulated scenarios. From the results we can see that it performs very well throughout all configurations that were considered in our evaluation. Moreover, we can see that for a given number of applications, the level of preference increases the more networks are available until it reaches a maximum and decreases again. This effect results from the fact that the calculated average does only include applications that were scheduled successfully to any network. Thus, the more capacity is available, the more applications might be served. At the point the level of preference decreases again, there is enough bandwidth available that even applications with lower priority might be scheduled to networks that have a higher preference.

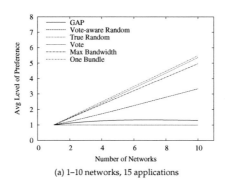

(a) 1–10 networks, 15 applications

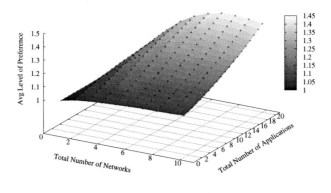

(b) GAP in different scenarios

Figure 5.31: Level of preference for varying numbers of networks and applications

Summary

To sum up, we can state that *GAP* performs very well with respect to our application-centered metrics. It is able to serve a high number of concurrent applications and provides a high level of compliance with respect to the application QoS requirements at the same time. The *Vote Scheduler* achieves the highest grade of quality with respect to the level of preference, but actually due to its nature it is only able to serve fewer applications at the same moment. The *One Bundle Scheduler* was able to schedule a very high number of applications as it minimizes the fragmentation of communication resources, but due to the spreading of application data flows across all available networks, it achieved bad results with respect to the adherence to application QoS requirements.

5.6.6 Efficient Use of Network Resources

A further issue relating to the performance of the different scheduling strategies is their efficiency in using available network resources. In our evaluation, we consider three metrics addressing this issue:

► the number of networks used for communications,

► the load of those networks being actively used, and

► the overall network utilization.

Number of Active Networks

The number of networks being actively used for communication is a two-edged sword. Actually, a scheduler should make use of as many networks as necessary and as few networks as possible. On the one hand, schedulers aim at serving as many application requests as possible. On the other hand, the use of each additional network results in additional costs in terms of monetary expenses and energy consumption. The actual weighting of both aspects is a matter of user preferences. The resulting effects will be separately evaluated in 5.6.8.

Figure 5.32 illustrates the proportion of the number of scheduling runs that resulted in a certain number of networks to be used for communication. The results for the *Max Bandwidth* and the *One Bundle Schedulers* are trivial throughout all scenarios. The former one always uses either none or one network, while the other one makes use of none or all available networks. Except for the *One Bundle Scheduler*, all other schedulers use on average between 0.72 and 0.92 networks in scenario (a). This mainly results from the low number of options that might be chosen. With an increased heterogeneity, the *True Random Scheduler* tends more and more to make use of all available networks. In scenario (c) it uses already 4.91 of 5 networks on average. This is a result of the higher number of applications and

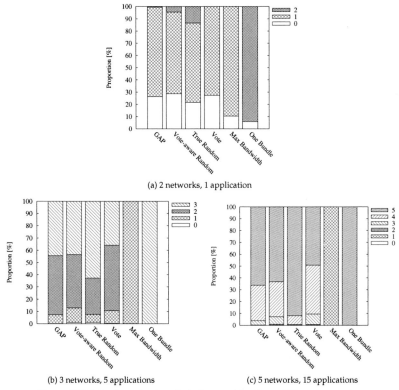

(a) 2 networks, 1 application

(b) 3 networks, 5 applications   (c) 5 networks, 15 applications

Figure 5.32: Number of networks being used for three different scenarios

the higher chance to allocate applications to all networks that comes along with this fact as shown in figure 5.33 (a). A general conclusion that we can derive from figures 5.32 and 5.33 is that *GAP* tends to use more networks than the *Vote Scheduler*. In scenario (c), *GAP* uses 4 or 5 networks in 96.12 % of the simulated scenarios. In contrast, for the *Vote Scheduler* this is the case in 90.52 % of the scenarios. The difference between both schedulers is even higher for the number of runs that end up with using 5 networks (66.20 % vs. 40.07 %). Table 5.13 summarizes the average proportion of the networks that are actually used for communication. It also includes the results for the *CPLEX* optimizations. As already seen in section 5.6.5, when looking at the number of scheduled applications, the results of *GAP* are between *CPLEX with K=0* and *CPLEX with K=500*. Again it becomes obvious that GAP tends to use more networks to serve a higher number of applications, as the results are much closer to that of *CPLEX with K=0* than to that of *CPLEX with K=500*.

Looking at the results for a fixed number of applications and a variable number of networks in figure 5.33 (b), the number of active networks grows faster for *GAP* than for the *Vote Scheduler*. This is actually a result of GAPs additional features that makes it possible to set up logical network bundles. Thus, even networks that may not be able to meet the requested resources of an application by oneself may contribute to such a bundle.

Scenario	GAP	Vote-aw. Rand.	True Rand.	Vote	Max Bw	One Bundle	CPLEX (K=500)	CPLEX (K=0)
(a)	37.14 %	37.95 %	46.00 %	36.36 %	44.82 %	94.06 %	40.49 %	32.30 %
(b)	78,95 %	76.44	84.69 %	74.96 %	33.30 %	99.99 %	59.20 %	82.96 %
(c)	92.43 %	91.03 %	98.25 %	87.80 %	20.00 %	100.00 %	69.88 %	94.02 %

Table 5.13: Average proportion of active networks

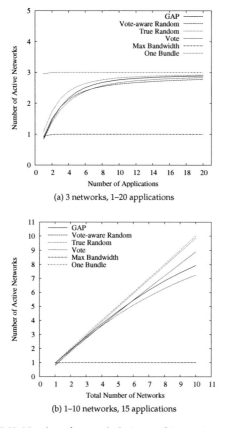

(a) 3 networks, 1–20 applications

(b) 1–10 networks, 15 applications

Figure 5.33: Number of networks being used in varying scenarios

Network Utilization

An aspect that goes along with the pure number of networks is the utilization of network resources. In our evaluation, we define the network utilization v as the proportion of the total available bandwidth provided by the available networks that is actually allocated to any applications:

$$v = 100 * \left(\frac{\sum_{j \in N} allocBw_j}{\sum_{j \in N} Bw_j} \right) \tag{5.19}$$

As a metric, the network utilization is intended to show how well a scheduler makes use of the capacity of those networks that are actively used for communication. The maximum achievable utilization within a certain scenario is limited by the bandwidth requests of the applications. Thus, the metric can be used to compare the relative efficiency of schedulers within a scenario, while the absolute values may vary between the scenarios. Moreover, the utilization is affected by the tradeoff between using network resources efficiently and reducing the overall costs.

Figure 5.34 shows the occurrence of certain values of average network utilization through all simulation runs as a cumulative distribution function. In scenario (a), both the *One Bundle Scheduler* and the *Maximum Bandwidth Scheduler* show the highest utilization. In section 5.6.5, we saw that both schedulers were able to schedule most applications in this scenario as they do not care about whether an application stated a network to be fully unsuited or not. This effect leads to the higher overall utilizations. The remaining schedulers show quite similar results. None of the schedulers achieve a utilization of 100 % in this scenario. This results from the scenario setup. There is only one application that needs to be scheduled and the requested bandwidth of this application does not exactly match to the total bandwidth of the two networks in all randomly generated scenarios. With increasing heterogeneity in scenarios (b) and (c) the different schedulers clearly differentiate from each other. As scenario (c) is intentionally modeled in such a way that the application bandwidth requirements exceed the available resources, it holds well as a benchmark for the overall efficiency of the schedulers. The best performance with respect to the utilization of networking resources is provided by the *One Bundle Scheduler*. It achieves a median overall network utilization of 63.37 % (b) and 96.84 % (c) respectively. As already mentioned before, this rests on the fact that the *One Bundle Scheduler* is intentionally designed to minimize the fragmentation of networking resources. However, the *One Bundle Scheduler* is directly followed by *GAP* that achieves a utilization of 44.93 % and 85.42 % in the respective scenarios. This is still considerably lower than the *One Bundle Scheduler*, but on the other hand, *GAP* has to account for various additional conditions that appear from the application-oriented QoS ratings. Looking only at scenario (c) where the application requests clearly exceed the available networking resources, we can state that *GAP* achieves a significantly higher utilization

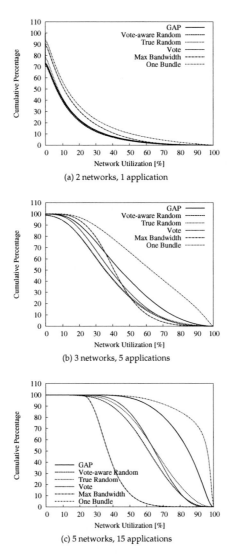

(a) 2 networks, 1 application

(b) 3 networks, 5 applications

(c) 5 networks, 15 applications

Figure 5.34: Utilization of network resources for three different scenarios

compared to the remaining schedulers. The *Vote Scheduler* reaches an overall utilization of 65.31 % which is 20.11 % lower than *GAP* and only compares to the results of the random schedulers.

Figure 5.35 shows the effect of a varying number of applications and networks on the network utilization. Here, we find our previous conclusion confirmed. The overall utilization increases with the number of applications. The maximum utilization of the *Max Bandwidth Scheduler* is limited by the network with the highest bandwidth in the modeled scenario. The utilization of the *One Bundle Scheduler* increases very fast and approaches a maximum of almost 100 %. Especially in the scenarios from 5 to 15 applications, *GAP* achieves a considerably lower utilization compared to the *One Bundle Scheduler*. On the other hand, it performs significantly better than the *Vote* or the *True Random Scheduler*. Both end up with quite comparable utilizations of 87.04 % and 83.56 %. The *Vote-aware Scheduler* achieves an even lower utilization than the *Vote* and *True Random Schedulers*.

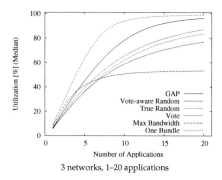

3 networks, 1–20 applications

Figure 5.35: Utilization of network resources for varying numbers of applications

Summary

We can summarize that the *One Bundle Scheduler* provides the highest efficiency in terms of network usage. This comes at the disadvantage of increased costs, as the scheduler uses always all available networks. Further, the *One Bundle Scheduler* implements an idealized strategy that will suffer from additional overheads for stream splitting and packet reordering in practice. *GAP* performs very well through the different scenarios and outperforms the remaining schedulers. The *Vote Scheduler* achieves an utilization that is only slightly higher than that of the *True Random Scheduler*.

5.6.7 Effects of Multipath Transfer and the Deferment of Application Requests

Up to now, we evaluated the general performance of the different approaches to network selection. Next, we turn to two specific characteristics of our approach which are:

► the bundling of networks for concurrent multipath transfer and

► the deferment of application requests.

In the following, we want to evaluate the effects that both mechanisms have on the results of the decision process.

Concurrent Multipath Transfer

Figure 5.36 illustrates the average number of network bundles per simulation run. In our scenarios, the value ranges between 0 and 1.33. When looking at the median and the 95 % quantile of the measurements, we can see that runs with more than four bundles are quite unlikely and more than 50 % of all runs end up with one or none bundle. At first glance, this value appears to be comparably low. However, it results from the fact that GAP first tries to schedule an application to one network before it examines possible configurations of bundles. Moreover, the QoS arbiter only sets up bundles using networks that are rated above a certain threshold. Thus, the solution space for finding suitable bundle configurations is

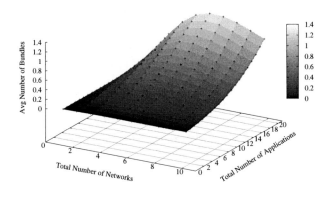

Figure 5.36: Average number of network bundles

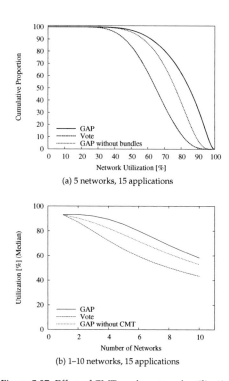

(a) 5 networks, 15 applications

(b) 1–10 networks, 15 applications

Figure 5.37: Effect of CMT on the network utilization

reduced. Moreover, especially applications with higher bandwidth demands benefit from the possibility to split data flows up. In our scenarios, the share of these applications is comparatively low.

Another interesting aspect that we can derive from the results is the fact that for a fixed number of applications there is a certain ratio of the number of available networks to the number of application requests, where the number of bundles forms a maximum. For lower number of networks, there are few options to set up bundles for CMT. At higher number of networks, additional resources are available that allow for scheduling applications to a single network.

To state the effects of network bundling on the efficiency of using network resources, figure 5.37 compares the achieved overall network utilization for *GAP without bundles* with that of *GAP* and the *Vote Scheduler*. Figure 5.37 (a) presents the cumulative distribution of the network utilization in 100 000 simulation runs for a scenario with 5 networks and 15 applications. The results indicate that when deactivating the option of network bundles, the utilization clearly falls off to the case where bundles are activated. The median of the utilization reduces from 85.42 % to 77.05 %. Thus, bundling increases the overall efficiency by about 8 %. However, *GAP without bundles* still performs better than the *Vote Scheduler*. The difference of about 12 % results from the smarter scheduling of applications and the fact that not only the "best" network is allocated to an application.

Figure 5.37 (b) shows the utilization depending on the total number of networks for a scenario with 15 applications. It emphasizes our findings from scenario (a). We can see that the results of *GAP without bundles* are always in the middle between those of *GAP* and the *Vote Scheduler*. The only exception for this is the scenario with one network, where all scheduler achieved similar results. Moreover, we find our previous results confirmed, as the distance between the *GAP* variants with and without bundles increases in the scenarios from 1 to 7 networks and decreases again if the number of networks is increased even further.

Deferment of Application Requests

The option to defer applications if there are not enough networking resources available was introduced for two reasons: To avoid overload situations and to enable applications to wait for better (e.g. cheaper) opportunities for data transfer.

We evaluate the effects of this deferment on the efficiency of *GAP* based on the overall network utilization. Figure 5.38 shows the network utilization for *GAP* with and without deferment as well as the *Vote Scheduler*. It becomes obvious that in the case where application deferment is switched off, there is a clearly higher chance of overload situations. The median of the network utilization increases from 85.42 % to 127.61 %. Figure 5.38 (b) shows the development of the network utilization for scenarios with an increasing number of applications. As it can be expected, the utilization increases linearly with the number of

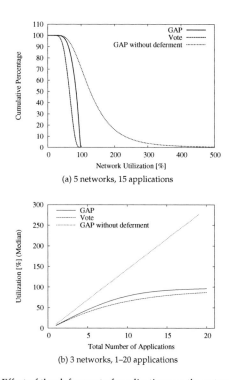

(a) 5 networks, 15 applications

(b) 3 networks, 1–20 applications

Figure 5.38: Effect of the deferment of applications on the network utilization

additional applications if no applications are deferred. In contrast, the scheduler variants with deferment go into saturation and approach the maximum limit of 100 %.

When abstaining from deferring any applications, the scheduler is able to assign each application to the network it prefers most. However, one side effect is that in the end none of the applications that use an overloaded network will get the resources that it requested. Thus, the quality of the decision results will clearly suffer, even with respect to a random scheduler.

5.6.8 Cost Reduction

Another parameter in GAP is the objective of cost reduction. In section 5.5.4 we described the implementation of a cost arbiter that aims at minimizing the number of active networks. This is done by giving a bonus to networks that are already in use. The effect of this bonus for the scheduling process is controlled by a weighting factor ω_c. In the following, we evaluate the effect of our implementation of cost reduction on the number of active networks and the adherence to application preferences for different values of ω_c.

Figure 5.39 shows how the number of active networks is affected by our approach to cost reduction. In (a) one can see that the proportion of decision outputs that end up with the use of all available networks, clearly decreases from 66.29 % to 49.22 % while the weight ω_c is changed from 0.0 to 1.0. At the same time, the proportions of the remaining configuration where 4 or less networks are being used increases. Thus, those decision outputs that result in the use of 4 networks increases by 12 %, while the number of results with 3 networks increases by 3 %. Even the further options with 1 or 2 networks increase marginally. Figure 5.39 (b) shows the effect of the value of ω_c in scenarios with a varying number of net-

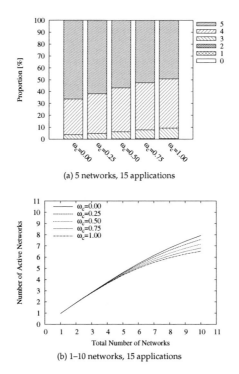

(a) 5 networks, 15 applications

(b) 1–10 networks, 15 applications

Figure 5.39: Effects of cost reduction on the number of active networks

works. One can see that the higher the number of available networks the higher the effect of the cost reduction. In the scenario with 15 applications and 10 networks it was possible to reduce the average number of active networks by about 1.4. This fact can be explained by the growing solution space and overall capacity. Both open up more room for optimizations of the decision output.

A disadvantage of our approach to cost reduction is that it reduces the number of active networks at the expense of the adherence to application preferences. As we only assign bonuses to networks which are already in use, we aim at increasing the utilization of those networks before the scheduler decides on using a further one. However, we actually do not limit the number of networks to be used actively and do not defer additional applications. Figure 5.40 shows the effect of increasing values of ω_c on the adherence to application pref-

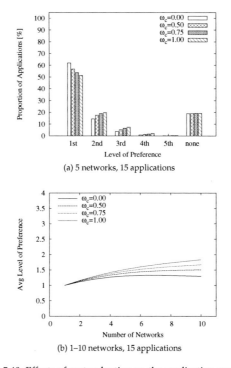

(a) 5 networks, 15 applications

(b) 1–10 networks, 15 applications

Figure 5.40: Effects of cost reduction on the application preferences

erences. It becomes apparent that the reduction of the results with 5 active networks by 17 % goes along with a reduction of the number of applications that are scheduled to the most preferred network by 10 %. Around 5 % more applications are scheduled to the second best network. The proportions for the third and fourth place increase as well by 3.7 % and 1.4 % respectively. Even the number of deferred applications increases marginally. When averaging the level of preference for all simulation runs, one can see that the average level increases from 1.30 ($\omega_c = 0.0$) to 1.52 ($\omega_c = 1.0$). This is still a very good result and far better than that of other benchmark schedulers without cost reduction as shown in section 5.6.5. Figure 5.40 (b) shows the average level of application preferences against a varying number of available networks. Again one can see that the relevance of the cost reduction factor increases clearly with the total number of networks.

Summing up, we can state that our implementation of cost reduction is actually able to reduce the number of networks being used. However, this comes at the costs of a slightly reduced adherence to application preferences. Thus, the actual weight of cost reduction in the decision process is a question of the tradeoff between network efficiency and costs. Nevertheless, the opportunities of this approach are bound, as it actually does not limit the total number of active networks at all. For such a behavior, the cost arbiter has to be extended by a cost budget that may account for both, monetary and energy constraints. However, this option will typically narrow the solution space for the decision process and, thus, reduce the performance in terms of the number of applications that can be served or the provided quality of experience. It can be expected that the performance of such an approach compares to that of a scenario with a lower number of networks.

5.6.9 Scalability

In addition to the different metrics for evaluating the actual decision result, we also analyzed the runtime performance of our implementation of *GAP*. Our main focus is the question of how well the scheduling approach scales with respect to an increasing number of applications and networks. The measurements have been done on a machine with Intel Xeon 3.2 GHz processor. We ensured that no concurrent processes affect the results of our measurements. In our evaluation, the runtime was measured using the POSIX function `clock_gettime()` and the Timer `PROCESS_CPUTIME_ID` [272]. The timer yields the amount of execution time for the scheduling process. The resolution of this timer is 1 ns, which was measured by using the POSIX function `clock_getres()`. We start our time measurement at the beginning of the scheduling process and determine the time period that it takes until the scheduler provides its final result. To obtain meaningful results, we measured the runtime for 10,000 measurement cycles with different scenario characteristics and averaged the results being obtained.

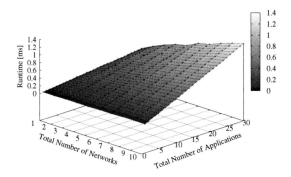

Figure 5.41: Runtime performance of GAP in different scenarios

These averaged results of our runtime measurements for scenarios with 1–10 networks and 1 – 30 applications are shown in figure 5.41. We can see that an increasing number of networks has only moderate effects on the runtime. In the scenario with 10 networks and 30 applications, the scheduling process takes only 1.4 ms on average. If the number of applications is increased, the runtime grows faster. This behavior results from the fact that the processing of additional applications is more time-consuming than the time it may require to handle an additional candidate network to which an application might be scheduled to. Our implementation must iterate though the whole list of applications, but may not check each network whether it provides enough resources to serve the application, as some networks are voted to be unsuitable and the scheduler takes the first network that matches to the application. However, in summary we can state that the increase of the runtime is always linear. Thus, GAP scales well with the number of networks and applications that have to be considered in the resource allocation process.

5.7   Discussion of the Results

A general result of our benchmark evaluation is that GAP performs very well with respect to both, the evaluation metrics in heterogeneous scenarios and the benchmark schedulers. Table 5.14 summarizes the evaluation results in a qualitative way.

With respect to the qualitative scoring, GAP achieved a high adherence to the results that were obtained by CPLEX. Compared to the other schedulers, it was able to allocate network resources to a high number of applications and providing a high adherence to application

Metric	GAP	Vote-aw. Rand.	True Rand.	Vote	Max Bw	One Bundle
Objective	++	o	--	+	--	--
# applications	++	o	o	o	-	++
Level of preference	+	o	--	++	--	--
Network utilization	++	o	o	o	-	++

Table 5.14: Qualitative summary of the evaluation results

requirements at the same time. Besides, it uses the available communication resources efficiently. The *Vote Scheduler* performs worse, as it lacks flexibility in actually choosing suitable networks for an application. The random schedulers generate decision results with a high fragmentation of network resources that increases with a higher heterogeneity of the scenarios. Moreover, they perform unsatisfactorily with respect to the application requirements. The *Maximum Bandwidth Scheduler* was intentionally designed to represent the way of how today's mobile devices implement the concept of ABC. The result shows that this approach may perform to some extend almost reasonable in scenarios with a low number of applications and networks. However, it reaches its limits quite fast. The *One Bundle Scheduler* achieved the highest efficiency as it considers the different available network as one logical transmission channel, but this comes at the disadvantage that this procedure does not allow for any differentiation of networks with respect to application requirements. Moreover, when using the *One Bundle Scheduler* in the field, it will suffer from additional overheads for reordering data. This will clearly have negative effects on the network capacities that can actually be used for user data transfer. In the way we implemented the scheduler for our evaluation, these aspects were neglected.

A second observation in our evaluation was that the option of combining networks to a bundle that can be used for concurrent multipath transfer brings definitely a benefit for the efficiency of mobile Internet access. In scenarios with a low number of networks this effect does not become clearly apparent. However, even here bundling enables the scheduler to serve applications with high demands on the required throughput. Network bundling gains a higher weight on decision output with an increasing number of networks and applications. We were able to show that an explicit deferment of application requests is necessary to provide at least some extend of guarantees such that applications are really able to make use of the allocated resources and to avoid that applications have to use networks that do not provide at least a minimum adherence to their requirements.

A third general observation we made in our evaluations is the fact that the benefit of smart decision strategies clearly depends on the size of the solution space. Especially when looking at the results on the number of active applications or the network utilization, we can see that the benefit of a smarter strategy like *GAP* clearly increases with the number of applications and the number of networks in the scenario. The main reason for this is the fact that even for randomized schedulers there is a high probability to find a suitable solution.

Although the evaluation results show that *GAP* performs well with respect to the other benchmark schedulers, there is still a potential for further improvements. First, in the way we implemented the functionality of bundling in *GAP*, it shows its benefits mainly in scenarios with a higher level of heterogeneity and where the available network resources are strongly limited. This is due to the fact that bundles are considered in the second-order after scheduling an application to a single network. However, implementing a more precise prediction on the effects of bundling to specific combinations of networks may allow for a better tradeoff between the additional overhead and the benefit to the decision output. This way, it might be possible to increase the weight of multipath transfer on the overall decision result. Second, we only implemented a smooth variant of cost reduction in *GAP* that aims at maximizing the loads of those networks that are already in use, but actually does not limit the total number of networks that are used. A more powerful cost reduction component may include further aspects as monetary and energy budgets, and thus allows for a more detailed consideration of these factors in the final decision. However, in the end a limitation of costs will basically result in a scenario with a lower number of available networks and again is conflictive with the aim to serve a high number of applications and to make effective use of network resources. Finally, the implementation of a better cost-benefit equation with respect to whether an application should be allocated to a network or not, may reduce the distance between *GAP* and the optimal solution of our formal problem statement. However, this requires a more detailed and differentiated modeling of the costs of each individual network.

To sum up, our quantitative evaluation shows that *GAP* brings clear advantages compared to other existing approaches to dynamic network selection. The additional options of bundling networks and deferring application requests have a clear contribution to that. The additional option to reduce costs by preferring networks that are already in use, allows for a moderate reduction of the number of networks and results only in a low reduction of the adherence to application requirements. Thus, *GAP* contributes to a higher efficiency in using mobile Internet by deliberating good tradeoffs between the different objectives and balancing the interest of the user as well as concurrent applications running on the mobile device. The actual parameterization of the process itself and the importance of particular objectives are subject to the interests of users and providers as well as the designated deployment scenario.

5.8 Summary

In this chapter, we presented our research work on a modular and flexible mechanism for dynamic and application-oriented network selection. In the first step, we discussed a set of QoS categories in mobile environments. We separated these categories into two classes. On the one hand we found technology-related categories of QoS characteristics that are strongly related to the communication performance of mobile Internet access and represent the resources that an application may use for its particular purpose. One the other hand, we identified a set of user-related QoS categories that depend on the level of quality a user expects to perceive. We concluded that not all of these QoS parameters are focused on the needs of an individual application, but some of them relate to cross-application aspects. Thus, we analyzed which aspects relate either to the domain of the application or the domain of all applications running on the device. In addition, we discussed the problem of tradeoffs that have to be made in the decision process. Especially, we focused on the aspects of conflicting objectives and on the question of how precisely a decision concept should model the communication environment, as a higher level of precision always comes at the cost of an increased complexity.

The findings on all of these aspects are integrated into the design of our concept for dynamic network selection. While previous research work only focused on either a fully application-oriented or a fully device-oriented decision approach, we combined both aspects and proposed a hybrid decision concept. One central building block of our approach is the arbitration technique. It allows for a modular and flexible integration of heterogeneous objectives. Afterwards, we introduced the design concepts and the algorithms being used in the two tiers of the muXer decision concept. Furthermore, we presented our prototype implementation of the decision concept that includes a set of basic decision objectives for the different QoS categories. A complete overview of the different modules in our prototype is shown in figure 5.42.

The evaluation compares the performance of our approach with that of other strategies that were proposed for network selection in related work. We found out that the muXer decision concept performs well will respect to multiple evaluation metrics relating to the aim of both meeting the decision objectives and making efficient use of the available network resources. It was shown that our *GAP* scheduler implements a reasonable tradeoff between the different optimization goals. We were able to show that the use of network bundles and the deferment of application requests in the case of constrained network resources increase the efficiency of network usage. The evaluation of the runtime performance showed that *GAP* scales well with an increasing number of networks and applications.

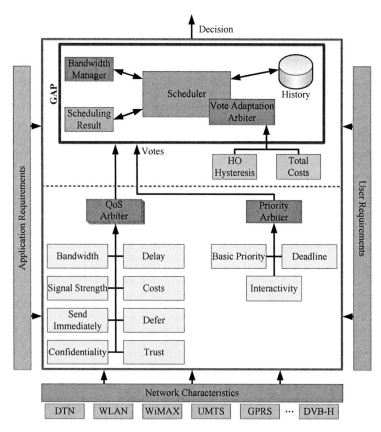

Figure 5.42: Complete overview on the prototype implementation

Chapter 6

Conclusions and Outlook

The Internet gained a high importance in people's daily life during the past years. With the advent of powerful mobile devices as, for instance, smartphones, netbooks, tablet computers, or even notebooks that are equipped with multiple network interfaces, the mobile use of Internet services grew drastically and opened up new business areas for applications and services. This growth will continue in the future or may even become stronger due to new innovations in terms of hard- and software.

One key aspect that is expected to boost the success of mobile Internet even further is the provision of ubiquitous access to Internet services and especially a seamless integration of heterogeneous networks, which provides a transparent selection of the best option for Internet access in any scenario. Thus, in the end a user should no longer be aware of how he gets access to the Internet. Such an approach requires a user-centric decision concept that comes with the flexibility to select the best communication path for each individual application.

6.1 Contributions

This thesis addresses the issue of using available communication resources more efficiently by providing each application with the resources that are actually required to meet its specific task. Our work was driven by the finding that existing approaches either implement solutions that neglect specific application demands, or that do not consider resource limitations of networks that are used concurrently by multiple applications on the device. In addition, the previously proposed concepts often lack on the flexibility of modeling arbitrary objectives for the decision process and are not able to use the existing communication capabilities to their full capacity. To overcome these deficiencies, we propose our muXer architecture for dynamic network selection. It is designed to provide a high level of flexibility to support arbitrary applications, networking technologies and decision objectives. It provides an application-oriented management of requirements and allows for making individual decisions on which networks to be used by a specific application.

One particular contribution of our work is the design of the overall system architecture. In addition, we made contributions to a seamless path management. Third, a main focus of our research work is put on the design of the decision process itself.

In the context of path management, we made the following contributions:

► the implementation of a path management approach with legacy support that enables vertical handovers using the Stream Control Transmission Protocol (SCTP);

► the analysis of the effects of vertical handovers on the throughput and the end-to-end delay that is experienced by applications;

► an analysis of the challenges of Concurrent Multipath Transfer (CMT) in heterogeneous communication environments;

► the enhancement of CMT mechanisms and their integration in SCTP to cope with challenging communication scenarios;

► the evaluation of potentials and limitations of CMT mechanisms in the context of heterogeneous communication scenarios.

Our general path management concept was designed to integrate functionalities at different layers of the ISO/OSI protocol stack. Based on a comparison of different mobility management approaches, we end up with the results that a transport layer approach for vertical handovers and multipath transfer meets our requirements best. For the implementation, we used SCTP as it inherently supports various features that would have been needed to be integrated into other protocols like TCP. In the context of vertical handovers, our particular interest was on the effects of handovers between networks with clearly different characteristics. Therefore, we evaluated the networking performance that is perceived by the application. Our findings show that the SCTP-based approach performs well in various scenarios and is able to adapt quickly to the characteristics of the new path. In addition, we were able to show that SCTP outperforms other approaches that manage mobility at the network layer and use TCP as transport protocol. As a second aspect, we analyzed the requirements on Concurrent Multipath Transfer in homogeneous and heterogeneous networking scenarios. To cope with these scenarios, we proposed XCMT that integrates several enhancements and modifications of SCTP to make it capable of multipath transfer. Here, we focused again on an evaluation of performance issues in homogenous and heterogeneous communication environments. We found out, that XCMT provides optimal results in scenarios where the bundled paths feature equal characteristics. In addition, it shows still very good results in certain typical networking scenarios that are close to the optimum and provides a valuable benefit to the option of using only the path with the highest bandwidth. Nevertheless, our evaluation also showed the general limitations of CMT mechanisms in heterogeneous scenarios. With increasing differences between the paths, there is a point where the efforts for reordering packets at the receiver exceed the benefit of the additional resources that are provided by the new path. Thus, the results that we obtained here in combination with additional work on the tolerance to network disruptions affirmed our ideas on integrating both issues into the network selection process to achieve a higher efficiency.

The path management is only one aspect in the muXer architecture. The core issue of this work is the decision process for selecting networks, which meets the application requirements on the one hand, but adheres to cross-application objectives as well. In this context we made the following contributions:

▶ a discussion of different QoS categories relating to the network selection problem and their importance to either individual applications or to all applications running on a device;

▶ a discussion of the need for decision tradeoffs that appear from conflicting objectives;

▶ the proposal of a highly modular and flexible decision concept that meets the aforementioned requirements;

▶ a proof-of-concept for the application-oriented arbitration phase that implements an individual rating of candidate networks and a demonstration of the general approach;

▶ the analysis of the problem on how to allocate network resources to applications in the best possible way;

▶ the proposal of the Global Arbitration Process (GAP) that follows a scheduling concept and allocates network resources based on the rating of networks and on application priorities;

▶ the evaluation of our approach with respect to other proposals in a variety of different communication scenarios.

The decision concept that is proposed in this thesis bases on an arbitration technique where multiple decision modules give their voting on the suitability of certain candidate networks. Each decision module focuses on one specific decision objective and can be implemented in an arbitrary way. Only the semantics of the interface to the arbiter that integrates the different ratings has to be defined. The decision modules run asynchronously from each other. Thus, the ratings may be updated in individual intervals. In addition, any objectives can be added or removed from the decision process easily. Such a modification is even possible for individual applications. A second tier in our decision process manages the actual allocation of network resources to the applications. It may implement further cross-application objectives and aims at using the available resources in an efficient way. We evaluated the performance of our approach in dependence of various metrics and compared it to other decision strategies that were proposed in the literature, as well as to random allocation strategies and to the optimum with respect to our problem statement.

To the best of our knowledge, there are no approaches in the literature prior to our proposals that provide either comparable evaluations on the performance of transport layer mechanisms for path management in heterogeneous communication environments or describe any comparable approach to network selection that features the aforementioned characteristics and functionalities.

The path management mechanisms and the decision concept are embedded in our muXer architecture that comes with further features like network monitoring and decision evaluation. We implemented a general concept for monitoring network characteristics that provides the basic features to map technology specific metrics onto generic network parameters to make different technologies comparable. Furthermore, we implemented basic mechanisms to predict possible candidate networks based on the current location and information that has been recorded during earlier traversals of the area. The implementation of a module that evaluates the final decisions and that improves the parameterization of the system was beyond the scope of this work. In summary, our framework provides a very flexible, comprehensive and efficient approach to dynamic network selection in heterogeneous communications ecosystems.

6.2   Future Work

The results that were achieved within this thesis provide an integrated approach to the implementation of an Always Best Connected (ABC) service. As usual, there is still room for further enhancements and optimizations. In the following, we give some examples for possible extensions of our muXer approach:

Content adaption: In some communication scenarios, it will not always be possible to serve all application requests. In these cases, application services may adapt to the limited resources that are available. Such an approach is almost simple for applications with elastic requirements like a file download, but might be more complex, for instance, to video streaming applications that require a certain bandwidth. Our network selection concept may consider the capabilities of such content adaptation techniques as further options in the decision process.

Self-optimization capabilities: The muXer architecture includes a separate module that is intended for implementing self-optimization capabilities. The implementation of such features may further improve the performance of the ABC service by tuning the system parameters and can help to better meet the preferences of a specific user.

Application requirements and decision objectives: Each application has its own specific requirements to the underlying network and certain communication characteristics will be more important than others. Our decision concept allows for an individual selection, parameterization and weighting of decision objectives for every application. However, further research is necessary on which parameter set matches the specific needs of certain applications.

Energy constraints: For mobile devices, the efficient use of the available energy budget is an important issue. Future work may propose the design of decision objectives that model these requirements in our decision process.

Alternative communication scenarios: In chapter 2, we described alternative communication scenarios like a mobile router in a bus or a swarm of mobile devices that make cooperative decisions on the use of networks. Although the modular design of the muXer architecture and of our decision process allow for a distributed implementation of the concept, the support of these alternative scenarios does still require additional services for sharing information on candidate networks and decisions as well as for managing the communication within the swarm or the bus. Furthermore, one might think about how muXer can interact with routing mechanisms in disruption tolerant store-carry-forward networks to get information on the data delivery characteristics through the network and on how data packets should be forwarded.

In addition, one might evaluate certain aspects of the decision process in more detail. Foremost, this may comprise the opportunities of using certain context information and mechanisms to predict the expected future availability of candidate networks and their impact on the efficiency of the decision process as well as the adherence to deadlines for application data transfers. In addition, a more detailed investigation on the performance of muXer in real world scenarios is required to parameterize the system. Such an evaluation must not only include aspects on how well application requirements are met, but should also focus on the Quality of Service that is experienced by the user. These results will help to determine optimization potentials for the practical use of muXer and ABC services in general.

Appendix A

SCTP Chunk Formats

The Stream Control Transmission Protocol (SCTP) [12] defines different types of so-called chunks that can be carried in an SCTP packet and contain either user data or control information. Figure A.1 illustrates the general format of an SCTP packet, which consists of a common SCTP header and one or multiple chunks. Each chunk has a header with a common structure and a chunk value that is individual for the respective chunk type. For the actual user data transfer, two chunk types are of major interest: the DATA chunk that encapsulates the actual user data and the SACK chunk that is used on the one hand to acknowledge data that arrived at the receiver and on the other hand to report DATA chunks that are missing at the receiver. Here, we introduce the format of these two chunks. For an introduction to the remaining chunk types we refer to the SCTP protocol definition in RFC 4960 [12].

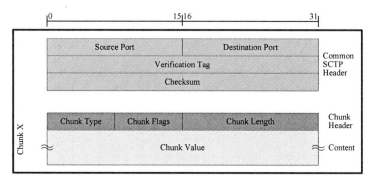

Figure A.1: The SCTP packet format

A.1   DATA Chunk

Figure A.2 illustrates the format of the DATA chunk that carries the application data . The chunk header contains three flags. If the U flag is set, it indicates that this DATA chunk is unordered and thus can be directly delivered to the application. The B and E flags are used in the case that the data chunk carries only a fragment of a user message. The B flags marks the first fragment of a message, while the E flag marks the last one.

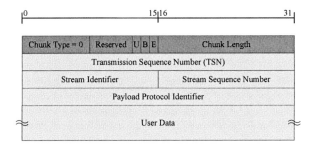

Figure A.2: The SCTP DATA chunk packet format

An important parameter in the DATA chunk is the *Transmission Sequence Number (TSN)*. It is used to uniquely identify a data chunk and thus to report whether a chunk has arrived at the receiver or is expected to be lost. Next, the *Stream Identifier* states the stream within the association to which the data belongs to. The *Stream Sequence Number* is another identifier relating to the respective stream. It extends the TSN and is used to provide an in-order delivery of DATA chunks within the stream. The *Payload Protocol Identifier* is not used by SCTP itself. Instead, it provides an option to inform applications or any other network entities about the kind of information that is carried within the DATA chunk. Finally, the *User Data* field contains the actual payload of the DATA chunk.

A.2   SACK Chunk

The SACK chunk is used by the remote peer to inform the sender about which DATA chunks have arrived and which ones are missing. It also starts with a common header. Next, the first SACK-specific field is the *Cumulative TSN Ack* point. It is set to the last TSN that has been received in-order at the receiving peer. Thus, all DATA chunks with TSN values up to the given sequence number are cumulatively acknowledged. Next, the *Advertised Receiver Window Credit* informs the remote peer about the remaining size of the local receive buffer. This parameter is followed by zero or more Gap Ack Blocks. They report any missing DATA chunks. Moreover, the SACK may report duplicate DATA chunks that arrived at the receiver. They are reported to the sender as well. Thus, first the packet format states two fields that indicate the *number of Gap Ack Blocks* and the *number of duplicate TSNs* that are sent with this chunk. These fields are followed first by the given number of Gap Ack Blocks. Each of these blocks is identified by a *Begin* and an *End* offset. The offset states the difference between the Cumulative TSN Ack and the TSNs of the respective DATA chunks at the beginning and the end of a Gap Ack Block. The report peer can assume all TSNs within a Gap Ack Block to be delivered correctly. Any TSNs between two Gap Ack Blocks or the Cumulative TSN and the first Gap Ack block are currently missing at the receiving peer. Finally, the list of Gap Ack blocks is followed by the list of *Duplicate TSNs* if any duplicate DATA chunks arrived at the receiver.

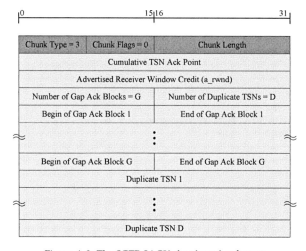

Figure A.3: The SCTP SACK chunk packet format

Appendix B

Implementation Details of XCMT

MuXer CMT (XCMT) integrates concurrent multipath transfer (CMT) functionalities into the Linux kernel SCTP module. The basis of our implementation is kernel version 2.6.23.1. In general, the core of the standard SCTP kernel module is a state machine that manages the protocol state and the events as well as a set of queues for the handling of data chunks. Figure B.1 illustrates these components.

Any data packets that are forwarded by the network layer protocol to the SCTP instance are added to the *inqueue*. Here, SCTP keeps track on which chunks have been received and controls the size of the receiver window. After processing the incoming data chunk, it is forwarded via the state machine to the *ulpqueue*, which is responsible for data reordering. The *ulpqueue* provides the interface to the socket API that is used by the applications. In the other direction, the data that comes from the applications is processed first in the state machine. From here, the chunk is injected into the *outqueue* that manages the whole flow and congestion control mechanisms, before it is forwarded to the network layer protocol.

As SCTP does only use one path for data transfer in each case, we had to enhance the existing mechanisms with the ability to use multiple paths in parallel. Moreover, we must integrate the scheduler that allocates messages to the different paths. Finally several modifications for the handling of retransmissions and for the monitoring of path characteristics were needed. The parts of the SCTP kernel module that have been modified are highlighted in figure B.1. The scheduling mechanisms were implemented in the *outqueue*. Here, we integrated the functionality to decide which path to use in `sctp_outq_flush()`. The handling of retransmissions is implemented in the same function. The mechanisms for adapting the scheduler with respect to the estimated level of reordering at the receiver are realized in a separate function `sctp_adjust_scheduler()` that is invoked from `sctp_outq_sack()`. Moreover, we provided enhancements to the congestion control functionalities to be able to use multiple paths in parallel. Further modifications relate to the procedure for handling missing chunks and the handling of selective acknowledgements. Finally, we inte-

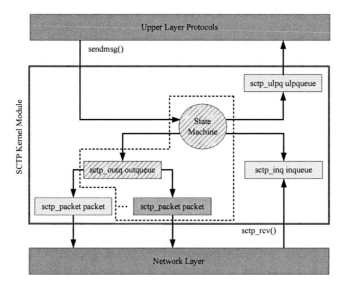

Figure B.1: Modifications in the SCTP kernel module

grated additional functions to monitor path characteristics. The approach for estimating the bandwidth of a path was implemented in a new `bandwidth_measure_timer` that invokes the new function `sctp_bandwidth_measure()` in periodic intervals. The loss probability is calculated in function `sctp_p_losses_measure()`. Finally, the estimation of round trip times for separate paths required changes in the functions `sctp_assoc_bh_rcv()` and `sctp_check_transmitted()`.

Appendix C

Implementation Details on the Measure-o-Mat Evaluation Suite

The Measure-o-Mat tool suite (Meomat) has been used for the evaluation of vertical handovers and concurrent multipath transfer in section 4.4. It comprises a set of programs and scripts that enable the automated procedure of measurements in our testbed and the evaluation of the raw data that has been gathered. Meomat was designed to measure the application-layer throughput and delay for a stream of data packets. In principle, the whole evaluation process is separated in two parts. First, data is sent from one peer to another one. Next, the receiving peer creates a timestamp for the messages that arrive and records the raw data. Finally, the results for different measurement runs are combined and analyzed.

The complete setup is depicted in figure C.1. It is made up by a sending and a receiving peer. Between both of them, we have two independent paths. The communication characteristics along each path are affected by the NistNet network emulator [234]. NistNet intercepts the IP packets in the Linux kernel and handles them according to a predefined set of rules that define certain network characteristics as, for instance, the bandwidth, the delay or the jitter of the communication path between two peers.

The *Meomat Client* and *Meomat Server* applications provide the basis for our tool suite. The former one controls the procedure of the measurement cycle and sends predefined data packets to the receiver. Each of these packets carries a timestamp that indicates when it was sent by the application. We developed multiple variants of this client that are intended for either evaluating handovers or concurrent multipath transfer. Moreover, they support the use of SCTP and TCP. The *Meomat Server* determines another timestamp when the message is received. Then, it copies both the timestamp and the address via which the packet was received into a memory buffer using memcpy operations [236]. After a measurement run is finished, the whole buffer is written to a file. By this procedure, we minimize any potential effects on our actual measurement results. To ensure that client and server work on the same

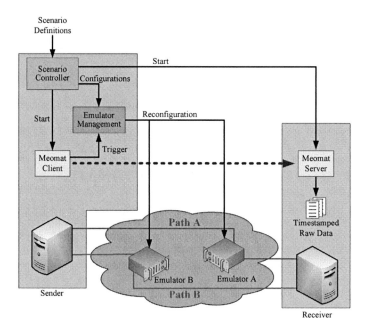

Figure C.1: Detailed overview of the Meomat setup

time basis, they are synchronized with the help of the Network Time Protocol (NTP) [235]. The offset between the time server and the local clocks of each host was typically lower than one millisecond.

C.1   Measurement Procedure

The overall measurement procedure is managed by the *Scenario Controller* script. It takes a set of scenario descriptions as input and executes them one by one. First, it configures the *Emulator Management*. This is a collection of scripts that are used to set certain scenario configurations of the network emulators. Second, it invokes the *Meomat Server* and afterwards the *Meomat Client* to start a new measurement cycle. The *Meomat Client* controls the procedure of a cycle that may consist of multiple runs in the same scenario setup. Before starting a measurement run, it triggers a reset of the network emulators. In the next step, it starts to send a given number of messages with a predefined payload size. Depending on the scenario that is investigated, the *Meomat Client* may initiate a handover or triggers changes of the network characteristics after sending a certain number of messages. Finally, the *Meomat Client* waits for some time before it starts another run. This period is used by the *Meomat Server* to dump the collected raw data into a file. At the end of a measurement cycle, the control path goes back to the *Scenario Controller* that executes the applications for evaluating raw data and finally preserves both the raw data and the statistics. Afterwards, it may prepare a new measurement cycle and the whole process starts anew.

C.2   Evaluation Procedure

For evaluating the raw data that was collected during the measurement runs, we developed tools to analyze the data with respect to certain metrics and to plot the results that have been obtained. In the context of our evaluations, we focused on three aspects:

► delay,

► throughput, and

► path statistics.

For each of these characteristics we implemented a so-called *Meomat Reader* as illustrated in figure C.2. It processes the raw data of the single runs with respect to a specific aspect and averages the result over all runs in a measurement cycle. Following, we describe how the results are determined.

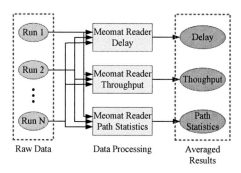

Figure C.2: Meomat evaluation tools

C.2.1 Delay

The *Meomat Reader Delay* calculates the end-to-end delay that was experienced by the application. For this, each message is tagged with two timestamps. The first one is the time t_{snd} to which the application passes the message to the socket API. The timestamp is determined by calling the POSIX function `gettimeofday()` at the client. Afterwards, the value is copied into the buffer for the message payload using `memcpy()` and directly passed to the socket API via calling `sendmsg()`. As already mentioned before, the second timestamp t_{recv} is determined when the packet is received by the *Meomat Server*. Again, we use `gettimeofday()` to obtain the current time and store this information together with the whole message. As both host are synchronized with an accuracy of typically lower 1 ms, we can use these timestamps to determine the end-to-end delay d of a packet i by simply subtracting the timestamps from each other:

$$d_i = t_{recv_i} - t_{snd_i} \quad . \tag{C.1}$$

The average delay across different runs j of the measurement cycle is determined for the absolute position i of a packet in the constant sequence of messages being sent during the measurement procedure:

$$d_{avg_i} = \frac{1}{R} \sum_{j=1}^{R} d_i \quad , \tag{C.2}$$

where R is the total number of runs in a measurement cycle.

C.2.2 Throughput

The throughput is defined as the amount of data that was received during certain time intervals. Thus, our *Meomat Reader Throughput* takes one part of the output generated by the *Meomat Reader Delay* and determines the amount of data that was received during a predefined interval. The first interval is started with the time the first packet is received at the server. The reader remembers the remaining time in the interval and picks the next packet. It checks whether this packet fits into the interval. If this is true, the message payload is added to the amount of data being received during the interval and the remaining time of the interval is reduced accordingly. Otherwise, the amount of data for the current interval is stored and a new interval is opened. Now, the algorithm checks whether the respective packet fits into this new interval. In the end, we have a list of time intervals each having the length l and the amount of data s that was delivered during interval k. Thus, the final throughput amounts to:

$$tp_k = \frac{l_k}{s_k} \tag{C.3}$$

C.2.3 Path Statistics

The *Meomat Reader Path Statistics* iterates through the gathered information on along which addresses packets were received. Thus, it is able to count the number packets for each path and determines an average for all runs.

Appendix D

Parameterization of the QoS Arbiter

In section 5.4.3 we introduced our prototype of the *QoS Arbiter* and presented eight basic decision module that were implemented as a proof of concept. We pointed out that an accurate design of decision modules will require an in-depth analysis of the parameters for each objective and the effects of different network characteristics on the performance of an application, which is beyond the scope of this work. Instead, we implemented a set of exemplary decision modules to demonstrate the general principle of the arbitration process. All functions that are used in these modules are based on plausibility assumptions. In the following, we provide the details of these functions. The maximum and minimum vote values are defined to 127 and -128 respectively.

D.1 Bandwidth

Input

- ► the requested bandwidth bw_{req}
- ► the tolerated bandwidth bw_{tol}
- ► the bandwidth provided by the network bw_{net}

Output

- ► the bandwidth vote v_{bw}

Function

$$
v_{bw} =
\begin{cases}
min\left(127 \cdot \left(\dfrac{2}{1 + e^{\left(-4 \cdot \frac{(bw_{net} - bw_{tol})}{bw_{req} - bw_{tol}}\right)}} - 1\right), 127\right) & bw_{net} \geq bw_{tol} \\[4em]
max\left(-128 + \left(128 \cdot \dfrac{1}{e^{\left(3 \cdot \frac{bw_{tol} - bw_{net}}{bw_{tol} - (0.9 \cdot bw_{tol})}\right)}}\right), -128\right) & bw_{net} < bw_{tol}
\end{cases}
$$

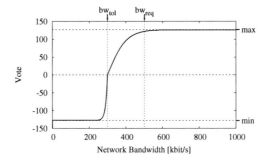

Figure D.1: Voting on bandwidth requirements

D.2 Delay

Input

- ▶ the requested delay d_{req}
- ▶ the tolerated delay d_{tol}
- ▶ the delay provided by the network d_{net}

Output

- ▶ the delay vote v_d

Function

$$
v_d = \begin{cases}
min\left(127 \cdot \left(\dfrac{2}{1 + e^{\left(-4 \cdot \frac{(d_{tol} - d_{net})}{d_{tol} - d_{req}}\right)}} - 1 \right), 127 \right) & d_{net} \leq d_{tol} \\[4em]
max\left(-128 + \left(128 \cdot \dfrac{1}{e^{\left(3 \cdot \frac{d_{net} - d_{tol}}{(1.1 \cdot d_{tol}) - d_{tol}}\right)}} \right), -128 \right) & d_{net} > d_{tol}
\end{cases}
$$

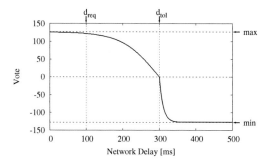

Figure D.2: Voting on delay requirements

D.3 Signal Strength

Input

▶ the normalized signal strength of a network SSI

▶ the signal strength trend in the past T

▶ the tolerance of an application to risky decisions L_r

Output

▶ the signal strength vote v_{ss}

Function

$$SSI_{eff} = SSI - 0.1 - 0.1 \cdot (1 - L_r)$$
$$v_{ss_{signal}} = 255 \cdot \left(-1 \cdot (1 - SSI_{eff})^3 + 1\right) + (-128)$$
$$v_{ss_{trend}} = 127 \cdot 3 \cdot T$$

$$v_{ss} = \begin{cases} -127 & SSI_{eff} \leq 0 \\[3em] min\left(max\left(-128, \left(0.7 \cdot v_{ss_{signal}} + 0.3 \cdot v_{ss_{trend}}\right)\right), 127\right) & SSI_{eff} > 0 \end{cases}$$

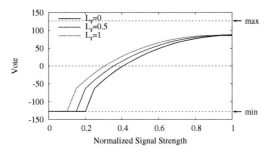

(a) Variation of the application's risk level

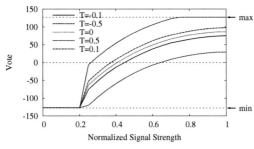

(b) Variation of the signal strength trend

Figure D.3: Voting on the network's signal strength

D.4 Defer

Input

- ▶ the deadline for beginning a data transmission t_{dead}
- ▶ the estimated time to connecting to a network t_{con}
- ▶ the level of an application's tolerance to disruptions L_{dt}

Output

- ▶ the defer vote v_{defer}

Function

$$v_{defer_{dt}} = 255 \cdot L_{dt} + (-128)$$

$$v_{defer_{con}} = 127 \cdot \left(\frac{2}{1 + \frac{-6 \cdot (t_{dead} - t_{con})}{200}} - 1 \right)$$

$$P = \begin{cases} 0 & \text{network is available} \\ 1 & \text{network is predicted to apprear} \end{cases}$$

$$v_{defer} = \begin{cases} 0 & P = 0 \\ max \left(min \left(127, \left(0.6 \cdot v_{defer_{con}} + 0.4 \cdot v_{defer_{dt}} \right) \right), -128 \right) & P = 1 \end{cases}$$

D.5 Send Now

Input

- ▶ the deadline for beginning a data transmission t_{dead}
- ▶ the estimated time to connecting to a network t_{con}

Output

- ▶ the *send now* vote $v_{sendnow}$

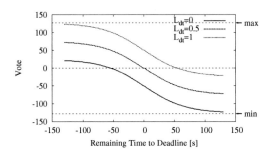

Figure D.4: Voting on candidate networks for deferring an application request

Function

$$
v_{snd} = \begin{cases} 0 & \text{predicted network} \\[2mm] 127 & \text{no predicted network} \land t_{dead} < 0 \\[2mm] 127 \cdot \dfrac{1}{e^{(0.02 \cdot t_{dead})}} & \text{no predicted network} \land t_{dead} \geq 0 \end{cases}
$$

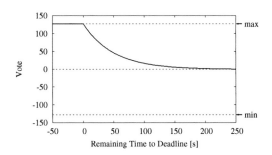

Figure D.5: Voting using a network that is available

D.6 Confidentiality

Input

▶ the required level of confidentiality L_{creq}

▶ the level of confidentiality provided by the network L_{cnet}

Output

▶ the *confidentiality* vote v_{conf}

Function

$$
v_{conf} = \begin{cases} 0 & L_{c_{req}} \text{ is undefined} \\ 127 & L_{c_{net}} \geq L_{c_{req}} \\ -128 & L_{c_{net}} < L_{c_{req}} \end{cases}
$$

D.7 Trust

Input

▶ the required level of trust L_{treq}

▶ the level of trust provided by the network L_{tnet}

Output

▶ the *trust* vote v_{trust}

Function

$$
v_{trust} = \begin{cases} 0 & L_t \text{ is undefined} \\ 127 & L_{t_{net}} \geq L_{t_{req}} \\ -128 & L_{t_{net}} < L_{t_{req}} \end{cases}
$$

D.8   Costs

Input

► the rate for network access R

► the level to which a volume budget is already used L_{bud}

► the costs of network usage L_{cost}

Output

► the *costs* vote v_{cost}

Function

$$v_{cost} = \begin{cases} 0 & R \text{ is undefined} \\[2ex] 127 & R = FREE \vee R = FLAT \\[2ex] (0.75 \cdot 127 - (-128)) \cdot \left((-L_{bud}^3) + 1\right) + (-128) & R = BUDGET \\[2ex] (0.75 \cdot 127 - (-128)) \cdot \frac{1}{e^{(0.1 \cdot L_{cost})}} + (-128) & R = ONDEMAND \end{cases}$$

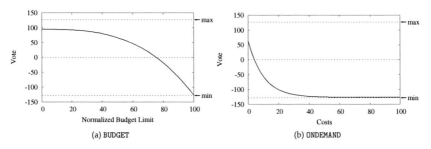

Figure D.6: Voting on candidate networks for deferring an application request

Bibliography

[1] E. Gustafsson, A. Jonsson, "Always Best Connected," IEEE Wireless Communications, vol. 10, pp. 49 – 55, February 2003.

[2] J. Eisl, J. Höller, S. Uno, R. A. Calvo, "Towards Modular Mobility Management in Ambient Networks," Proceedings of the 1st ACM Workshop on Dynamic Interconnection of Networks (DIN '05), Cologne, Germany, pp. 43 – 47, September 2005.

[3] Deutsche Telekom AG, "Deutsche Telekom Investor Day, On Our Way To A New DT - Fix - Transform - Innovate," Presentation held by René Obermann, March 2010 `http://www.download-telekom.de/dt/StaticPage/83/29/12/dtag_investorentag_praesentation_obermann.pdf_832912.pdf` visited in April 2010.

[4] Bundesverband Informationswirtschaft, Telekommunikation und neue Medien e.V., "Connected Worlds," BITKOM Studie, March 2010 `http://www.bitkom.org/files/documents/bitkom-praesentation_connected_worlds_01_03_2010.pdf`, visited in April 2010.

[5] JiWire, Inc., "JiWire Global Wi-Fi Finder," `http://www.jiwire.com` visited in april 2010.

[6] H. Hartenstein, K. P. Laberteaux, "A Tutorial Survey on Vehicular Ad Hoc Networks," IEEE Communications Magazine, vol. 46, pp. 164 – 171, June 2008.

[7] J. Ott, "Delay Tolerance and the Future Internet," Proceedings of the 11th International Symposium on Wireless Personal Multimedia Communications (WPMC '08), Lapland, Finland, September 2008.

[8] Apple Inc., "Homepage of the Apple iPhone," `http://www.apple.com/iphone/` visited in April 2010.

[9] AdMob, "Mobile Metrics Report," February 2010 `http://metrics.admob.com/wp-content/uploads/2010/03/AdMob-Mobile-Metrics-Feb-10.pdf`, visited in April 2010.

[10] S. Lahde, L. Wolf, "Dynamic Network Selection for Robust Communications – Why Disruption Tolerance Matters," Proceedings of the 4th ACM International Workshop on Mobility in the Evolving Internet Architecture (MobiArch '09), Krakow, Poland, June 2009.

[11] S. Lahde, M. Doering, L. Wolf, "Dynamic Transport Layer Handover for Heterogeneous Communication Environments," Computer Communications – Special Issue on Concurrent Multipath Transport, vol. 30, pp. 3232 – 3238, November 2007.

[12] E. R. Stewart, "Stream Control Transmission Protocol," Internet Engineering Task Force Request for Comments 4960, September 2007 http://tools.ietf.org/html/rfc4960.

[13] S. Lahde, M. Wegner, L. Wolf, "Efficient Network Selection in Heterogeneous Communication Scenarios using Arbitration," Proceedings of the 11th IEEE International Symposium on a World of Wireless, Mobile and Multimedia Networks (WoWMoM 2010), Montreal, QC, Canada, June 2010.

[14] GSM Association and Europe Technologies Ltd, "GSM World Coverage 2009," http://www.gsmworld.com/roaming/GSM_WorldPoster2009A.pdf', 2009 visited in May 2010.

[15] Telekom Deutschland GmbH, "Funkversorgung im Inland," http://www.t-mobile.de/funkversorgung/inland/ visited in July 2010, [German].

[16] Bluetooth SIG, Inc., "Bluetooth Specification Version 2.1 + EDR," July 2007.

[17] Bluetooth SIG, Inc., "Bluetooth Specification Version 3.0 + HS," April 2009.

[18] Ecma International, "High Rate Ultra Wideband PHY and MAC Standard," Standard ECMA-368, December 2008.

[19] The Institute of Electrical and Electronics Engineers, "IEEE 802.15 WPAN Terahertz Interest Group (IGthz)," http://www.ieee802.org/15/pub/IGthz.html visited in May 2010.

[20] The Institute of Electrical and Electronics Engineers, "IEEE Standard for Information Technology – Telecommunications and Information Exchange Between Systems – Local and Metropolitan Area Networks – Specific Requirements Part 11: Wireless LAN Medium Access Control (MAC) and Physical Layer (PHY) Specifications," IEEE Std 802.11-2007, June 2007.

[21] Wolfsburg AG, "Wireless Wolfsburg," http://www.wireless-wolfsburg.de/ visited in October 2010.

[22] Google Inc., "Google WiFi for Mountain View," http://wifi.google.com/ visited in October 2010.

[23] Mairie de Paris, "Paris Wi-Fi," http://www.paris.fr/portail/pratique/Portal.lut?page_id=7799 visited in October 2010.

[24] The Institute of Electrical and Electronics Engineers, "Standard for Information Technology – Telecommunications and Information Exchange Between Systems – Local and Metropolitan Area Networks – Specific Requirements – Part 11: Wireless LAN Medium Access Control (MAC) & Physical Layer Specifications Enhancements for Higher Throughput," IEEE 802.11n-2009, October 2009.

[25] Bundesamt für Sicherheit in der Informationstechnik, "Drahtlose Kommunikationssysteme und ihre Sicherheitsaspekte," Report, September 2009 https://www.bsi.bund.de/cae/servlet/contentblob/487312/publicationFile/42808/drahtkom_pdf.pdf, visited in Feburary 2010 [German].

[26] The Institute of Electrical and Electronics Engineers, "IEEE Standard 802.11e/D13.0, Draft Supplement to Standard for Telecommunications and Information Exchange between Systems-LAN/MAN Specific Requirements – Part 11: Wireless Medium Access Control and Physical Layer Specifications: Medium Access Control Enhancements for Quality of Service," April 2005.

[27] The Institute of Electrical and Electronics Engineers, "IEEE Standard for Local and Metropolitan Area Networks – Part 16: Air Interface for Broadband Wireless Access Systems," IEEE Std 802.16-2009, May 2009.

[28] S. Ahmadi, "Introduction to Mobile WiMAX Radio Access Technology: PHY and MAC Architecture," Presentation at University of California, Santa Barbara, December 2006 http://www.mat.ucsb.edu/~ggroup/ahmadiUCSB_slides_Dec7.pdf, visited in May 2010.

[29] M. Paolini, "WiMAX Performance in the Clear Network in Portland," Report, January 2009 http://www.senzafiliconsulting.com/resources/clear-network-portland.php, visited in May 2010.

[30] IEEE Computer Society, "IEEE Standard for Local and Metropolitan Area Networks – Part 20: Air Interface for Mobile Broadband Wireless Access Systems Supporting Vehicular Mobility – Physical and Media Access Control Layer Specification," IEEE Std 802.20-2008, August 2008.

[31] M. Klerer, "Introduction to IEEE 802.20 – Technical and Procedural Orientation," Presentation, March 2003 `http://www.ieee802.org/20/P_Docs/IEEE%20802.20% 20PD-04.pdf`, visited in May 2010.

[32] C. Cordeiro, K. Challapali, D. Birru, S. Shankar N, "IEEE 802.22: An Introduction to the First Wireless Standard Based on Cognitive Radios," Journal of Communications, vol. 1, pp. 38 – 47, April 2006.

[33] M. Bechler, "Internet Integration of Vehicular Ad Hoc Networks," Berlin: Logos Verlag, 2004.

[34] S. Lahde, M. Doering, W.-B. Pöttner, G. Lammert, L. Wolf, "A Practical Analysis of Communication Characteristics for Mobile and Distributed Pollution Measurements on the Road," Wireless Communications and Mobile Computing, vol. 7, pp. 1209 – 1218, December 2007.

[35] Swisscom AG, "Mobile Unlimited," `http://www.swisscom.ch/res/internet/ mobilessurfen/mobile-unlimited/index.htm?languageId=en` visited July 2009.

[36] P. Pöyhönen, J. Markendahl, O. Strandberg, "Analysis of User Experience of Access Selection in Multi-operator Environments," Proceedings of the 3rd International Conference on Systems and Networks Communications (ICSNC '08), Sliema, Malta, pp. 27 – 32, October 2008.

[37] P. Pöyhönen, D. Hollos, H. Tang, O. Blume, R. Aguero, K. Pentikousis, "Analysis of Load Dependency of Handover Strategies in Mobile Multiaccess Ambient Networks," Proceedings of the 12th IEEE Symposium on Computers and Communications (ISCC 2007), Santiago, Portugal, pp. MW–15 – MW–20, July 2007.

[38] J. Brandt, L. Wolf, "Multidimensional Transcoding for Adaptive Video Streaming," Proceedings of the 17th International Workshop on Network and Operating Systems Support for Digital Audio and Video (NOSSDAV'07), Urbana, IL, USA, June 2007.

[39] J. Rosenberg, H. Schulzrinne, G. Camarillo, A. Johnston, J. Peterson, R. Sparks, M. Handley, E. Schooler, "SIP: Session Initiation Protocol," Internet Engineering Task Force Request for Comments 3261, June 2002 `http://tools.ietf.org/html/ rfc3261`.

[40] H. Schulzrinne, E. Wedlund, "Application-layer Mobility Using SIP," ACM SIGMOBILE Mobile Computing and Communications Review, vol. 4, pp. 47 – 57, July 2000.

[41] H. Zhu, M. Li, I. Chlamta, B. Prabhakaran, "A Survey of Quality of Service in IEEE 802.11 Networks," IEEE Wireless Communications, vol. 11, pp. 6 –14, August 2004.

[42] B. Landfeldt, T. Larsson, Y. Ismailov, A. Seneviratne, "SLM, A Framework for Session Layer Mobility Management," Proceedings of the Eight International Conference on Computer Communications and Networks (ICCCN '99), Boston, MA , USA, pp. 452 – 456, October 1999.

[43] J. Kristiansson, P. Parnes, "Application-layer Mobility support for Streaming Real-time Media," Proceedings of the IEEE Wireless Communications and Networking Conference (WCNC 2004), Atlanta, GA ,USA, pp. 268 – 273, March 2004.

[44] A. Popescu, D. Ilie, D. Erman, M. Fiedler, K. de Vogeleer, "An Application Layer Architecture for Seamless Roaming," Proceedings of the Sixth International Conference on Wireless On-Demand Network Systems and Services (WONS 2009), Snowbird, UT, USA, pp. 212 – 220, February 2009.

[45] D. A. Maltz, P. Bhagwat, "MSOCKS: An Architecture for Transort Layer Mobility," Proceedings of the 17th Annual Joint Conference of the IEEE Computer and Communications Societies (INFOCOM 1998), San Francisco, CA, USA, pp. 1037 – 1045, April 1998.

[46] J. Border, M. Kojo, J. Griner, G.Montenegro, Z. Shelby, "Performance Enhancing Proxies Intended to Mitigate Link-Related Degradations," Internet Engineering Task Force Request for Comments 3135, June 2001 http://tools.ietf.org/html/rfc3135.

[47] A. Bakre, B. R. Badrinath, "I-TCP: Indirect TCP for Mobile Hosts," Proceedings of the IEEE International Conference on Distributed Computing Systems, Vanvouver, Canada, pp. 136 – 143, May 1995.

[48] Z. J. Haas, P. Agrawal, "Mobile-TCP: An Asymmetric Transport Protocol Design for Mobile Systems," Proceedings of the IEEE International Conference on Communications (ICC '97), Montreal, QC, Canada, pp. 1054 – 1058, June 1997.

[49] A. C. Snoeren, H. Balakrishnan, "An End-to-End Approach to Host Mobility," Proceedings of the 6th Annual International Conference on Mobile Computing and Networking (MobiCom '00), Boston, MA, USA, pp. 155 – 166, August 2000.

[50] M. Riegel, M. Tuexen, "Mobile SCTP," Internet Engineering Task Force Internet Draft draft-riegel-tuexen-mobile-sctp-09.txt, November 2007 http://tools.ietf.org/html/draft-riegel-tuexen-mobile-sctp-09, work in progress.

[51] S. Fu, M. Atiquzzaman, L. Ma, W. Ivancic, Y.-J. Lee, J. S. Jones, S. Lu, "TraSH: A Transport Layer Seamless Handover for Mobile Networks," Technical Report OU-TRNL-04-100, School of Computer Science, University of Oklahoma at Norman, December 2004.

[52] S. Fu, L. Ma, M. Atiquzzaman, "Architecture and Performance of SIGMA: A Seamless Handover Scheme for Data Networks," Proceedings of the IEEE International Conference on Communications (ICC '05), Seoul, South Korea, May 2005.

[53] I. Aydin, W. Seok, C.-C. Shen, "Cellular SCTP: A Transport-Layer Approach to Internet Mobility," Proceedings of the 12th International Conference on Computer Communications and Networks (ICCCN 2003), Dallas, TX, USA, pp. 285 – 290, October 2003.

[54] R. Moskowitz, P. Nikander, P. Jokela, T. R. Henderson, "Host Identity Protocol," Internet Engineering Task Force Request for Comments 5201, April 2008 http://tools.ietf.org/html/rfc5201.

[55] P. Nikander, T. R. Henderson, C. Vogt, J. Arkko, "End-Host Mobility and Multihoming with the Host Identity Protocol," Internet Engineering Task Force Request for Comments 5206, April 2008 http://tools.ietf.org/html/rfc5206.

[56] C. E. Perkins, "IP Mobility Support for IPv4," Internet Engineering Task Force Request for Comments 3344, August 2002 http://tools.ietf.org/html/rfc3344.

[57] D. B. Johnson, C. E. Perkins, J. Arkko, "Mobility Support in IPv6," IETF Request for Comments 3775, June 2004 http://tools.ietf.org/html/rfc3775.

[58] S. Sharma, I. Baek, T.-C. Chiueh, "OmniCon: A Mobile IP-based Vertical Handoff System for Wireless LAN and GPRS Links," Proceedings of the International Workshop on Network Design and Architecture (IWNDA 2004), Montreal, QC, Canada, pp. 779 – 798, August 2004.

[59] L. Suciu, J.-M. Bonnin, K. Guillouard, T. Ernst, "Multiple Network Interfaces Management for Mobile Routers," Proceedings of the International Conference on Intelligent Transportation Systems Telecomunications (ITST '05), Brest, France, pp. 347 – 351, June 2005.

[60] V. Devarapalli, R. Wakikawa, A. Petrescu, P. Thubert, "Network Mobility (NEMO) Basic Support Protocol," Internet Engineering Task Force Request for Comments 3963, January 2005 http://tools.ietf.org/html/rfc3963.

[61] L.-J. Chen, T. Sun, M. Gerla, "USHA: A Practical Handoff Solution," Proceedings of the First International Conference on Multimedia Service Access Networks (MSAN'05), Orlando, FL, USA, pp. 83 – 87, June 2005.

[62] M. Bechler, B. Hurler, V. Kahmann, L. Wolf, "A Management Entity for Improving Service Quality in Mobile Ad-Hoc Networks," Proceedings of the International Confer-

ence on Wireless LANs and Home Networks (ICWLHN 2001), Singapore, December 2001.

[63] M. Lee, G. Kim, S. Park, S. Jun, J. Nah, O. Song, "Efficient 3G/WLAN Interworking Techniques for Seamless Roaming Services with Location-Aware Authentication," Proceedings of Networking 2005, vol. 3462 of Lecture Notes in Computer Science, Waterloo, Canada, pp. 370 – 381, Springer Verlag Berlin/Heidelberg, May 2005.

[64] H.-H. Choi, O. Song, D.-H. Cho, "A Seamless Handoff Scheme for UMTS-WLAN Interworking," Proceedings of the IEEE Global Telecommunications Conference (GLOBECOM '04), Dallas, TX, USA, pp. 1559 – 1564, November 2004.

[65] H. Park, S. Yoon, T. Kim, J. Park, M. Do, J. Lee, "Vertical Handoff Procedure and Algorithm between IEEE 802.11 WLAN and CDMA Cellular Network," Proceedings of the Seventh CDMA International Conference (CIC '02), Seoul, pp. 103 –112, October 2002.

[66] Y. Liu, C. Zhou, "A Vertical Handoff Decision Algorithm (VHDA) and a Call Admission Control (CAC) policy in integrated network between WiMax and UMTS," Proceedings of the Second International Conference on Communications and Networking in China (CHINACOM '07), Shanghai, China, pp. 1063 – 1068, August 2007.

[67] The Institute of Electrical and Electronics Engineers, "IEEE Standard for Local and Metropolitain Area Networks – Part 21: Media Independent Handover Services," IEEE Std 802.21-2008, January 2009.

[68] 3rd Generation Partnership Project (3GPP), Technical Specification Group GSM/EDGE, Radio Access Network, "Generic Network Access – Stage 2 (Release 9)," 3GPP TS 43.381, December 2009.

[69] Kineto Wireless Inc., "SMART WI-FI," http://www.umatoday.com visited in May 2010.

[70] T. Ishikawa, S. Hanaoka, M. Kataoka, M. Yano, S. Nisimura, "Basic Simulation Result of Inter System Handover for Cognitive Radio," Proceedings of the International Conference on Future Generation Communication and Networking (FGCN 2007), Jeju-Island, Korea, pp. 270 – 273, December 2007.

[71] T. J. Hacker, B. D. Athey, B. Noble, "The End-to-End Performance Effects of Parallel TCP Sockets on a Lossy Wide-Area Network," Proceedings of the 16th International Parallel and Distributed Processing Symposium (IPDPS '02), Fort Lauderdale, FL, USA, pp. 434 – 443, April 2002.

[72] H. Sivakumar, S. Bailey, R. L. Grossman, "PSockets: The Case for Application-level Network Striping for Data Intensive Applications using High Speed Wide Area Networks," Proceedings of the ACM/IEEE Conference on Supercomputing (SC '00), Dallas, TX, USA, November 2000.

[73] H.-Y. Hsieh, R. Sivakumar, "pTCP: An End-to-End Transport Layer Protocol for Striped Connections," Proceedings of the 10th IEEE International Conference on Network Protocols (ICNP '02), Paris, France, pp. 24 – 33, November 2002.

[74] M. Zhang, J. Lai, A. Krishnamurthy, L. Peterson, R. Wang, "A Transport Layer Approach for Improving End-to-End Performance and Robustness Using Redundant Paths," Proceedings of the USENIX Annual Technical Conference (ATEC '04), Boston, MA , USA, pp. 99 – 112, June 2004.

[75] D. Andersen, H. Balakrishnan, F. Kaashoek, R. Morris, "Resilient Overlay Networks," Proceedings of the 18th ACM Symposium on Operating Systems Principles (SOSP '01), Chateau Lake Louise, Banff, Canada, pp. 131 – 145, October 2001.

[76] J. Iyengar, K. Shah, P. Amer, R. Stewart, "Concurrent Multipath Transfer Using SCTP Multihoming," Proceedings of the International Symposium on Performance Evaluation of Computer and Telecommunication System (SPECTS '04), San Jose, CA, USA, July 2004.

[77] J. R. Iyengar, P. D. Amer, R. Stewart, "Concurrent Multipath Transfer Using SCTP Multihoming Over Independent End-to-End Paths," IEEE/ACM Transactions on Networking, vol. 14, pp. 951 – 964, October 2006.

[78] A. Argyriou, V. Madisetti, "Bandwidth Aggregation with SCTP," Proceedings of the IEEE Global Telecommunications Conference (GLOBECOM '03), San Francisco, CA, USA, pp. 3716 – 3721, December 2003.

[79] G. Ye, T. N. Saadawi, M. Lee, "IPCC-SCTP: An Enhancement to the Standard SCTP to Support Multi-homing Efficiently," Proceeding of the IEEE International Conference on Performance, Computing, and Communications (IPCCC '04), Phoenix, AZ, USA, pp. 523 – 530, April 2004.

[80] A. E. Al, T. Saadawi, M. Lee, "A Transport Layer Load Sharing Mechanism for Mobile Wireless Hosts," Proceedings of the Second IEEE Annual Conference on Pervasive Computing and Communications Workshops (PerCom '04), Orlando, FL, USA, pp. 87 – 91, March 2004.

[81] F. Perotto, C. Casetti, G. Galante, "SCTP-based Transport Protocols for Concurrent Multipath Transfer," Proceedings of the IEEE Wireless Communications and Net-

working Conference (WCNC 2007), Hong Kong, Special Administrative Region of the People's Republic of China, pp. 2969 – 2974, March 2007.

[82] S. Mascolo, L. A. Grieco, R. Ferorelli, P. Camarda, G. Piscitelli, "Performance Evaluation of Westwood+ TCP congestion control," Performance Evaluation, vol. 4, pp. 93 – 111, January 2004.

[83] M. Fiore, C. Casetti, G. Galante, "Concurrent Multipath Communication for Real-Time Traffic," Computer Communications, vol. 30, pp. 3307 – 3320, November 2007.

[84] R. R. Stewart, M. A. Ramalho, Q. Xie, M. Tuexen, P. T. Conrad, "Stream Control Transmission Protocol (SCTP) Partial Reliability Extension," Internet Engineering Task Force Request for Comments 3758, May 2004 http://tools.ietf.org/html/rfc3758.

[85] D. S. Phatak, T. Goff, "A Novel Mechanism for Data Streaming Across Multiple IP Links for Improving Throughput and Reliability in Mobile Environments," Proceedings of the 21th Annual Joint Conference of the IEEE Computer and Communications Societies (INFOCOM 2002), New York, NY USA, pp. 773 – 781, June 2002.

[86] J. Ott, D. Kutscher, "A Disconnection-tolerant Transport for Drive-thru Internet Environments," Proceedings of the 24th Annual Joint Conference of the IEEE Computer and Communications Societies (INFOCOM 2005), Miami, FL, USA, pp. 1849 – 1862, March 2005.

[87] J. Ott, P. Ylikoski, N. Seifert, C. Carroll, N. Wallbridge, O. Bergmann, D. Kutscher, "The CHIANTI Architecture for Robust Mobile Internet Access," Proceedings of IEEE International Symposium on a World of Wireless, Mobile and Multimedia Networks & Workshops (WoWMoM 2009), Kos, Greece, pp. 1 – 9, June 2009.

[88] V. Paxson, M. Allman, "Computing TCP's Retransmission Timer," Internet Engineering Task Force Request for Comments 2988, November 2000 http://tools.ietf.org/html/rfc2988.

[89] T. Goff, J. Moronski, D. Phatak, V. Gupta, "Freeze-TCP: A True End-to-End TCP Enhancement Mechanism for Mobile Environments," Proceedings of the 19th Annual Joint Conference of the IEEE Computer and Communications Societies (INFOCOM 2000), Tel-Aviv, Israel, pp. 1537 – 1545, March 2000.

[90] W. R. Stevens, "TCP/IP Illustrated,", vol. I Addison Wesley, 1994.

[91] K. Brown, S. Singh, "M-TCP: TCP for Mobile Cellular Networks," ACM SIGCOMM Computer Communication Review, vol. 27, pp. 19 – 43, October 1997.

[92] M. Bechler, S. Jaap, L. Wolf, "An Optimized TCP for Internet Access of Vehicular Ad Hoc Networks," Proceedings of Networking 2005, Waterloo, Ontario, Canada, May 2005.

[93] K. L. Scott, S. Burleigh, "Bundle Protocol Specification," Internet Engineering Task Force Request for Comments 5050, November 2007 http://tools.ietf.org/html/rfc5050.

[94] M. Ratola, "Which Layer for Mobility? – Comparing Mobile IPv6, HIP and SCTP," Seminar on Internetworking, Helsinki University of Technology, April 2004.

[95] W. M. Eddy, "At What Layer Does Mobility Belong?," IEEE Communications Magazine, vol. 42, pp. 155 –159, October 2004.

[96] I. F. Akyildiz, J. Xie, S. Mohanty, "A Survey of Mobility Management in Next-Generation All-IP-Based Wireless Systems," IEEE Wireless Communications, vol. 11, pp. 16 – 28, August 2004.

[97] M. Atiquzzaman, A. S. Reaz, "Survey and Classification of Transport Layer Mobility Management Schemes," Proceedings of the IEEE 16th International Symposium on Personal, Indoor and Mobile Radio Communications (PIMRC 2005), pp. 2109 – 2115, September 2005.

[98] J.-M. Kim, J.-W. Jang, "Low Latency Vertical Handover Using MIH L2-Trigger Algorithm in Mobile IP Networks," Proceedings of the 5th International Symposium on Parallel and Distributed Processing and Applications (ISPA 2007), vol. 4742 of Lecture Notes in Computer Science, Niagara Falls, Canada, pp. 707 – 718, Springer Verlag Berlin/Heidelberg, August 2007.

[99] H. Bing, C. He, L. Jiang, "Performance Analysis of Vertical Handover in a UMTS-WLAN Integrated Network," Proceedings of the 14th IEEE Personal, Indoor and Mobile Radio Communications (PIMRC 2003), Beijing, China, pp. 187–191, September 2003.

[100] Q. Zhang, C. Guo, Z. Guo, W. Zhu, "Efficient Mobility Management for Vertical Handoff between WWAN and WLAN," IEEE Communications Magazine, vol. 41, pp. 102 – 108, November 2003.

[101] G. P. Pollini, "Trends in Handover Design," IEEE Communications Magazine, vol. 34, pp. 82 – 90, March 1996.

[102] European Telecommunications Standards Institute (ETSI), "Digital Cellular Telecommunications System (Phase 2+) (GSM);Radio subsystem link control (GSM 05.08 version 8.4.1 Release 1999)," ETSI EN 300 911 V8.4.1 (2000-10), October 2000.

[103] M. Ylianttila, R. Pichna, J. Vallstrom, J. Makela, A. Zahedi, P. Krishnamurthy, K. Pahlavan, "Handoff Procedure for Heterogeneous Wireless Networks," Proceedings of the Global Telecommunications Conference (GLOBECOM '99), Rio de Janeiro, Brazil, pp. 2783 – 2787, December 1999.

[104] M. Ylianttila, M. Pande, J. Makela, P. Mahonen, "Optimization Scheme for Mobile Users Performing Vertical Handoffs between IEEE 802.11 and GPRS/EDGE Networks," Proceedings of the IEEE Global Telecommunications Conference (GLOBECOM '01), San Antonio, TX, USA, pp. 3439 – 3443, November 2001.

[105] M.Ylianttila, J. Mäkelä, P. Mähönen, "Supporting Resource Allocation With Vertical Handoffs in Multiple Radio Network Environment," Proceedings of the 13th IEEE International Symposium on Personal, Indoor and Mobile Radio Communications (PIMRC 2002), Lisbon, Portugal, pp. 64 – 68, September 2002.

[106] K. Pahlavan, P. Krishnamurthy, A. Hatami, M. Ylianttila, J.-P. Makela, R. Pichna, J. Vallstron, "Handoff in Hybrid Mobile Data Networks," IEEE Personal Communications, vol. 7, pp. 34 – 47, April 2000.

[107] K.-S. Jang, J.-S. Kim, H.-J. Shin, D.-R. Shin, "A Novel Vertical Handoff Strategy for Integrated IEEE802.11 WLAN/CDMA Networks," Proceedings of the Fourth Annual ACIS International Conference on Computer and Information Science (ICIS '05), Las Vegas, NV, USA, pp. 616 – 621, December 2005.

[108] A. H. Zahran, B. Liang, A. Saleh, "Signal Threshold Adaptation for Vertical Handoff in Heterogeneous Wireless Networks," Mobile Networks and Applications, vol. 11, pp. 625 – 640, August 2006.

[109] C. Casetti, C.-F. C. andRoberta Fracchia, M. Meo, "Autonomic Interface Selection for Mobile Wireless Users," IEEE Transactions on Vehicular Technology, vol. 57, pp. 3666 – 3678, November 2008.

[110] R. Fracchia, C. Casetti, C.-F. Chiasserini, M. Meo, "WiSE: Best-Path Selection in Wireless Multihoming Environments," IEEE Transactions on Mobile Computing, vol. 6, pp. 1130 – 1141, October 2007.

[111] 3rd Generation Partnership Project (3GPP), "3G TS 23.107 QoS Concept and Architecture," Technical Specification, 1999.

[112] G. Fan, X. Lu, "Novel Service Oriented Handoffs in Heterogeneous Wireless Networks," Proceedings of the Second International Conference on Quality of Service in Heterogeneous Wired/Wireless Networks (QSHINE '05), Orlando, FL, USA, p. 38, August 2005.

[113] A. Westerinen, J. Schnizlein, J. Strassner, M. Scherling, B. Quinn, S. Herzog, A. Huynh, J. Perry, S. Waldbusser, "Terminology for Policy-Based Management," Internet Engineering Task Force Request for Comments 3198, November 2001 http://tools.ietf.org/html/rfc3198.

[114] B. Moore, E. Ellesson, J. Strassner, A. Westerinen, "Policy Core Infomration Model – Version 1 Specification," Internet Engineering Task Force Request for Comments 3060, February 2001 http://tools.ietf.org/html/rfc3060.

[115] N. Damianou, A. K. Bandara, M. Sloman, E. C. Lupu, "A Survey of Policy Specification Approaches," Technical Report, Imperial College of Science, Technology and Medicine, April 2002.

[116] J. D. Moffett, M. S. Sloman, "Policy Hierarchies for Distributed Systems Management," IEEE Journal on Selected Areas in Communications, vol. 11, pp. 1404 – 1414, December 1993.

[117] J. C. Strassner, "Policy-Based Network Management: Solutions for the Next Generation," Seattle: Morgan Kaufman Publishers, 2003.

[118] K. Murray, R. Mathur, D. Pesch, "Intelligent Access and Mobility Management in Heterogeneous Wireless Networks Using Policy," Proceedings of the 1st International Symposium on Information and Communication Technologies (ISICT '03), Dublin, Irland, pp. 181–186, September 2003.

[119] P. A. A. Gutierrez, I. Miloucheva, "Automated QoS Policy Adaptation for Heterogeneous Access Network Environments," Proceedings of Second International Conference on Systems and Networks Communications 2007 (ICSNC '07), Cap Esterel, France, August 2007.

[120] S. Avallone, P. D. Gennaro, I. Miloucheva, S. Rao, M. Roth, "NETQOS: Policy Based Management of Heterogeneous Networks for Guaranteed QoS," Proceedings of the QoS 2006 Workshop, Coimbra, Portugal, May 2006.

[121] S. Avallone, S. D'Antonio, S. P. Romano, "A Semantic Approach to Policy-based Management: Linking Policies to Ontologies," Proceedings of the International Conference on Wireless Information Networks and Systems (WINSYS 2007), Barcelona, Spain, pp. 311 – 317, July 2007.

[122] J. Strassner, D. Raymer, S. Samudrala, "Providing Seamless Mobility Using the FOCALE Autonomic Architecture," Proceedings of the 7th International Conference on Next Generation Teletraffic and Wired/Wireless Advanced Networking (NEW2AN '07) (Y. Koucheryavy, J. Harju, A. Sayenko, eds.), vol. 4712 of Lecture

Notes in Computer Science, Saint-Petersburg, Russia, pp. 330 – 341, Springer Verlag Berlin/Heidelberg, September 2007.

[123] S. Russell, P. Norvig, "Artificial Intelligence: A Modern Approach," Prentice Hall, 2nd ed., December 2002.

[124] H. B. Keller, "Maschinelle Intelligenz," Braunschweig: Vieweg Verlag, 2000.

[125] L. A. Zadeh, "Fuzzy Sets," Information and Control, vol. 8, pp. 338 – 353, June 1965.

[126] L. A. Zadeh, "Fuzzy Logic and Approximate Reasoning," Synthese, vol. 30, pp. 407 – 428, September 1975.

[127] L. A. Zadeh, "Fuzzy Sets and Applications: Selected Papers by L.A. Zadeh," John Wiley & Sons, 1987.

[128] MathWork Inc, "Fuzzy Logic Toolbox 2 – User's Guide, Release 2007a," Natick, MA, USA, March 2007.

[129] E. Mamdami, S. Assilina, "An Experiment in Linguistic Synthesis with a Fuzzy Logic Controller," International Journal of Man-Machine Studies, vol. 7, pp. 1–13, January 1975.

[130] T. Takagi, M. Sugeno, "Fuzzy Identification of Systems and its Applications to Modeling and Control," IEEE Transactions on Systems, Man, and Cybernetics, vol. 15, pp. 116 –132, February 1985.

[131] C.-Y. Chang, H.-J. Wang, H.-C. Chao, J. H. Park, "IEEE 802.11 Handoff Latency Improvement Using Fuzzy Logic," Wireless Communications and Mobile Computing, vol. 8, pp. 1201–1213, November 2008.

[132] H. Liao, L. Tie, Z. Du, "A Vertical Handover Decision Algorithm Based on Fuzzy Control Theory," Proceedings of the First International Multi-Symposiums on Computer and Computational Sciences (IMSCCS '06), Zhejiang, China, pp. 309 – 313, June 2006.

[133] J.-L. Wang, C.-W. Chen, "Knowledge-Based Intelligent Information and Engineering Systems,", vol. 4252 of Lecture Notes in Computer Science, ch. Fuzzy Logic Based Mobility Management for 4G Heterogeneous Networks, pp. 888 – 895 Berlin / Heidelberg: Springer Verlag, 2006.

[134] A. Wilson, A. Lenaghan, R. Malyan, "Optimising Wireless Access Network Selection to Maintain QoS in Heterogeneous Wireless Environments," Proceedings of the Wireless Personal Multimedia Communications 2005 (WPMC '05), Aalborg, Denmark, pp. 1236 – 1240, September 2005.

[135] M. Bechler, L. Wolf, "Fuzzy Logic Based Handoffs in Vehicular Ad Hoc Networks," Proceedings of the 2nd Workshop on Intelligent Transportation (WIT 2005), Hamburg, Germany, March 2005.

[136] W. Zhang, "Handover Decision Using Fuzzy MADM in Heterogeneous Networks," Proceedings of the IEEE Wireless Communications and Networking Conference (WCNC 2004), Atlanta, GA USA, pp. 653 – 658, March 2004.

[137] C.-J. Lin, I.-T. Tsai, C.-Y. Lee, "An Adaptive Fuzzy Predictor Based Handoff Algorithm for Heterogeneous Network," Processings of the IEEE Annual Meeting of the Fuzzy Information Processing Society (NAFIPS '04), Banff, AB, Canada, pp. 944 – 947, June 2004.

[138] A. Majlesi, B. H. Khalaj, "An Adaptive Fuzzy Logic Based Handoff Algorithm for Interworking Between WLANs and Mobile Networks," Proceedings of the 13th IEEE International Symposium on Personal, Indoor and Mobile Radio Communications (PIMRC '03), Beijing, China, pp. 2446 –245, September 2002.

[139] P. Chan, R. Sheriff, Y. Hu, P. Conforto, C. Tocci, "Mobility Management Incorporating Fuzzy Logic for a Heterogeneous IP Environment," IEEE Communications Magazine, vol. 39, pp. 42 – 51, December 2001.

[140] X. Haibo, T. Hui, Z. Ping, "A Novel Terminal-controlled Handover Scheme in Heterogeneous Wireless Networks," Computers & Electrical Engineering, vol. 36, pp. 269 – 279, March 2010.

[141] S. Horrich, S. B. Jamaa, P. Godlewski, "Adaptive Vertical Mobility Decision in Heterogeneous Networks," Proceedings of the Third International Conference on Wireless and Mobile Communications (ICWMC '07), Guadeloupe, French Caribbean, p. 44, March 2007.

[142] L. Giupponi, R. Agustí, J. Pérez-Romero, O. Sallent, "A Fuzzy Neural JRRM in a Heterogeneous Scenario Supported by Prediction Strategies for Horizontal and Vertical Handovers," Proceedings of the IEEE International Conference on Fuzzy Systems (FUZZ-IEEE '06), Vancouver, BC, Canada, pp. 655 – 662, July 2006.

[143] L. Giupponi, R. Agustí, J. Pérez-Romero, O. Sallent, "Joint Radio Resource Management algorithm for multi-RAT networks," Proceedings of the IEEE Global Telecommunications Conference (GLOBECOM '05), St. Louis, MO, USA, pp. 3851 – 3855, November 2005.

[144] Q. Guo, J. Zhu, X. Xu, "An Adaptive Multi-criteria Vertical Handoff Decision Algorithm for Radio Heterogeneous Network," Proceedings of the IEEE International Conference on Communications (ICC 2005), pp. 2769 – 2773, May 2005.

[145] R. Agusti, O. Sallent, J. Perez-Romero, L. Giupponi, "A Fuzzy-Neural Based Approach for Joint Radio Resource Management in a Beyond 3G Framework," Proceedings of the First International Conference on Quality of Service in Heterogeneous Wired/Wireless Networks (QSHINE 2004), Los Alamitos, CA, USA, pp. 216 – 224, October 2004.

[146] S. Haykin, "Neural Networks: A Comprehensive Foundation," Prentice Hall, 2nd ed., 1998.

[147] E. Alpaydin, "Introduction to Machine Learning," The MIT Press, 2004.

[148] A. Mehbodniya, J. Chitizadeh, "An Intelligent Vertical Handoff Algorithm for Next Generation Wireless Networks," Proceedings of the Second IFIP International Conference on Wireless and Optical Communications Networks (WOCN 2005), Dubai, United Arab Emirates, pp. 244 – 249, March 2005.

[149] F. Zhu, J. McNair, "Multiservice Vertical Handoff Decision Algorithms," EURASIP Journal on Wireless Communications and Networking, vol. 2006, pp. 52 – 52, April 2006.

[150] F. Zhu, J. McNair, "Optimizations for Vertical Handoff Decision Algorithms," Proceedings of the IEEE Wireless Communications and Networking Conference (WCNC 2004), Atlanta, GA, USA, pp. 867 – 872, March 2004.

[151] N. Nasser, A. Hasswa, H. Hassanein, "Handoffs in Fourth Generation Heterogeneous Networks," IEEE Communications Magazine, vol. 44, pp. 96 – 103, October 2006.

[152] G. Nyberg, C. Ahlund, T. Rojmyr, "SEMO: A Policy-based System for Handovers in Heterogeneous Networks," Proceedings of the International Conference on Wireless and Mobile Communications (ICWMC '06), Bucharest, Romania, pp. 62 – 62, July 2006.

[153] O. Ormond, J. Murphy, G.-M. Muntean, "Utility-based Intelligent Network Selection in Beyond 3G Systems," Proceedings of the IEEE International Conference on Communications 2006 (ICC '06), Istanbul, Turkey, pp. 1831 – 1836, June 2006.

[154] O. Ormond, P. Perry, J. Murphy, "Network Selection Decision in Wireless Heterogeneous Networks," Proceedings of the IEEE 16th International Symposium on Personal, Indoor and Mobile Radio Communications (PIMRC 2005), Berlin, Germany, pp. 2680 – 2684, September 2005.

[155] L.-J. Chen, T. Sun, B. Chen, V. Rajendran, M. Gerla, "A Smart Decision Model for Vertical Handoff," Proceedings of the 4th ANWIRE International Workshop on Wireless Internet and Reconfigurability, Athens, Greece, May 2004.

[156] H. J. Wang, R. H. Katz, J. Giese, "Policy-Enabled Handoffs Across Heterogeneous Wireless Networks," Proceedings of the Second IEEE Workshop on Mobile Computer Systems and Applications (WMCSA '99), New Orleans, LA, USA, pp. 51 – 60, February 1999.

[157] O. Ormond, J. Murphy, G.-M. Muntean, "Economic Model for Cost Effective Network Selection Strategy in Service Oriented Heterogeneous Wireless Network Environment," Proceedings of the 10th IEEE/IFIP Network Operations and Management Symposium (NOMS 2006), Vancouver, QC, Canada, April 2006.

[158] E. Stevens-Navarro, V. W. Wong, "Comparison between Vertical Handoff Decision Algorithms for Heterogeneous Wireless Networks," Proceedings of IEEE 63rd Vehicular Technology Conference (VTC 2006-Spring), Melbourne, Australia, pp. 947 – 951, May 2006.

[159] F. Bari, V. C. Leung, "Automated Network Selection in a Heterogeneous Wireless Network Environment," IEEE Network, vol. 21, pp. 34 – 40, January 2007.

[160] T. L. Saaty, "The Analytic Hierarchy Process: Planning, Priority Setting, Resource Allocation," McGraw-Hill, 1980.

[161] T. L. Saaty, "Fundamentals of the Analytic Hierarchy Process," RWS Publications, 2000.

[162] X. Guan, R. Tang, S. Bai, D. Yoon, "Enhanced Application-Driven Vertical Handoff Decision Scheme for 4G Wireless Networks," Proceedings of the International Conference on Wireless Communications, Networking and Mobile Computing, 2007 (WiCom 2007), Shanghai, China, pp. 1771–1774, September 2007.

[163] T. Ahmed, K. Kyamakya, M. Ludwig, "Context-Aware Decision Model for Vertical Handover in Heterogeneous Networks," Proceedings of the 1st IEEE International Conference on Next-Generation Wireless Systems (ICNEWS 2006), Dhaka, Bangladesh, pp. 103 –107, January 2006.

[164] J. Deng, "Introduction to Grey System Theory," The Journal of Grey System, vol. 1, pp. 1 – 24, November 1989.

[165] Q. Song, A. Jamalipour, "An Adaptive Quality-of-Service Network Selection Mechanism for Heterogeneous Mobile Networks," Wireless Communications and Mobile Computing, vol. 5, pp. 697 – 708, September 2005.

[166] Q. Song, A. Jamalipour, "Network Selection in an Integrated Wireless LAN and UMTS Environment using Mathematical Modeling and Computing Techniques," IEEE Wireless Communications, vol. 12, pp. 42 – 48, June 2005.

[167] P. Stuckmann, R. Zimmermann, "European Research on Future Internet Design," IEEE Wireless Communications, vol. 16, pp. 14 – 22, October 2009.

[168] P. Pacyna, J. Godzdecki, K. Loziak, A. Jajszczyk, "Mobility Across Multiple Technologies – The Daidalos Approach," Interdisciplanary Information Sciences, vol. 12, pp. 127 – 132, October 2006.

[169] S. E. Deering, R. M. Hinden, "Internet Protocol, Version 6 (IPv6) – Specification," Internet Engineering Task Force Request for Comments 2460, December 1998 http://tools.ietf.org/html/rfc2460.

[170] T. Strauf, "Mobile Endgeräte mit Mehrfach-Netzanbindung Protokoll-Unterstützung auf Basis von Mobilem IPv6," Proceedings of the 3rd Braunschweiger Symposium Informationssysteme für mobile Anwendungen (IMA '06), Braunschweig, Germany, October 2006 [German].

[171] S. Sargento, R. Sarrô, R. Duarte, P. Stupar, "Seamless Mobility Architecture Supporting Ad-Hoc Environments," Proceedings of the Seventh International Conference on Networking (ICN '08), Cancun, Mexico, pp. 137 – 144, April 2008.

[172] M. Wetterwald, F. Filali, C. Bonnet, D. Nussbaum, L. Gauthier, A. M. Hayar, A. Banchs, C. J. Bernardos, M. Liebsch, T. Melia, C. Lafouge, J. Ribeiro, "A Flexible Framework for the Support of Heterogeneous Wireless Networks," Proceedings of the 15th IST Mobile & Wireless Communications Summit, Myconos, Greece, June 2006.

[173] S. McBurney, E. Papadopoulou, N. Taylor, H. Williams, "Adapting Pervasive Environments Through Machine Learning and Dynamic Personalization," Proceedings of the 2008 IEEE International Symposium on Parallel and Distributed Processing with Applications (ISPA '08), Sydney, Australia, pp. 395 – 402, December 2008.

[174] N. Niebert, M. Prytz, A. Schieder, N. Papadoglou, L. Eggert, F. Pittmann, C. Prehofer, "Ambient Networks: A Framework for Future Wireless Internetworking," Proceedings of the 61st IEEE Vehicular Technology Conference (VTC 2005-Spring), Stockholm, Sweden, pp. 2969 – 2973, May 2005.

[175] A. Gunnar, B. Ahlgren, O. Blume, L. Burness, P. Eardley, E. Hepworth, J. Sachs, A. Surtees, "Access and Path Selection in Ambient Networks," Proceedings of the 16th IST Mobile and Wireless Communications Summit, Budapest, Hungary, July 2007.

[176] R. Calvo, A. Surtees, J. Eisl, M. Georgiades, "Mobility Management in Ambient Networks," Proceedings of the 65th IEEE Vehicular Technology Conference (VTC2007-Spring), Dublin, Ireland, pp. 894 – 898, April 2007.

[177] Z. Feng, V. Le, P. Zhang, "A Seamless Vertical Handover Scheme for End-to-End Reconfigurability Systems," Proceedings of the IEEE Vehicular Technology Conference (VTC 2008-Spring), Marina Bay, Singapore, pp. 2152 –2156, May 2008.

[178] L. Giupponi, R. Agusti, J. Perez-Romero, O. S. Roig, "A Novel Approach for Joint Radio Resource Management Based on Fuzzy Neural Methodology," IEEE Transactions on Vehicular Technology, vol. 57, pp. 1789 –1805, May 2008.

[179] L. Giupponi, R. Agusti, J. Perez-Romero, O. Sallent, "A Fuzzy Neural JRRM in a Heterogeneous Scenario Supported by Prediction Strategies for Horizontal and Vertical Handovers," Proceedings of the IEEE International Conference on Fuzzy Systems, Vancouver, BC, Canada, pp. 655 – 662, September 2006.

[180] L. Giupponi, R. Agustí, J. Pérez-Romero, O. Sallent, "A Framework for JRRM with Resource Reservation and Multiservice Provisioning in Heterogeneous Networksbono," Mobile Networks and Applications, vol. 11, pp. 825 – 846, December 2006.

[181] M. Bonola, S. Salsano, A. Polidoro, "UPMT: Universal Per-Application Mobility Management Using Tunnels," Proceeding of the IEEE Global Telecommunications Conference (GLOBECOM 2009), Honolulu, HI, USA, November 2009.

[182] M. Khan, A. Toker, C. Troung, F. Sivrikaya, S. Albayrak, "Cooperative Game Theoretic Approach to Integrated Bandwidth Sharing and Allocation," International Conference on Game Theory for Networks (GameNets '09), Istanbul, Turkey, pp. 1 – 9, May 2009.

[183] G. Gehlen, E. Weiss, S. Lukas, C.-H. Rokitansky, B. Walke, "Architecture of a Vehicle Communication Gateway for Media Independent Handover," Proceedings of the 3rd International Workshop on Intelligent Transportation (WT2006), Hamburg, Germany, pp. 205 – 209, March 2006.

[184] R. Kroh, A. Held, M. Adlinger, R. Keller, T. Lohmar, E. Kovacs, "High-Quality Interactive and Broadband IP Services for the Vehicle on the Net – The COMCAR Approach," Proceedings of the 7th World Congress on Intelligent Transport Systems, Torino, Italy, November 2000.

[185] L. Christodouplides, T. Sammut, R. Tönjes, "DRiVE Towards Systems Beyond 3G," Proceedings of the 5th World Multi-Conference on Systemics, Cybernetics and Informatics (SCI '01), Orlando, FL, USA, July 2001.

[186] R. Tönjes, P. Benkö, J. Ebenhard, M. Frank, T. Göransson, W. Hansmann, J. Huschke, T. Lohmar, T. Paila, F. Sällström, W. Stahl, L. Xu, "Architecture for a Future Generation Multi-Access Wireless System with Dynamic Spectrum Allocation," Proceedings of the IST Mobile Communications Summit, Galway, Ireland, October 2000.

[187] P. Rodriguez, R. Chakravorty, J. Chesterfield, I. Pratt, S. Banerjee, "MAR: A Commuter Router Infrastructure for the Mobile Internet," Proceedings of the 2nd International Conference on Mobile Systems, Applications, and Services (MobiSys '04), Boston, MA, USA, pp. 217 – 230, June 2004.

[188] P. Gutierrez, I. Miloucheva, D. Wagner, C. Niephaus, A. Flizikowski, N. V. Wambeke, F. Armando, C. Chassot, S. Romano, "NETQOS Policy Management Architecture for Flexible QoS Provisioning in Future Internet," Proceedings of the Second International Conference on Next Generation Mobile Applications, Services and Technologies (NG-MAST '08), Cardiff, Wales, UK, pp. 53 – 58, September 2008.

[189] J. Jähnert, H.-W. Kim, "The Moby Dick Approach Towards 4G Networks," Proceedings of the Next Generation Teletraffic and Wired/Wireless Advanced Networking Conference (NEW2AN '04), St. Petersburg, Russia, February 2004.

[190] M. Zitterbart, K. Weniger, O. S. et. al., "IPonAir - Drahtloses Internet der Nächsten Generation," Praxis der Informationsverarbeitung und Kommunikations (PIK) Themenheft, December 2003 [German].

[191] M. Siebert, B. Xu, E. Weis, B. Bayer, D. Sivchenki, T. Banniza, K. Wünstel, S. Wahl, R. Sigle, R. Keller, A. Dekorsy, M. Bauer, M. Soellner, J. Eichinger, C. Gan, F. Pittmann, R. Kühne, M. Schläger, I. Baumgart, R. Bless, S. S. and, "ScaleNet - Converged Networks of the Future," Information Technology, vol. 48, p. 5, October 2006.

[192] K. Lai, M. Baker, "Measuring Bandwidth," Proceedings of the IEEE International Conference on Computer Communications (INFOCOM '99), New York, NY, USA, pp. 235 – 245, March 1999.

[193] C. Dovrolis, P. Ramanathan, D. Moore, "What Do Packet Dispersion Techniques Measure?," Proceedings of the 20th IEEE International Conference on Computer Communications (INFOCOM '01), Anchorage, Alaska, USA, pp. 905 – 914, April 2001.

[194] A. J. Nicholson, Y. Chawathe, M. Y. Chen, B. D. Noble, D. Wetherall, "Improved Access Point Selection," Proceedings of the 4th International Conference on Mobile Systems, Applications and Services (MobiSys '06), Uppsala, Sweden, pp. 233 – 245, June 2006.

[195] J. Sachs, R. Aguero, K. Daoud, J. Gebert, G. P. Koudouridis, F. Meago, M. Prytz, T. Rinta-aho, H. Tang, "Generic Abstraction of Access Performance and Resources for

Multi-Radio Access Management," Proceedings of the 16th IST Mobile and Wireless Communications Summit, Budapest, Hungary, pp. 1 – 5, July 2007.

[196] G. Lampropoulos, A. K. Salkintzis, N. Passas, "Media-Independent Handover for Seamless Service Provision in Heterogeneous Networks," IEEE Communications Magazine, vol. 46, pp. 64 – 71, January 2008.

[197] A. J. Nicholson, B. D. Noble, "BreadCrumbs: Forecasting Mobile Connectivity," Proceedings of the 14th ACM International Conference on Mobile Computing and Networking (MobiCom '08), San Francisco, CA, USA, pp. 46 – 57, September 2008.

[198] Telekom Deutschland GmbH, "Hotspot Locator," http://www.t-mobile.de/hotspot/locator/ visited in January 2010, [German].

[199] J. Pang, B. Greenstein, M. Kaminsky, D. McCoy, S. Seshan, "Wifi-Reports: Improving Wireless Network Selection with Collaboration," Proceedings of the 7th international conference on Mobile systems, applications, and services (MobiSys '09), Kraków, Poland, pp. 123 – 136, June 2009.

[200] The MadWifi Project, "Homepage," http://madwifi-project.org/ visited in January 2010.

[201] Kismet, "Homepage," http://www.kismetwireless.net/ visited in January 2010.

[202] J. K. Rosenblatt, "DAMN: A Distributed Architecture for Mobile Navigation," Phd thesis, The Robotics Institute, CMU, January 1997 CMU-RI-TR-97-01.

[203] L. Budzisz, R. Ferrús, A. Brunstrom, K.-J. Grinnemo, R. Fracchia, G. Galante, F. Casadevall, "Towards Transport-layer Mobility: Evolution of SCTP Multihoming," Computer Communications, vol. 31, pp. 980 – 998, May 2008.

[204] A. Pentland, R. Fletcher, A. Hasson, "DakNet: Rethinking Connectivity in Developing Nations," IEEE Computer, vol. 37, pp. 78 – 83, January 2004.

[205] M. Doering, S. Lahde, J. Morgenroth, L. Wolf, "IBR-DTN: An Efficient Implementation for Embedded Systems," Proceedings of the Third ACM Workshop on Challenged Networks (CHANTS '08), San Francisco, CA, USA, pp. 117 – 120, September 2008.

[206] S. J. Koh, Q. Xie, S. D. Park, "Mobile SCTP (mSCTP) for IP Handover Support," Internet Engineering Task Force Internet Draft draft-sjkoh-sctp-mobility-04.txt, October 2005 http://tools.ietf.org/id/draft-sjkoh-msctp-01.txt, work in progress.

[207] P. Lei, L. Ong, M. Tuexen, T. Dreibholz, "An Overview of Reliable Server Pooling Protocols," Internet Engineering Task Force Request for Comments 5351, September 2008 http://tools.ietf.org/html/rfc5351.

[208] P. Mockapetris, "Domain Names - Concepts and Facilities," Internet Engineering Task Force Request for Comments 1034, November 1987 http://tools.ietf.org/html/rfc1034.

[209] P. Vixie, S. Thomson, Y. Rekhter, J. Bound, "Dynamic Updates in the Domain Name System (DNS UPDATE)," Internet Engineering Task Force Request for Comments 2136, April 1997 http://tools.ietf.org/html/rfc2136.

[210] T. Dreibholz, A. Jungmaier, M. Tüxen, "A New Scheme for IP-based Internet-Mobility," Proceedings of the 28th Annual IEEE International Conference on Local Computer Networks (LCN '03), Bonn/Königswinter, Germany, pp. 99 – 108, October 2003.

[211] J.-W. Jung, Y.-K. Kim, H.-K. Kahng, "SCTP Mobility Highly Coupled with Mobile IP," Telecommunications and Networking - Proceedings of the 11th International Conference on Telecommunication (ICT 2004), vol. 3124 of Lecture Notes in Computer Science, Fortaleza, Brazil, pp. 671 – 677, Springer Verlag Berlin/Heidelberg, August 2004.

[212] J. F. Kurose, K. W. Ross, "Computer Networking – A Top-Down Apporach Featuring the Internet," Pearson Education, 2nd ed., 2003.

[213] The Cooperative Association for Internet Data Analysis (CAIDA), "CAIDA Data - Overview of Datasets, Monitors, and Reports," http://www.caida.org/data/overview/ visited in April 2010.

[214] R. Stewart, Q. Xie, K. Morneault, C. Sharp, H. Schwarzbauer, T. Taylor, I. Rytina, M. Kalla, L. Zhang, V. Paxson, "Stream Control Transmission Protocol," Internet Engineering Task Force Request for Comments 2960, October 2000 http://tools.ietf.org/html/rfc2960.

[215] L. Ong, J. Yoakum, "An Introduction to the Stream Control Transmission Protocol (SCTP)," Internet Engineering Task Force Request for Comments 3286, May 2002 http://tools.ietf.org/html/rfc3286.

[216] R. R. Stewart, "List of SCTP Implementations," http://www.sctp.org/implementations.html visited in March 2010.

[217] M. Tuexen, "Stream Control Transmission Protocol (SCTP)," http://www.sctp.de/sctp.html visited in March 2010.

[218] M. Scharf, S. Kiesel, "Head-of-line Blocking in TCP and SCTP: Analysis and Measurements," Proceedings of the IEEE Global Telecommunications Conference (GLOBECOM '06), San Francisco, CA, USA, November 2006.

[219] T. Peng, C. Leckie, K. Ramamohanarao, "Survey of Network-Based Defense Mechanisms Countering the DoS and DDoS Problems," ACM Computing Surveys (CSUR), vol. 39, pp. 1 – 42, April 2007.

[220] K.-J. Grinnemo, A. Brunstrom, "Performance of SCTP-controlled Failovers in M3UA-based SIGTRAN Networks," Proceedings of the Advanced Simulation Technologies Conference (ASTC), Applied Telecommunication Symposium (ATS), Arlington, VA, USA, pp. 86 – 91, April 2004.

[221] J. Eklund, K.-J. Grinnemo, S. Baucke, A. Brunstrom, "Tuning SCTP Failover for Carrier Grade Telephony Signaling," Computer Networks, vol. 54, pp. 133 – 149, January 2010.

[222] L. Budzisz, R. Ferrus, K.-J. Grinnemo, A. Brunstrom, F. Casadevall, "An Analytical Estimation of the Failover Time in SCTP Multihoming Scenarios," Proceedings of the IEEE Wireless Communications and Networking Conference (WCNC '07), Hong Kong, Special Administrative Region of the People's Republic of China, pp. 3929 – 3934, March 2007.

[223] L. Budzisz, R. Ferrus, F. Casadevall, "SCTP Multihoming Performance in Dynamically Changing Channels with the Influence of Link-Layer Retransmissions," Proceedings of the 64th IEEE Vehicular Technology Conference (VTC 2006-Fall), Montreal, QC, Canada, September 2006.

[224] J. Eklund, "Performance of Network Redundancy Mechanisms in SCTP," Technical Report 48, Karlstad University, 2005.

[225] A. L. Caro Jr., P. D. Amer, R. R. Stewart, "End-to-end Failover Thresholds for Transport Layer Multihoming," Proceedings of the IEEE Military Communications Conference (MILCOM '04), Monterey, CA, USA, pp. 99 – 105, October 2004.

[226] M. Mathis, J. Mahdavi, S. Floyd, A. Romanow, "TCP Selective Acknowledgment Options," Internet Engineering Task Force Request for Comments 2018, October 1996 http://tools.ietf.org/html/rfc2018.

[227] M. Allman, V. Paxson, W. Stevens, "TCP Congestion Control," Internet Engineering Task Force Request for Comments 2581, April 1999 http://tools.ietf.org/html/rfc2581.

[228] M. Allman, S. Floyd, C. Partridge, "Increasing TCP's Initial Window," Internet Engineering Task Force Request for Comments 3390, October 2002 http://tools.ietf.org/html/rfc3390.

[229] R. R. Stewart, Q. Xie, M. Tüxen, S. Maruyama, M. Kozuka, "Stream Control Transmission Protocol (SCTP) Dynamic Address Reconfiguration," Internet Engineering Task Force Request for Comments 5061, September 2007 http://tools.ietf.org/html/rfc5061.

[230] R. Stewart, K. Poon, M. Tuexen, V. Yasevich, P. Lei, "Sockets API Extensions for Stream Control Transmission Protocol (SCTP)," Internet Engineering Task Force Internet Draft draft-ietf-tsvwg-sctpsocket-22.txt, March 2010 http://tools.ietf.org/html/draft-ietf-tsvwg-sctpsocket-22, work in progress.

[231] I. Gaponova, "Concurrent Multipath Transfer for Heterogeneous Networks," Master Thesis, Technische Universität Braunschweig, Institute of Operating Systems and Computer Networks, July 2008.

[232] M. Allman, W. M. Eddy, S. Ostermann, "Estimating Loss Rates With TCP," ACM SIGMETRICS Performance Evaluation Review, vol. 31, pp. 12 – 24, December 2003.

[233] M. Carson, D. Santay, "NIST Net: A Linux-based Network Emulation Tool," ACM SIGCOMM Computer Communication Review, vol. 33, pp. 111 – 126, July 2003.

[234] US National Institute of Standards and Technology, "NIST Net Homepage," http://www-x.antd.nist.gov/nistnet/ visited in March 2010.

[235] D. L. Mills, "Network Time Protocol (Version 3) – Specification, Implementation and Analysis," Internet Engineering Task Force Request for Comments 1305, March 1992 http://tools.ietf.org/html/rfc1305.

[236] M. Doering, "Transport Layer Handover for Heterogeneous Communication Systems," Diploma Thesis, Technische Universität Braunschweig, Institute of Operating Systems and Computer Networks, June 2006.

[237] M. H. Marko Jurvansuu, Jarmo Prokkola, P. Perälä, "HSDPA Performance in Live Networks," Proceedings of the IEEE International Conference on Communications (ICC '07), Glasgow, Scotland, UK, pp. 467–471, June 2007.

[238] P. Benko, G. Malicsko, A. Veres, "A Large-scale, Passive Analysis of End-to-End TCP Performance over GPRS," Proceedings of the 23th Annual Joint Conference of the IEEE Computer and Communications Societies (INFOCOM 2004), pp. 1882 –1892, March 2004.

[239] R. Chakravorty, I. Pratt, "Performance Issues with General Packet Radio Service," Journal of Communications and Networks (JCN), vol. 4, pp. 266 – 281, 2002.

[240] L. Budzisz, R. Ferrus, F. Casadevall, P. Amer, "On Concurrent Multipath Transfer in SCTP-Based Handover Scenarios," Proceedings of the IEEE International Conference on Communications (ICC '09), Dresden, Germany, June 2009.

[241] D. Chalmers, M. Sloman, "A Survey of Quality of Service in Mobile Computing Environments," IEEE Communications Surveys, vol. 2, pp. 2 – 10, April 1999.

[242] International Telecommunication Union Telecommunication Standardization Sector (ITU-T), "Vocabulary for Performance and Quality of Service," Recommendation P.10/G.100 (2006) Amendment 2 (07/08), July 2008.

[243] N. Muhammad, D. Chiavelli, D. Soldani, M. Li, "QoS and QoE Management in UMTS Cellular Systems,", ch. Chapter 1: Introduction, pp. 1–8 John Wiley & Sons, Ltd, 2006.

[244] K. Kilkki, "Quality of Experience in Communications Ecosystem," Journal of Universal Computer Science, vol. 14, no. 5, pp. 615 – 624, 2008.

[245] Atheros Communications, Inc., "Power Consumption and Energy Efficiency Comparisons of WLAN Products," White Paper, May 2003 http://atheros.com/pt/whitepapers/atheros_power_whitepaper.pdf, visited in Feburary 2010.

[246] u-blox AG, "N711 –GSM/GPRS/EDGE modem reference design," Product Summary, 2009 http://www.u-blox.com/images/downloads/Product_Docs/N711_Product_Summary.pdf, visited in Feburary 2010.

[247] u-blox AG, "N721 – GSM/GPRS/EDGE/HSDPA modem reference design," Product Summary, 2009 http://www.u-blox.com/images/downloads/Product_Docs/N721_Product_Summary.pdf, visited in Feburary 2010.

[248] J. Bardwell, "You Believe You Understand What You Think I Said ... – The Truth About 802,11 Signal and Noise Metrics," White Paper, 2004.

[249] J. Bardwell, "Converting Signal Strength Percenatge to dBm Values," White Paper, November 2002.

[250] Wi-Fi Alliance, "Wi-Fi Protected Access Specification," 2004 http://www.wi-fi.org, visited in Feburary 2010.

[251] C. Çelik, İnci Sariçiçek, "Tabu Search for Parallel Machine Scheduling with Job Splitting," Proceeding og the sixth International Conference on Information Technology: New Generations (ITNG '09), Las Vegas, NV , USA, pp. 183 – 188, April 2009.

[252] Z.-L. Chen, "Simultaneous Job Scheduling and Resource Allocation on Parallel Machines," Annals of Operations Research, vol. 129, pp. 135 – 153, July 2004.

[253] L. Epstein, R. van Stee, "Online Scheduling of Splittable Tasks," ACM Transactions on Algorithms, vol. 2, pp. 79 – 94, January 2006.

[254] C.-Y. Lee, G. Yu, "Parallel-machine Scheduling under Potential Disruption," Optimization Letters, vol. 2, pp. 27 – 37, January 2008.

[255] K. Li, S. Yang, "Non-identical Parallel-machine Scheduling Research with Minimizing Total Weighted Completition Times: Modells, Relaxations and Algorithms," Applied Mathematical Modelling, vol. 33, pp. 2145 – 2158, April 2009.

[256] R. Logendran, B. McDonell, B. Smucker, "Scheduling Unrelated Parallel Machines with Sequence-dependent Setups," Computers & Operations Research, vol. 34, pp. 3420 – 3438, November 2007.

[257] S.-O. Shim, Y.-D. Kim, "A Branch and Bound Algorithm for an Identical Parallel Machine Scheduling Problem with a Job Splitting Property," Computers & Operations Reseach, vol. 35, pp. 863 – 875, March 2008.

[258] D. N. Thahar, F. Yalaoui, C. Chu, L. Amodeo, "A Linear Programming Approach for Identical Parallel Machine Scheduling with Job Splitting and Sequence-dependent Setup Times," International Journal of Production Economics, vol. 99, pp. 63 – 73, January–February 2006.

[259] A. Grigoriev, M. Sviridenko, M. Uetz, "Machine Scheduling with Resource Dependent Processing Times," Mathematical Programming: Series A and B, vol. 110, pp. 209 – 228, March 2007.

[260] M. Skutella, "Convex Quadratic and Semidefinite Programming Relaxations in Scheduling," Journal of the ACM (JACM), vol. 48, pp. 206 – 242, March 2001.

[261] T. H. Cormen, C. E. Leiserson, R. L. Rivest, "Introduction To Algorithms," MIT Press, 1990.

[262] A. Colorni, M. Dorigo, V. Maniezzo, "Distributed Optimization by Ant Colonies," Proceedings of ECAL91 - European Conference on Artificial Life, Paris, France, pp. 134 – 142, December 1991.

[263] G. B. Dantzig, "Linear Programming and Extensions," Princeton, N.J., USA: Princeton University Press, 1963.

[264] R. J. Dakin, "A Tree-search Algorithm for Mixed Integer Programming Problems," The Computer Journal, vol. 8, no. 3, pp. 250 – 255, 1965.

[265] M. Padberg, G. Rinaldi, "A Branch-and-Cut Algorithm for the Resolution of Large-Scale Symmetric Traveling Salesman Problems," SIAM Review, vol. 33, pp. 60 – 100, March 1991.

[266] J. A. Stankovic, M. Spuri, K. Ramamritham, G. Buttazzo, "Deadline Scheduling for Real-Time Systems - EDF and Related Algorithms," Springer, 1st ed., October 1998.

[267] R. Steinmetz, K. Nahrstedt, "Multimedia Systems," Springer, 1st ed., April 2004.

[268] IBM, "IBM ILOG CPLEX – Product Homepage," http://www.ibm.com/software/integration/optimization/cplex/ visited in Feburary 2010.

[269] P. Stuckmann, N. Ehlers, B. Wouters, "GPRS Traffic Performance Measurements," Proceedings of the 56th IEEE Vehicular Technology Conference (VTC 2002-Fall), Vancouver, BC, Canada, pp. 1289 – 1293, September 2002.

[270] A. L. Wijesinha, Y. Song, M. Krishnan, V. Mathur, J. Ahn, V. Shyamasundar, "Throughput Measurement for UDP Traffic in an IEEE 802.11g WLAN," Proceedings of the 6th International Conference on Software Engineering, Artificial Intelligence, Networking and Parallel/Distributed Computing and First ACIS International Workshop on Self-Assembling Wireless Networks (SNPD/SAWN 2005), Baltimore, MD, USA, pp. 220 – 225, May 2005.

[271] A. Silvennoinen, M. Hall, S.-G. Häggman, "The Effect of Terminal Movement on the Performance of IEEE 802.11 g Wireless LAN Systems in Simulated Radio Channels," Wireless Personal Communications, vol. 41, pp. 487 – 505, June 2007.

[272] "The Open Group Base Specifications Issue 7 and IEEE Std 1003.1-2008," 2004 http://www.opengroup.org/onlinepubs/9699919799/functions/clock_gettime.html visited in Feburary 2010.